EDMUND A. OPITZ

RELIGION AND CAPITALISM:

ALLIES, NOT ENEMIES

ARLINGTON HOUSE   NEW ROCHELLE, N.Y.

Library of Congress Catalog Card Number: 72-101955

SBN: 87000–079–9

MANUFACTURED IN THE UNITED STATES OF AMERICA

RELIGION AND CAPITALISM:

ALLIES, NOT ENEMIES

Contents

Preface

THE LATE RICHARD HENRY TAWNEY, EMINENT BRITISH
Fabian and Laborite, delivered the Holland Memorial Lectures at
King's College, London, in 1922. They were published in 1926 as
Religion and the Rise of Capitalism, a book which has had an
immense vogue. The Holland Lectures for 1949 were delivered by
Canon V. A. Demant, appearing three years later in book form as
Religion and the Decline of Capitalism. The present volume might
almost have been entitled *Religion and the Restoration of Capital-
ism,* except that the connotations I attach to the word "capitalism"
would be unacceptable to Tawney and Demant.

The confusion over terminology is well illustrated by a letter
which Demant received from George Bernard Shaw when the
1949 lecture series was announced. "Capitalism, far from decaying," writes Shaw, "has been carried to unpredecented magnitudes
in the Tennessee Valley and elsewhere, and is culminating in state
capitalism, alias communism, socialism, Fabianism. . . ." Intelligible discourse is impossible if words may be twisted to mean whatever the speaker wishes. Shaw, it may be inferred from the above
sentence, understands capitalism to mean large scale enterprise,
whether carried on under private or state auspices. Tawney and
Demant, both of whom are in the British Socialist tradition, accept
this dubious terminology, and add some thoughts of their own.
Capitalism, in their view, is the secular world outlook that has
spread over the West since the Reformation; it is the factory

system, the overweening pursuit of material advantage, the erosion of community ties, popular government; it is a rehearsal which sets the stage for socialism. Capitalism, in short, is the sum total of the impediments which prevent man from building himself a heaven on earth, and its overthrow is invested with religious sanctions.

My understanding of capitalism is quite different. I understand capitalism to mean the free economy, the market. Economics has to do with the efficient allocation of the planet's scarce goods so that human wants are met in the order of their urgency, and with a minimum wastage of time, energy, and resources. People's buying habits provide the clues needed by entrepreneurs to tell them what to produce, and in what quantities, colors, sizes, and so on. The goods people actually produce and consume in a given era will depend on several factors: the geographical setting, the level of technological and related skills, popular taste, the prevailing ethical code, the religious outlook. Economic habits will be altered as these several factors change for better or worse. Their unfettered interplay constitutes the market economy, provided—and this is a critical proviso—the society is free.

If a society enjoys political liberty a certain pattern of economic activity will be precipitated, depending on historical circumstances and the factors cited above. This pattern is capitalism, the posture assumed by economic actions when men are free; this is the free economy, and it doesn't have to be made to work, it works of its own accord unless it is prevented from functioning.

The free economy—or economic liberty—is an idea at the same level of importance as free speech or freedom of the press. Now, no one accuses the believer in free speech of endorsing gossip, slander, or demagogic oratory. Nor is the champion of freedom of the press accused of endorsing everything that appears in print— unintelligible poetry, bad novels, uplift literature, socialist tracts, pornography. But the believer in economic liberty is often accused of defending every evil, illegal, tasteless action that occurs in the business sector of society. The accusation is gratuitous. In point of fact, economic liberty is justified by the same arguments, *mutatis mutandis*, that justify intellectual and religious liberty.

These, then, are some of the themes to be expanded in the pages that follow. The book deals also with one aspect of the contemporary ecclesiastical sphere, the penchant of certain church officials to make dubious pronouncements on economic and political issues in the name of the Church. Christian social action, as it is called today, has the effect of making the Church subordinate to transient schemes for reforming society, and Christian Socialism is a contradiction in terms. But there are connections between Christianity and the free economy, and it will be our task to trace them.

It is a pleasure to acknowledge my indebtedness to the authors whose words are cited herein, and I am grateful to their publishers who freely granted permission to quote. My best thanks also to Mr. Theodore Lit, then senior editor of Arlington House, who broached the idea for this book. My main debt, however, is to my secretary, Mrs. R. H. Norrell, whose persistent nagging gradually overcame this author's inertia.

Introduction

THIS BOOK DEALS WITH THE PROBLEM OF THE PROPER ORDER-
ing of our economic affairs within the framework supplied by
Christian values. The science of economics does not come
equipped with a built-in value system, nor do economic activities
as such generate one. Economics, its most eminent practitioners
inform us, is a value-free science; it is a science of means, not one
of ends.[1] The economist as economist does not tell people how
they ought to behave, or what ends they ought to pursue. He
accepts whatever goals or values people profess and merely tries
to figure out the most efficient and direct means for attaining the
stated goals or values. It is not the economist's province to help
people decide between guns and butter, between houses and automobiles and education; but once they decide what they want, his
job is to tell them how to economize on means so that they may
attain the ends they seek with minimum wastage of scarce resources.

A science which proclaims itself value-free presupposes that
someone is paying sufficient attention to the value structure to
maintain it in good repair. For man is a valuing, freely choosing,

---

1. Von Mises, *Human Action*, p. 10. "It is true that economics is a theoretical science
and as such abstains from any judgment of value. It is not its task to tell people what ends
they should aim at. It is a science of the means to be applied for the attainment of ends
chosen, not, to be sure, a science of the choosing of ends. Ultimate decisions, the valuations
and the choosing of ends, are beyond the scope of any science. Science never tells a man
how he should act; it merely shows how a man must act if he wants to attain definite ends."

decision-making creature. He is constantly seeking to do good, as he understands it, and avoid that which he regards as evil. He is forever rating his preferences, always seeking the better alternative. The moralist and the religionist are concerned with the question of what values men ought to honor, with the highest good for man, with shaping and reshaping the current system of values into harmony with evolving insights into human nature and destiny. The branch of philosophy which deals with values is known as axiology, and while the economist is content merely to record men's preferences and their implications, the axiologist argues that men ought to prefer some things to others. Neither discipline can function in isolation; ends and means cannot be pried apart in real life. The specialist in means counts on someone else to handle the problem of ends, and those who deal in the realm of ends need those able to fit appropriate means to the chosen end.[2]

Numerous books and pamphlets on Christian Socialism have been written during the past century. Associations and parties have been founded to further the view that when Christianity is applied to the social problems of an industrial society, the result equates with socialism. A war cry of the English Christian Socialists in the 1880s was "Christianity is the religion of which Socialism is the practice." It was argued by a leader in this movement, the Reverend Stewart D. Headlam, that the Church Catechism may be regarded as a manual of socialism. There are still Christian Socialists, but in a society that has adopted the major planks of the Socialist Party, there is no longer a need for a minority to insist on what the majority takes for granted.

Christian Socialism—when the imperatives of a socialist order are understood—is a contradiction in terms, as will be demonstrated during the course of this book; it is rank folly. But any attempt to confound Christian Socialism by constructing a hybrid of the same order—Christian Capitalism—would be a similar piece of folly.

In short, the answer to Christian Socialism is not to wave the flag for Christian Capitalism. In general, opponents of the Christian Socialist movement have not been guilty of identifying their

2. Oakeshott, *Rationalism in Politics*, p. 248. "Moral conduct is art, not nature; it is the exercise of an acquired skill. But the skill here is not that of knowing how to get what we want with the least expenditure of energy, but knowing how to behave as we *ought* to behave: the skill, not of desiring, but of approving and of doing what is approved."

religious faith with a particular formula for organizing economic
and political life. There has never been an organized Christian
Capitalist movement, and no slogan has ever appeared saying that
Christianity is the religion of which capitalism is the practice. The
argument has been advanced, however, that acceptance of the
main features of the Christian philosophy implies a free society
and a limited government, with economic affairs organized in
terms of the market; and this book spells out that argument at
some length.

Only like things may be profitably compared, and a moment's
thought convinces us that Christianity and capitalism[3] do not
belong to the same order of things. Christianity is a total philosophy of life, offering a reading of human nature and destiny in terms
of its version of the ultimate nature of the cosmos—the conviction
that the universe is intentional, and that man shares in God's
mighty purpose. Communism, likewise, proclaims itself to be a
total philosophy of life, one which rejects the Christian view of
men and things at every level. Capitalism, by contrast, is not an
ideology. Capitalism is a way of organizing economic life for the
efficient meeting of our creaturely and material needs, and this
necessarily implies a theory of government. Any political theory
which releases government from the traditional safeguards of individual liberty and gives it a free hand to direct and control the
economy is incompatible with capitalism. Capitalism, or the free
economy, is not a *Weltanschauung,* but—being in the realm of
means—it does need one. Since the time of Adam Smith, the free
economy has been championed by men who have not been able
to agree as to its metaphysics, the ultimate foundations on which
it is properly based. Some have been theists, others have not; but
all have accepted the main tenets of classical liberalism, whose
cultural values presupposed the traditional outlooks of Christendom. The free market way of organizing economic affairs did not
emerge in China, India, or Africa, but in the West. The cultural
values emerging out of Confucianism, Hinduism, or Animism did

3. I share Wilhelm Roepke's dislike of the term "capitalism." He writes, "As coined and
circulated by Marxism, the term has retained up to the present so much of its hate-filled
significance and class-struggle overtones that its usefulness for the purposes of scientific
discussion has become extremely questionable. In addition, it provides us with only a very
vague notion of the real essence of our economic system. Instead of promoting understanding, it merely arouses the emotions and obscures the truth." *Economics of the Free Society,*
p. 259.

not supply the basic ingredients for the initial appearance of the free economy, nor has the market way of life been successfully transplanted to these cultures. Capitalism was an offshoot of the eighteenth-century Enlightenment; the Enlightenment presupposes the Scientific Revolution and the breakup of medieval society during the sixteenth and seventeenth centuries; which in turn presupposes the heritage of the classical and biblical worlds.

The modern world was launched at the time of the French Revolution, confident of its ability to conquer the natural world and to organize the economic and political spheres on terms supplied from within those spheres. The improvement of man's material circumstances, and the perfect adaptation of man to society and society to nature was the goal. Religion, on the other hand, is premised on the conviction that a divine order transcends and interpenetrates the orders of nature and society. This faith was pretty well displaced from the nineteenth-century view of life, and it is a negligible concern of the modern temper. Communism is based squarely on the denial of an otherworldly dimension in human affairs; it promises a redemption of the social order strictly in terms of this world, a utopia at the end of history.[4]

There are able studies which relate the rise of capitalism to antecedent religious conditions of the proper sort; corollary studies explore the emergence of Marxism out of the secularism of the nineteenth and twentieth centuries. Nevertheless, there are still some who argue that capitalism functions optimally within a secularist ethos. When men turn their back on spiritual values, it is urged, they deal more competently with their material concerns. Otherworldly considerations, argue these economists, are excess baggage in the workaday world, rendering consumers that much less efficient in their striving to better their economic circumstances. The overriding aim of every man is, after all, to advance his own material wellbeing, and any effort on his part to meet dubious spiritual claims is wasted energy and a needless handicap. Merely demonstrate to the people that the market economy means more material comforts for the masses of men and they will eagerly embrace capitalism.

4. "In an age prepared for by nearly 2,000 years of Christianity," writes Bertram Wolfe, "but in which the faith of millions has grown dim and the altar seemed to them vacant of its image, Marxism arose to offer a fresh vision. . . . History was to be given a new meaning, a new goal, and a new end in Time. . . . At last man would become as God, master of his own destiny, maker of his own future, conscious architect of his world."

The modern world finds this line of argument singularly unconvincing, and so do I. Everyone who has scanned the literature of economics since Smith is aware that this science has been expanded, refined, and popularized decade by decade. But the greater the progress of economic science the less secure has the market economy become, not only in distant parts of the earth where it was taken by Westerners, but even in its homeland. The United States, once regarded as the capitalist nation par excellence, is now the world's model welfare state. A planned economy, this book will argue, is almost impossible to avoid, given a secular ethos; whereas Christian values, properly understood and implemented by the appropriate economic and political means, generate the free society and the market economy.

A planned economy is integral to Communism, and a planned economy is the antithesis of the market economy, or capitalism. By the same token, the opposite of Communism is not capitalism; like may be compared only with like. Communism may be properly contrasted only with things of a like order, and this means only with competing world views. These competing world views are the great religions, which, practically speaking, mean Christianity and Judaism for people of our culture. Several times in the course of world history, large numbers of people have come to share a *Weltanschauung* and to participate in its cultic manifestations. Thus we have the great faiths of mankind; Buddhism, Christianity, Confucianism, Hinduism, Islam, and Judaism, with an appropriate culture stemming from each. Pondering the mystery of existence, each of these religions posits a divine order that transcends this world of time and space (an inward order, in the case of Buddhism); a realm of Being in contrast to this world of change and decay, the realm of becoming.

Communism, too, offers its faithful a *Weltanschauung*, one that pretends to be scientific. The Marxian world view differs from that of the historic religions by rejecting the reality of things not seen. Communism is a peculiar sort of religion, being based on a denial of that which every previous religion has affirmed, namely, God, the divine ground of existence. The world view of Communism is wholly earthbound, and includes the planning of economic life as a necessary feature, along with totalitarian political controls. Suppose that we reject this world view on every level, and embrace its opposite. This commits us, on the economic level, to the market economy; and on the political level, to the limited state of classical liberal theory. But where does it leave us on the philosophical level?

It leaves one group, which vociferously champions capitalism, right with the Marxists. These people are dogmatic atheists, proclaiming that man's life is the standard, individual self-interest the motor. Other exponents of the free market soft pedal the atheism, regarding religious affiliation as a matter of taste and, in any event, irrelevant to the improvement of man's material circumstances. The consensus is that an earthly utopia is within man's capacity to achieve, and that men will achieve it by the simple expedient of turning the market loose so as to maximize their productive activities. When this happens, abundance will be achieved and men will live happily ever after.

The intellectual baggage of an era, its mythologies and its things taken for granted, are shared by most men of the period. The idea of inevitable progress has been an article of faith in the modern world, and it is part of the creed of most contemporary champions of the free market. Day by day in every way things are getting better and better, and by and by when society is organized for maximum production men will attain the full happiness of which they are capable, in an earthly paradise. The paradox is that this is a conclusion impossible to reach from the premises of economic science. The economist's basic task has to do with the planet's scarce goods, which must be parceled out somehow to creatures urged on by insatiable needs and wants. In the economist's vocabulary, a thing is a good if someone wants it, and it is an economic good if there is not enough of it to go around. Economics is the discipline that deals with goods in short supply. But scarce resources are only half the problem. Scarcity would be a problem even if man were the kind of creature who is as easily satisfied with half a loaf, or with a single slice of bread, as with the whole. But no, he wants the whole loaf, and when he has that he wants a jug of wine, a book of verses, ad infinitum. Man is a creature of insatiable wants, which are quieted only by death. This is the other, the active half of the economist's problem. The allocation of scarce resources among creatures whose demands are without limit poses a problem which is forever insoluble. This is perhaps what Roepke is getting at when he declares that "Economics should be an anti-ideological, anti-utopian, disillusioning science."[5]

When he is candid, the economist must address his contemporaries somewhat as follows: "Scarcity is a built-in feature of human life on this planet. There are institutionally organized, artificial scarcities of this or that commodity, and I can help you get rid of these; but no conceivable organization or reorganization of society will ever result in abundance—except relatively speaking. The market economy is more productive than any alternative, but that is the best I can promise you. To the end of time you will never have enough. No one is to blame for this; it is in the nature of the human condition that this is so. This is a fact of life."

As a sales pitch aimed at a generation that is incurably romantic, this is not guaranteed to move the product. Everybody "knows," and has "known" ever since the French Revolution, that man's proper end is the perfected temporal life of man, and that the brave new world is just around the next corner but one. Men might take diametrically opposed views as to the appropriate means for reaching this goal, but that the goal was within human reach hardly anyone denied. The popular solution is to harness new techniques in science and technology to democratic political processes. Turning everything over to the market is the other answer. The plain truth of the matter, revealed by economic analysis, runs head-on into the ideology of inevitable progress toward the kingdom of heaven on earth—and the ideology triumphs almost every time.

And so it must, unless we raise our sights. Man is undeniably part of the natural order; most of the laws of physics and chemistry that apply to things and to the lesser creatures apply also to him. Man is also involved in a social order, and part of what each man is or becomes is due to the cultural influences playing on him from his society. This much no one can deny. But does man also participate in a third order, radically differing from the other two, the divine order? If so, and if he is at home in his eternal nature, then the defeats in this life can be taken in stride; he does not expect an earthly utopia, and the utterances of the economists on this point square with his expectations. In the absence of this religious conviction, however, the belief in unending material progress will tend to take over, as it has done in modern times. The plain

5. Roepke, *The Humane Economy*, p. 150.

teaching of economics about pemanent scarcity can find no lodgment in the mentality which embraces one panacea after another and waits expectantly for the earthly utopia to arrive.

The religious conviction of a divine order comes to us in the West from the faith of the Bible. Christianity is not a religion of pure spirituality. God is a Spirit, but his creature, man, who is enjoined to "worship Him in spirit and in truth," is emphatically not a disembodied soul. Man is not merely a spiritual being; he is a spiritual being who eats, feels the cold, suffers pain, seeks to order his communities, and works to improve his material estate. The individual person is in the physical body and in society because God created him this kind of creature; and because God does nothing in vain, some cosmic purpose is served by our involvement in things earthly as well as by our participation in things spiritual. Augustine observed that "we are here schooled for life eternal," which means, I take it, that optimum biological, social, and personal life in the City of Man is our training ground for possible citizenship in the City of God. Fulfill the requirements of the former and we may get the latter as an undeserved bonus.

PART ONE

CHAPTER 1

Christian Socialism: A Profile

THE GROWTH OF POLITICAL LIBERTY IN THE WEST IS ATTRIBUT-able, in large measure, to the cultural transformations effected over the centuries by the religious faith of the West. This is not to say that those who struggled to be free could always count on church-men as allies; all too frequently, alas, the Church was leagued with the secular authorities in suppressing popular bids for individual and group immunities against governmental power. But those who fought for freedom in society had learned from their faith that the God of the Bible willed liberty for His creatures, and so they demanded conditions of outer freedom to match the inner liberty stressed in the Gospels.

Opposition to the powers of the world, based on a claim to natural liberty, came to a head on this continent in the eighteenth century. The colonial churches played a significant role in the real American revolution, a revolution in ideas which sought to give form and political structure to the concept of individual rights under a Sovereign Creator. The European movements of libera-tion during the period of the Enlightenment, while avowedly secu-lar, took much of their ethical emphasis and idealism from Christianity. The colonists were influenced by the Enlightenment, but resisted its anticlericalism. Anticlericalism develops as a senti-ment or a party wherever the Church goes officially into the poli-tics of a nation.

The colonists didn't have to contend with a politicalized

Church, and later wrote the First Amendment to prevent such a development. The eighteenth-century pulpit in America stood staunchly for freedom. ("The Americans," wrote Alexis de Tocqueville, "combine the notions of Christianity and liberty so intimately in their minds that it is impossible to make them conceive the one without the other."[1]

The framers of our basic political documents and the people for whom they spoke were end products of the long religious and cultural heritage of Christendom. They willed religious, political, and social liberty as a necessary corollary of their religious commitment, and our relatively free society was, in part, a projection of the teaching of the colonial churches.

The free society is now under alternating siege and attack from several quarters. The tide that once flowed in the direction of human emancipation has turned, and now moves in the opposite direction, toward a collectivized existence in which individual lives are submerged for the greater glory of the State. It is bad enough that there are powerful secular movements working toward this end, each with a devoted or fanatical following—communism, fascism, welfarism, and others. But it is worse that influential segments of the Church now add religious sanction to the secular trend toward the monolithic State. The spiritual wellsprings of the American revolutionary idea, its churches, now appear to be feeders of an antifreedom ideology. There are historical antecedents for this, but not in America. "In France," wrote Tocqueville, "I had almost always seen the spirit of religion and the spirit of freedom marching in opposite directions. But in America I found they were intimately united and that they reigned in common over the same country."[2] This appears to be true no longer. Influential ecclesiastical voices swell the chorus of collectivism and put the churches on record against the free society. This is what is so disconcerting to the average church member, as well as to students of the problem.

No nation has fully lived up to the principles it aspires to, and the United States is no exception. But in the aspirations of this country there converged such ancient ideals as personal liberty, the rule of law, constitutional government, private property, and

1. Tocqueville, *Democracy in America*, p. 306.
2. Ibid., p. 308.

freedom of economic enterprise. All of these, indeed, are facets of a single concern: that no man shall be another's victim. The aspirations which were, to some extent at least, embodied in our institutions, had a carrier—the Church. Religious convictions about man's inviolable soul, the sanctity of private conscience, and the belief that man's final allegiance is to God rather than to any state or collective spelled out, on the social level, the ideals of equal justice before the law, limited government, and individiual rights. This meant a gradual widening of the average man's area of political and economic freedom. The original American equation had a built-in religious dimension; our premises about the nature and destiny of man, our understanding of right and wrong, the code governing our manners and customs all came to us as part of our religious heritage. "Religion," Tocqueville said of our ancestors, ". . . is the first of their political institutions."[3]

Human nature being what it is, we expect to see an embarrassing gap between profession and practice. The high quality of the American dream has not prevented American politicians from behaving much like politicians elsewhere; it has not prevented American businessmen from seeking political favors at the expense of their competitors; it has not prevented Americans from joining pressure groups in order to get something for nothing; and ordinary citizens exhibit a kill-the-umpire mentality in many departments of life. All this we could more or less take in our stride. These deviations from our aspirations and standards were criticized throughout the nineteenth century from the platform and pulpit as violations of the American dream of liberty and justice for all. But no longer. What we once did from lack of principle we are now doing on principle.

At the heart of the nineteenth-century malpractices was the opening of the public treasury to private interests: taxes for all, subsidies for a selected few. The twentieth-century refinement is to reduce our principles to the level of our malpractices. Heavy taxes on everyone, followed by selective political redistribution of wealth is the operational procedure of the welfare state, just as it is the operational procedure of every other variety of collectivism: communism, fascism, new dealism, and all the rest.

Modern collectivism is deadlier than old-fashioned tyranny by

3. Ibid., p. 305.

reason of being a "democratic despotism." Modern collectivism
has its roots in the eighteenth century, as did classical liberalism.
The early advocates of collectivism believed that theirs was a
movement of liberation, a logical completion of the emancipating
fervors of the Enlightenment. To assess the reasons why this early
idealism inevitably turned sour and brought forth the bitter fruit
of twentieth-century totalitarianism would take us far afield. This
has happened, however. These movements which have so brutal-
ized modern life still attract a few intelligent and sensitive men
because they contain enticing ingredients left over from their origins. These ingredients, however, now exert no more influence on
direction or results than is exerted on the tides by a bright pebble
caught up in a breaking wave and flung on a beach. "Leviathan
lives and moves before our eyes," writes Alfred Cobban about this
phenomenon, "all the more dangerous because in infancy he was
called liberty."[4]

A pronouncement or resolution on some vexed economic or
political question issues from church body or council. A typical
reaction is, "Why doesn't the Church stick to its knitting and stop
meddling in politics?" Such a reaction is more the mark of exasperation than a comment about the proper relation between religion
and culture. The exasperation is due, in part, to the fact that the
pronouncements are so often lacking in expertise and finesse; and
in part, because they are issued with fake thunder and a "Made
on Sinai" label, even though they may be obviously partisan and
carry echoes of some party line or current fad.

Disillusionment with this kind of ecclesiastical preoccupation is
articulately voiced in an old editorial in *Fortune* magazine, written
by a layman. "The first result is," he writes, "a rise in materialism.
If the Churches merely come down to our level we will lack
spiritual guidance in meeting our material problems. Second, so
long as the Church pretends, or assumes to preach, absolute values, but actually preaches relative and secondary values, it will
merely hasten this process of disintegration. . . . The voice of the
Church today, we find, is the echo of our own voices. And the
result of this experience, already manifest, is disillusionment. . . .
The way out is the sound of a voice, not our voice, but a voice
coming from something not ourselves, in the existence of which

4. Cobban, *In Search of Humanity*, p. 193.

we cannot disbelieve. It is the earthly task of the pastors to hear this voice, to cause us to hear it, and to tell us what it says. If they cannot hear it, or if they fail to tell us, we, as laymen, are utterly lost. Without it we are no more capable of saving the world than we were of creating it in the first place."

This contains a tall order, obviously, and in fairness to church-men and church bodies it must be said that they conceive their resolutions and pronouncements, adequately publicized and brought to the attention of lawmakers, as a discharge of Christian responsibility in and to society. Politics, they would say, *is* the church's business, or part of it. They are quite wrong, of course. Religion is the Church's business, and a just order in society is one of the Church's concerns. Is there a way to resolve the impasse between the social actionist position and its critics who urge the Church to stick to spiritual matters? As a matter of fact there is, for each of the above positions is partly right in what it affirms, partly wrong in what it denies. A signpost pointing beyond this impasse is offered in the following observation by the late Dean Inge: "The advance of civilization is, in truth, a sort of by-product of Christianity—not its chief aim; but we can appeal to history to support us that this progress is most stable and genuine when it is a by-product of a lofty and unworldly idealism."[5]

Christianity has been accurately called a religion of world and life affirmation. Christianity is not "other worldly" even though it does stress the dimension of eternity. Its Founder could not reduce the number of commandments below two; the first expressing a man's obligations toward God, the second toward his neighbor. Thomas Aquinas rendered this as follows: "Man has a natural inclination toward knowing the truth about God, and toward living in society."

Christianity, in short, has cultural as well as personal signifi-cance. Historically it seeped into the morals, manners, laws, insti-tutions, ideals, and customs of the West to transform Europe into Christendom. The contemporary Catholic theologian, Josef Pieper, has characterized Western culture as "theologically grounded worldliness."

The most obvious outward trend in religion in this century is caught by such words as "consolidation," "unification," and

5. Inge, *Personal Religion and The Life of Devotion*, p. 84.

"merger." Getting together makes a good deal of sense in some cases. If a denominational split was originally precipitated by a theological quarrel, now patched up, there's no reason for not joining forces. A new denomination formed to accommodate immigrants who spoke only a foreign language has little excuse for separate existence when the present communicants speak nothing but English. We tend to be embarrassed by the silly denominational rivalries of a former day and rightfully seek new ways of Christian cooperation, which we can do, while still recognizing that liturgical and theological differences are meaningful to those concerned.

The unification movement goes beyond the closing of irrational divisions, however, beyond mere cooperation between Christians; it is largely in the hands of centralizers who view the large, monolithic church body as a means for effecting revolutionary change. These churchmen appear to believe that we can advance toward the Kingdom by constructing the kind of compact ecclesiastical structure which would convert Protestantism from a scattering of churches and denominations into a Voice to be reckoned with politically. The result is the ecumenical movement and the World Council of Churches. In the United States, it is the National Council of Churches. An official statement of the World Council of Churches reads: "One of the major forces which have drawn and held the Churches together in the ecumenical movement has been the necessity of their uniting in thought and action on the vast political, economic, and social problems of the modern world." Much the same set of incentives operated to launch the Federal Council of Churches in 1908, precursor of the National Council. Describing the beginnings of this organization, former Dean Liston Pope of Yale Divinity School writes approvingly of the social reform movements in this country early in the century and observes that "the Federal Council of Churches, in 1908, reflected these purposes and gave institutional form to efforts for their realization." The National Council of Churches carries on in much the same vein. During this half century each of the major denominations has spawned an official social action agency, each one premised on the notion that the free society has failed, and committed to the proposition that our basic need is for political controls on economic life. This church-sponsored program was similar to that of the Socialist Party, of which many influential churchmen are members.

This twentieth-century movement in the churches did not happen overnight. Two Church of England clergymen, F. D. Maurice and Charles Kingsley launched a movement called Christian Socialism in 1848, the year of *The Communist Manifesto*. Marx, in this document, referred to the rival movement in derisive terms: "Christian Socialism is but the holy water with which the priest consecrates the heartburnings of the aristocrat." The Social Gospel took its rise in the United States after the Civil War. Numerically, its adherents were never a significant percentage of Protestant clergymen, and many of these were not parish ministers. Relatively few laymen in the churches had any inkling of what was going on behind the ecclesiastical scenes until 1948.

The ecumenical movement had its inception in 1910, but it was not until 1948 that the World Council of Churches had its formative meeting in Amsterdam. Here the century-old social actionist trend surfaced for all to see. "The Church should make clear that there are conflicts between Christianity and capitalism," reads a portion of one report. The churches should aim at a middle ground "something like the regime which the Labor Party is working out in Great Britain," a spokesman said.

The report kicked up a considerable stir, and it served to call attention to things that students of the subject had known all along —that articulate and skillful men, strategically located in official church bodies, on seminary faculties, and in editorial offices were pushing the socialist or semi-socialist line, especially during the bleak 1930s. A few were attracted to Communism.

Early in 1934 a social-interest questionnaire was sent to 100,499 clergymen. Replies were received from 20,870. Of this number 51 percent favored a "drastically reformed capitalism," and 28 percent or nearly 6,000 clergymen declared in favor of socialism. One hundred and twenty-three ministers favored the establishment of Communism of the Russian variety in America.

In the August 19, 1953, issue of *The Christian Century*, Reinhold Niebuhr wrote an article entitled "Communism and the Clergy." The piece was occasioned by a statement by Bishop Oxnam which made a sweeping denial of Communist influence in the churches. "Such a statement causes difficulties," said Niebuhr, "because there are in fact Communist sympathizers and fellow travelers in the Church. I wonder whether Bishop Oxnam ought not to have admitted this more freely. . . ."

Niebuhr goes on to assert, "it must be affirmed that there have never been many explicit Stalinists in the churches. . . . Nevertheless, there are a few and we ought to admit it." How does the seemingly incongruous union between Stalinism and Christianity occur, we ask, and Niebuhr answers, "The pathetic clerical Stalinism could not have developed except against the background of a very considerable Marxist dogmatism in the 'liberal' wing of Protestant Churches."

How shall we explain this "very considerable Marxist dogmatism" among certain liberal Protestants? The horror of Orwell's 1984 society was not the meticulous tyranny of Big Brother nor the occasional tortures; the real horror lay in the fact that Big Brother's victims came through their ordeals loving Big Brother! There is a monstrous kind of fascination in power; powerful men and movements exert an obscene attraction on those who scramble to be where the wave of the future is cresting. Communism, from the date of its political ascendancy in Russia in 1918 to its domination over much of the world today, represents a success story of sorts. And success is hard to argue with. A successful movement or philosophy exerts a gravitational pull on those who want to be where the action is, and so there are many who seek an accommodation between Communism and Christianity. This is not to be confused with a détente between the Soviet Union and the United States, or a carving out of respective spheres of influence between the two nations. That is another matter, importantly but peripherally related to a projected philosophical rapprochement between two seemingly antithetical world views.

Marx and Engels embraced atheism with religious devotion, and the promulgation of atheism continues to be the established "religion" of the Communist state. Given the premises, there would seem to be good ground for the antireligious thrust of Communism. If dialectical materialism is a valid explanation of the nature of things, then the propositions of high, spiritual religion are false. If every man owes first allegiance to the State, then the doctrine that a man's primary loyalty is to God is treasonable. If the life of each social unit is to be politically planned for him, then the masses must be disabused of the idea that each person has inherent, God-given rights and responsibilities for his own life. If each man's life is for others and for the State, there can be no tolerance for the contrary belief that God has made us for Himself and the proper ordering of our souls is an obligation we owe Him. Communism embraces the idea of inevitable linear progress and holds out the promise of an earthly paradise for the faithful, to be achieved within history by human, mainly political, agencies. Christian thought, on the other hand, maintains that man is involved in a transcendent dimension, and although the Christian seeks a more just social order here and now, he is not to expect fulfillment except in that other order of reality beyond time and beyond space.

On all counts, then, Christianity and Communism are polar opposites; it may be said that they are enemies. We are not speaking here of military or battlefield enemies, but of two sets of ideas which contradict each other at every point and at every level. Should a member of the Communist Party suffer an automobile accident, it goes without saying that the Christian has an obligation to bind up his wounds or render such other aid as the immediate situation calls for. But love for the enemy most assuredly does not call for an accommodation to ideas deemed false. Marxian Communism is a false philosophy (to say nothing of its practice); it is a misreading of the universe and man's place therein, it misconceives the nature of man and his destiny, its politics are despotic and its economics unproductive. Nevertheless, it's "On with the Dialogue!" insofar as many Catholic and Protestant theologians are concerned. There are outstanding exceptions, of course. The renowned Johns Hopkins archeologist and Biblical scholar, W. F. Albright, has no illusions about the nature of Communism, or of what would happen to Christianity if some sort of rapprochement were effected: "Christianity," he writes, "stands today at one of the most critical junctures of history, facing in Communism its deadliest foe since the end of pagan Rome." But there are other theologians who plaintively ask, as did the president of the nation's wealthiest seminary: "Why must they conclude that there is a conflict between Christianity and Communism?"

Protestant, Catholic, and secular intellectuals warmly received Roger Garaudy, a leading French Communist theoretician during his visit to the United States several years ago, when he spoke at eight universities. Garaudy, at the moment, is the most sought after Communist for those who wish to engage in a "dialogue," and for all one knows Garaudy may honestly believe that some sort of *modus vivendi* is possible between Christian theologians and Party theoreticians; or, he may be trying to con these church-men. Likewise, those Christians who seek a "dialogue" may well be mistaken as to the nature of Communism—and/or Christianity.

But if there is illusion at this summit level, the conflicting reali-ties stand forth pretty clearly at the level where people live. The International Documentation and Information Centre in Holland (INTERDOC) reprints an article from the Russian paper *Kommu-nist*, No. 15, October, 1965. It is entitled "Individual Treatment of the Faithful Through Atheist Propaganda," by A. Judin, party committee secretary of the city of Schuja. The article is addressed to the need for more skillful evangelism on the part of propagan-dists for atheism. Although "the religious ideology has always been the anti-pole to a scientifically founded ideology, represented by communism," there still remain some religious remnants in the land of the Soviets, and one hears their counterarguments. "Unfor-tunately, the preparation of a part of our propagandists and agita-tors for atheist work is very unsatisfactory; they are not familiar with the modern manifestation of religion and its capacity to adapt itself to the new trend of the times." The propagandist must, therefore, develop his intellectual skills, but in addition he "must show much tact and sincere interest in the lot of the person, if he wants to be successful in his atheist work."

The argument is concluded when Mr. Judin "underlines the communist atheist thesis, that religion undermines morals and, through the bonds to a higher authority outside humanity, alien-ates man from an active participation in the interests and duties of his environment." The antithesis between Communist and Christian theory could not be more clearly revealed. "Religion undermines morals!" In Marxian theory, the moral man is one who carries out party orders without flinching, even though the orders might involve murder, theft, and lies. In Christian theory, the moral man seeks to carry out God's will and obey His com-mandments to shun murder, theft, and false witness. The second portion of Mr. Judin's indictment involves the order of a man's priorities. The Christian is told to seek first the Kingdom of God, and his conscience directs him to obey God rather than men when the two conflict. But for the Communist, "the party of humanity" and national solidarity come before all else, and for the true Communist, there *is* nothing else.

Niebuhr, the theologian is often at odds with Niebuhr, the reformer. It would not be surmised from his observations quoted above that one of the principal contributors to this "considerable Marxist dogmatism in the 'liberal' wing of the Protestant churches" has been Niebuhr himself. He has called Marxism ". . . the only possible property system compatible with the necessities of a technical age." He wrote this in 1935, but the book has recently been republished, presumably with his sanction.

Niebuhr rejects the moonshine of Marxian metaphysics, even while embracing Marx's economic and political nostrums. But it is indeed a fact that Communist economic and political practices do things to people, on principle, which can be "justified" only by a materialistic view of man. The individual does not count, in Marxist "theology"; he has no inherent right to his own personal goals. In its sociology, as a consequence, he is regarded as a mere unit to be manipulated on behalf of some "five-year plan" or other national goal. Communism, in other words, is all of a piece; adopt its metaphysics and, in a technological age, we get the planned-from-the-top-down society. Start on the social level by putting any collectivist principle into operation and it breeds more of the same until eventually the society becomes fully collectivized. The many parts of society are delicately interrelated; start by fixing the price of a quart of milk and the glass industry will be told what it must charge for bottles, the wages of delivery men must be regulated, the dairy industry controlled, and so on, until the logical result, in time, is the totally regimented economy, or socialism. "Compulsory labor, with death as the final penalty, is the keystone of Socialism," wrote George Bernard Shaw, in *Labor Monthly*, October, 1921. What must be done to people deliberately, as public policy, under collectivism can be rationalized only by some form of materialism which discounts the intrinsic worth of the individual person.

Communism has been called a Christian heresy. The point is not well taken. If one must talk in these terms he is on safer ground if he affirms that liberalism is a Christian heresy and Communism is a liberal heresy. In any event, the mentality which prevails in social action circles is willing to allow that Communism is a permissible deviation for a mid—twentieth—century Christian. A similar mentality once sanctioned the split level living which permitted a man to be an earnest Christian with one part of himself and a kindly slave holder with all the rest. This tolerance was naively voiced by Theodore Gill when he was an editor of *The Christian Century.* Addressing the Czech theologian, Hromadka, a leading Christian apologist for the Soviet regime, he referred to ". . . those of us who knew your passionately conscientious commitment to Marxist analysis and prescriptions and who knew you well enough never to question your Christian integrity in these commitments." Someday, perhaps, the same tolerance will be extended to those whose Christian integrity still inspires their devotion to political and economic liberty.

The "very considerable Marxist dogmatism" to which Niebuhr refers, coupled with the lust to appear politically relevant and socially significant, has lured many theologians and churchmen into competition for the post of court chaplain to the New Deal–Great Society trend.

The dean of the Pacific School of Religion writes that he and many of his associates were members of the Socialist Party during the 1930s, convinced that the New Deal didn't go far enough. But "looking back now (1956) we can at last appreciate that the Democratic New Deal which we so heartily despised was getting done exactly what we really wanted to have done."

The dean of Boston University School of Theology, writing in *The Socialist Call,* calls attention to the "amazing correlation between the social ideals lifted up by the churches and the positions taken in the platforms of the political parties." The social ideals of the churches "tended, where deviations were clear, toward the Socialist position." When these social ideals are finally clothed with reality, writes the late Alexander Miller of Stanford University in a little book entitled *The Christian Significance of Karl Marx,* the Christian will rejoice "that by the mechanism of government he can feed the hungry, clothe the naked, and love his brethren in practical ways." We may have all this and heaven too, according to a Canadian theologian writing in the symposium entitled *Towards the Christian Revolution,* edited by Scott and

Vlastos: "Until Christians learn to understand and apply the lessons of Marxism," he declares, "they cannot enter the Kingdom of Heaven." (p. 139)

All men of good will want to remove impediments that might hinder people from bettering their circumstances. Students of the subject of wages—the sum total of economic satisfactions—agree with Ludwig von Mises that "The only means to raise wage rates is to raise the productivity of labor by increasing the per-head quota of capital invested and improving the methods of production. . . . There are no means by which the general standard of living can be raised other than by accelerating the increase of capital as compared with population." A general increase in social wellbeing is one thing, and religion should applaud progress along these lines; quite different is church support mustered behind special privilege, behind the economic enhancement of one segment of society at the expense of other groups or to the detriment of society as a whole. This is what has occurred in the case of the churches and the labor union monopolies. The uncritical support which many churchmen lavish upon the drive for power by union leaders reveals the extent to which some theologians are willing to shelve economic, political, ethical, and even religious considerations whenever required in order to further a doctrinaire program of social reform. "I do not like to see the clergy," wrote the Very Reverend William Ralph Inge, "who were monarchists under a strong monarchy, and oligarchs under the oligarchy, tumbling over each other in their eagerness to become court chaplains to King Demos. The black-coated advocates of spoliation are not a nice lot."[6]

The alliance between labor union officials and churchmen comes to a sort of head in the National Council of Churches General Committee of the Department of the Church and Economic Life which contains, in addition to churchmen of liberal political views, no fewer than eighteen salaried union officials! Just how impartial is "In Search of Maturity in Industrial Relations," a recent National Council booklet on the steel strike? How nonpartisan is it possible to make any of the N.C.C. deliverances on the social problems that bedevil us when they issue from a department so biased?

Official church bodies have long lent their support to unionism,

6. Inge, *Vale*, p. 88.

in the mistaken belief that the key to economic progress is not increased production, but increased organization. The special interests of union labor are identified with the general interests of society by many men in the ecclesiastical hierarchy. John C. Bennett points out that ". . . the large scale economic group to which the churches during the last half century have given most support is the labor movement . . . This interest in the labor movement has been characteristic of the national leaders of the denominations, of the Federal Council of Churches, and of others who have been most articulate in interpreting Christian social ethics."

Our current labor union problems stem in large measure from the legal privileges and immunities granted to unions in a series of national laws beginning with the Norris–LaGuardia Act of 1932. In an effort to protect themselves against labor union abuses, several states have passed so-called Right-to-Work laws. It is possible to discuss the efficacy of these laws to accomplish their intended purpose, but it reveals the slant of mind of prominent churchmen on this matter to see how the matter is approached by a very vocal Methodist Bishop. Among those who sponsor Right-to-Work laws, said the late Bishop G. Bromley Oxnam, are "greedy and undemocratic powers . . . The public is being deceived by the machinations of these stupid men." Right-to-Work laws, he concluded, "are a dangerous proposal, conceived in hypocrisy, and proclaimed in Pharasaic deceit." They are, adds Dean Walter Muelder of Boston University School of Theology, "a virtual conspiracy of the crafty, the ignorant, or the misguided."

This is the use of the smear technique, it exhibits a complete lack of Christian charity, and its effect is to prevent any intelligent discussion of the pressing problem of irresponsible union power.

In addition to the strength that union labor displays in official church circles, it also operates in ecclesiastical circles unofficially. There is, for instance, The Religion and Labor Council of America, Inc. This is an interfaith organization with Catholic, Jewish, and Protestant clergymen on its board. It publishes both a monthly and a weekly, and sponsors conferences at which union spokesmen present their case to clergymen and seminar students. And labor has its own program to influence churchmen. Oldtime social actionist Charles Webber, who was ordained Minister to Labor by Bishop Oxnam, operates out of an office in the new AFL-CIO building in Washington. As a result of these efforts unionism is sometimes invested with messianic significance. The Methodist Bishops in 1955, in an Episcopal Address to the General Conference, regretted that "all too few churchmen see in labor a worldwide movement that means a new social order as truly as the coming of the machine meant the passing of feudalism."

The real meaning of unionism, and the false premises on which its tactics are based, are spelled out elsewhere to my satisfaction; the ends it proclaims cannot be attained by the means it employs. They are a modern version of the old system of political privilege —statutory advantage for itself at the nation's expense. But even if the labor movement were soundly based, economically, ethically, and politically, it should not be singled out by the Church for special favor; and neither, of course, should business, or agriculture, or any other segment of society. "It is of crucial importance that the Church, acting corporately, should not commit itself to any particular policy," wrote the late Archbishop of Canterbury, William Temple. "The Church is committed to the everlasting Gospel and to the Creeds which formulate it; it must never commit itself to an ephemeral program of detailed action."[7] This is the crux of the matter.

Religion must not turn its back on the common concerns of life, nor allow itself to be spiritualized out of all relevance to the issues of freedom, justice, and mercy, nor allow evil to go unrebuked. But this is far different from the all too common practice of identifying the Church's mission with a program of reform which is temporary at best, and at worst, introduces elements into political life which are destructive of such gains as we have made in the direction of "liberty and justice for all."

The methods of religion are not the methods of politics. Religion renews and elevates society by enhancing the quality of personal life, by recalling men to a true sense of what it means to be human, by quickening the individual conscience, by increasing our sensitivity to the full range of our environment. But some churchmen are tempted to shortcircuit this process. They come to believe that if they can only control, or at least guide, affairs of state by manipulating the political machinery, religion can make its weight felt directly in human affairs—even though men themselves re-

7. Temple, *Christianity and Social Order*, pp. 18–19.

main unregenerate. A classic study of an instance of such self-deception is *Grey Eminence*, by Aldous Huxley. Father Joseph thought he could do "God's deeds by means of the French" and wound up by turning a devil's brood loose in Europe in the shape of the Thirty Years' War.

The Fifth World Order Conference called by the National Council of Churches in Cleveland, November 18–21, 1958, released a message whose words on Red China continue to kick up a storm. "With reference to China," reads the message, "Christians should urge reconsideration by our government of its policy in regard to the Peoples' Republic of China. While the rights of the people of Taiwan and Korea should be safeguarded, steps should be taken toward the inclusion of the Peoples' Republic of China in the United Nations and for its recognition by our government. Such recognition does not imply approval. These diplomatic relations should constitute a part of a much wider relationship between our peoples." We Christians, says the message, "cannot sit complacently and hopefully behind the moral subterfuge which divides the world into 'good and bad' peoples, waiting for the bad ones to be converted to our position."

It is right for the Church to conceive the work of reconciliation as one of its tasks—but it should be consistent. If it urges us to love Mao, why has it not urged us to love Franco and the late Mr. Trujillo? If it is now wrong in 1970, to divide the world into good and bad peoples, why wasn't this practice wrong in 1941? Some sincere pacifists and others did urge American neutrality and nonintervention in World War II, but the main thrust of social actionist clergymen was directed toward getting their countrymen into the fight. *The Christian Century*, under C. C. Morrison, took a noninterventionist position, so the opposition, headed by Reinhold Niebuhr and John C. Bennett founded *Christianity and Crisis* as a sounding board for their war cries. The twentieth anniversary issue of this latter periodical bearing the date, February 6, 1961, contains a history of the paper written by Robert T. Handy, a Union Seminary professor. He describes the group which started the journal as men "who held a generally liberal position in social and political matters," and who joined forces "in seeking America's entrance into the war." There are, it appears, good totalitarians and bad ones; after we have killed off the bad totalitarians, then the good ones, who now control so much of the globe, become "a human reality with which we must live," as Dr. Bennett tells us. Well, live and let live is a time-tested rule of thumb, and a pretty good recipe for getting along in this world. But if it is offered to us now as revealed truth, why was the revelation of twenty-seven years ago so different?

No love was lost on the Batista regime in Cuba; things were so bad that it was hard to conceive of any change that would not be for the better. But the inconceivable, apparently, has happened. Batista once had Castro in jail and let him go; Castro is not making the same mistake as regards any present or future opposition. The cold-blooded executions which have been taking place by the hundreds and at his orders make a mockery of legal procedure. But the selective conscience which politically minded churchmen bring into play at the slightest provocation refuses to be affronted by these slayings. A *Christian Century* editorial more than a year after Castro's coup was headlined: "Bad Public Relations Plague the Cubans." The executioners, after all, are just doing a job, but the reporters who tell the American public what goes on in Cuba are giving the Castro regime a black eye!

The same issue carries an article by the veteran leftist journalist, Carleton Beals, entitled "Cuba in Revolution." The editorial heading reads: "Cuba's regime is showing great restraint in dealing with Batista criminals. Let the U.S. beware of turning that restraint into violence!" Mr. Beals does not deny that hundreds of people have been disposed of before firing squads, but in extenuation of this horror he refers to the United States, "where the legal processes have become so complicated and devious that a poor man is lucky if he secures justice." Furthermore, concludes Mr. Beals, if Castro falters in his executions "then the Cuban people, at present showing such remarkable restraint, will act, and their action will not be pretty." The politicalized religious mind, voicing such sentiments as these, has lost whatever title it may have had to speak to or for the conscience of our time.

No one can live up to the hard Gospel injunction to love our enemies, but even to fall short of this goal is a long way from an attitude which defends, and even seems to delight in, bloodletting and revenge.

The liberation movement in the modern world came to its fullest fruition in this country. To secure the widest possible scope for individual self-expression in creative and productive action it sought to limit government to those delegated and specified duties which would secure individual liberty within the agreed upon rules. The federal republic whose structure and functions are set forth in the Constitution is to be understood mainly in these terms. The strict limitation of government provides for an area of freedom in society within which men take care of their material needs by a system of bargaining, contract, and free exchange. "The market" is simply a label for the system which uses free choice in buying and selling as a means of making economic decisions; it is the tactic of liberty applied to the workaday world. Within the network of market arrangements each man is rewarded according to the value his fellows place upon his offerings of goods and services. This reward is his "wage." Human nature being what it is, every man will tend to feel that his own wage is too low, whereas other folks' prices are too high. Most people develop a reality sense on this point; others never do, and consequently go through life seeking some "fair advantage" over their fellows to restore what they regard as an imbalance.

Economic activity is fundamental to human existence. A Robison Crusoe could get along without politicking, but if he did not work he would die of hunger and exposure. Out of economic activity emerges the concept of rights to property and claims to service around which many political battles are fought. Economics, on the surface, deals with prices, production, and the operations of the market as determined by the buying habits of every one of us. In reality, however, economics is concerned with the conservation and stewardship of the earth's scarce goods: human energy, time, material resources, and natural forces. These goods-in-short-supply are our birthright as creatures of this planet. Use them wisely, as natural piety dictates and common sense confirms—that is, providently and economically—and human wellbeing is the result. Ignore the realities in this area, as we have done in our time, and a host of evils follows. We might be able to live with economic ills if we didn't think we could cure them with political nostrums, but our political efforts aimed at mopping up the consequences of economic mistakes head us in the direction of the Total State.

Every collectivist ideology—from the welfare state idea to totalitarian Communism—is strung on a framework of economic error. People are prisoners of their beliefs, and so long as they cherish a wrong understanding of economics they will be appealed to by one form of collectivism or another. But when they embrace sound economics, collectivism will cease to be a menace, and we won't then have one clergyman in five believing, as revealed by an opinion poll, that total suppression of economic liberty implies no essential threat to religious liberty.

All movements that enhance the powers of the state correspondingly diminish the stature of the individual person. Big government means little people. Interestingly enough, we find a major theological movement of the modern world aimed at sharpening the contrast between man's impotence and God's omnipotence, stressing the world's emptiness and God's complete otherness or transcendence. Karl Barth stunned the theological world in 1919 with his commentary on the Epistle to the Romans. The movement he launched, called Neo-Orthodoxy or Continental Theology, attracted many able minds in this country and in Europe; it articulated the mood of despair and "failure of nerve" which settled down on the Western psyche in the wake of World War I.

The upshot of this thinking, as it applies to our problem, is to hammer home the point that man is helpless to effect his own salvation, which can result only from an arbitrary and overwhelming irruption of God's grace. Man is wholly corrupt, which means that his reason as well as his instincts are too depraved to catch even a glimpse of the natural laws of his being, and his will too weak to guide his life accordingly. He is, therefore, not a responsible being who needs freedom in order to realize his potential; he is an uprooted creature dominated by external forces. Freedom implies some measure of self-reliance, and to entertain the idea of self-reliance is to exhibit the sin of pride. The Apostle Paul could say, "Work out your own salvation with fear and trembling; for it is God who worketh in you both to will and to work, for his good pleasure." But after all, he lived in a very small country!

Much of Barth's thought bears the mark of a pendulum which has swung too far in one direction as a protest against an unwarranted faith in the unaided powers of man which led a nineteenth-century poet to sing, "Glory to man in the highest, for man is the master of things." The plain truth of the matter probably lies somewhere along the lines of a statement by Bishop Berggrav who wrote that ". . . man by nature simply does not have the potentialities of creating any ultimate good of and by himself," with "ultimate" being the operative term. In proximate matters, on the other hand, man's initiative can make a decisive difference in his own life and in his relationship with his fellows. By a just ordering of social life, for instance, we are, as Augustine put it, "schooled for life eternal." Injustice, by inference, can affect our eternal destiny.

The parallel trend in Christian ethical speculation leads to moral nihilism, causing Robert Fitch, Dean of the Pacific School of Religion, a minority voice in these matters, to observe: "It will be an interesting matter for later historians to determine the precise point at which ethics became obsolete in our Western culture. Whatever may be the answer to that question, we may be sure that the researchers will be entertained as they discover the way in which Protestant theology helped toward the obsolescence of ethics."

Protestant theology has contributed to ethical obsolescence in six ways, according to Dr. Fitch. First: Indiscriminate compassion. "The usual moral distinctions are simply drowned in a maudlin emotion in which we have more feeling for the murderer than for the murdered. . . ." The second device "obliterates all principle before the holiness of God." Third is the Christian sophisticate whose "big business is the attack on Puritanism and on bourgeois morality." The fourth device is to be so preoccupied with exploring the rich soil of spirituality from which ethics spring that the formulation of any explicit moral principles is neglected. The fifth gambit is to deride any clean-cut program of ethical endeavor as a "return to salvation by works." The sixth contribution to ethical obsolescence is what might be called "an ethic of Christian togetherness," stressing fellowship at the expense of principles.

Recent ecclesiastical developments have taken place against a secular backdrop peculiar to the modern age. It is notoriously risky to characterize a period by a series of labels. One can do no more with labels than catch the mood or drift of an age, and recognize that individual men here and there are exceptions. With these qualifications in mind, it is safe to say, I believe, that the modern mind and mood represent the convergence of secularism, materialism, individualism-nationalism, rationalism, and futurism or the idea of inevitable progress. These ideas are taken for granted by many of our contemporaries, forming the ingredients of their unexamined premises. They can be described somewhat as follows:

Secularism: The mood of our time is to discount the reality of a spiritual order; the natural world is all there is and the improvement of material circumstances is the goal of life.

Individualism-nationalism: Man ceases to regard himself as a person and comes to think of himself as a mere individual unit of the nation-state—all intermediate, natural human groupings being abolished.

Rationalism: Parts of the universe may be presently unknown, the rationalist admits, but no parts are unknowable. Individual life and society can be perfectly grasped rationally, that is to say, perfectly correlated with verbal formulations and propositions. But if individual life and society can be rationally grasped they can be rationally altered. The Communist reduces "the-thing-in-itself" to "the-thing-to-us." Thus the universe is "limited and knowable"—and therefore "controllable."

Futurism: This reorganization may be a bit rough on contemporaries, but present sacrifice is a small price to pay for the perfect society of the future.

This set of ideas, or this mood, which has been gathering strength for the past century, confronts religion with a real challenge. Individual churchmen have resisted with vigor and courage; but ecclesiastical officialdom thinks to outflank the challenge by going along with the trend—with some of the results outlined earlier.

America and the world move in the direction of the democratic despotism foreseen by Tocqueville. The most advanced stage of this great social drift is represented by the "Peoples Democracies" of the Communist nations. Our forebears placed several kinds of restraint on political action in order to provide areas of individual immunity against governmental power, and our political machinery was designed to secure individuals in their God-given rights. This machinery was operated by fallible men and, of course, it fell short of the ideal, as human devices always do, and will continue to do till the end of time. Rights were overridden and privacy

invaded in America as elsewhere, but not on principle. Now we
are operating on a new principle: the political machinery is no
longer conceived to be an instrument of justice; it is regarded as
a device to distribute economic advantage and privilege to those
who capture it. When governmental machinery is so used it necessarily pares down or denies the rights of those who lose. This new
political pattern ill accords with representative, republican government. When the spoils of office reach a certain level it is fatuous
to expect that the power-hungry groups enjoying them will be
pried out of office by mere paper ballots. They will use their power
to consolidate their advantage, under the old forms perhaps, but
with a different spirit. In such a society the churches are driven
toward an eventual decision; act as a prop to the regime, or go
underground. Only in a society with free institutions and a limited
government can the Church be fully the Church.

It is the aim of many Protestant churchmen to put the Church
officially on record as sponsor for the movement which, in this
country, has produced the welfare state. To the extent that any
church puts most of its eggs into a collectivist basket, it absolutizes
the relative and temporary. It impairs the primary responsibility
of high religion, which is to recall men to a proper sense of their
creaturehood and destiny so that they may order their souls aright.
Civilization is a happy by-product of spiritual activity but cannot
be its direct goal, and because the Kingdom of God is beyond
history, the true Church must expect to forever confront political
and social institutions in an atmosphere of encounter and tension.
"If the Church marries the spirit of this age," wrote Dean Inge,
"she will be a widow in the next."

CHAPTER 2

The Church and the World

IT IS THE BASIC PREMISE OF EVERY ONE OF THE HIGHER RELI-
gions that man, as well as being involved in society and nature,
participates in an order of events which transcends nature and
history. Man is a social being. Men are members of one or another
of the historic cultures or societies; they are, in other words, Westerners or Orientals, or some other; and within the great cultures
they are French, or English, or American; they are members of
groups and infragroups right down to the little platoon wherein
each of us finds his niche. Man is also part of nature, subject to the
laws of physics, chemistry, and biology, akin to the planetary stuff
of which all creatures are formed. The social and natural orders
have an obvious claim on man, and the truly reigious purview
includes them even as it goes beyond them to posit a sacred or
divine order—a realm of being as contrasted with the realms of
becoming. The divine ground of the universe is God, the Eternal.

Theologians of nearly all schools are of one mind here, and the
matter is well put by one of the best known of contemporary
theologians, the late Paul Tillich: "Man together with all things,
comes from him who has put all things under man's feet. Man is
rooted in the same Ground in which the universe with all its
galaxies is rooted. This it is that gives greatness to everything,
however small it may be, to the atoms as well as to the plants and
animals; and this makes small all things, however great—the stars
as well as man. It gives significance to the seemingly insignificant;

it gives significance to each individual man and to mankind as a whole. This answer quiets the anxiety about our smallness no less than it quells the pride in our greatness. Nor is this answer biblical only, Christian only, religious only. Its truth is felt by all of us when we become conscious of our predicament, namely, that we are not by ourselves, that our presence upon this earth is not of our own doing. We are brought into existence and formed by the same power that bears up the universe and the earth and everything upon it, a power in comparison with which we are infinitely small but our awareness of which makes us great among the creatures."[1]

Men are not at one moment social beings and, at another, children of nature; they are both simultaneously, and the whole is sustained and interpenetrated by the divine. This is, at any rate, the religious reading of things, and it is, of course, at odds with the reading that has largely prevailed since the Enlightenment. This latter ideal is the perfect adaptation of individuals to their societies, and of those societies to nature. This might be an adequate description of the beehive or termitary, but if the claims of religion are not unfounded, it is a dehumanizing goal for men. Man, that pilgrim of the absolute, has needs and potencies within him which cannot be realized within time, but only beyond history. His total environment includes the dimension which transcends this world of sense, and as he cuts himself off from this portion of his normal milieu maladjustments crop up at other levels of his existence. An anthropoid capable of adapting perfectly to society and nature is a creature something less than man. A man who would achieve the full measure of his potential must yield to those claims that the sacred order has on his being and nature, and as he does so he begins to discover the right order of priorities for the other spheres of his life. C. S. Lewis puts the matter this way: "It is since Christians have largely ceased to think of the other world that they have become so ineffective in this. Aim at Heaven and you get earth 'thrown in': aim at earth and you will get neither."[2]

1. Paul Tillich, in *Christianity and Crisis*, June 25, 1962.
2. *Mere Christianity*, p. 106
John Calvin's words are also worth recalling: "Man, in short, belongs both to earth and to heaven, to the temporal and the eternal, subject to the secular law and recipient of the eternal Gospel, a being capable both of reason and of faith. In the spiritual kingdom he is wholly free, in the temporal kingdom he is totally in bondage. He is both a member of the Church, the eternal Body of Christ, and subject to the temporal authority of secular

The mundane concerns of the daily round are not exclusively secular; they have a cosmic setting, and the Church is in the world translating this *Weltanschauung* into policy for everyday life in the political, social, and economic sectors. Most churches are local; their world is the parish, and their spiritual leaders are busy with pastoral duties: preaching, teaching, counselling, visiting the sick, burying the dead, and countless other tasks. But when the Church wishes to speak to the world, it organizes, first nationally and then on a world scale.

When ecclesiastics meet in council to speak to the world, what do they say? Short question, but any adequate answer to it would be of book length. Where would we start so as to pick up the near end of the thread of that answer? Any starting point has some measure of arbitrariness about it, but the founding meeting of the World Council of Churches in Amsterdam in 1948 is as convenient a point of entry into the problem as any. This well-remembered affair was attended by churchmen from many lands, and its pronouncements were blurted out, so to speak. Thus they more directly reveal the beliefs and feelings of the leadership of the ecumenical movement than later and more polished statements designed with the sensibilities of certain segments of the public in mind.

The overall theme of the Amsterdam Assembly was "Man's Disorder and God's Design." Public interest centered on the work of the third commission on "The Church and the Disorder of Society." It was the report of this Commission which affirmed that "The Christian Churches should reject the ideologies of both communism and *laissez faire* capitalism, and should seek to draw men away from the false assumption that these extremes are the only alternatives."

The words just quoted appear in the concluding paragraph of Section IV of the report. Now the words "communism" and "capitalism" are not merely descriptive words; they are emotionally loaded war cries—for one side or another—and each one carries a chain of connotations. Section IV tries to tell us what each of these words means to the Commission. It opens by saying that "Christians should ask why communism in its modern totalitarian

magistrates and laws. He is instructed in the temporal realm largely by reason, tradition, and the authority of the great minds of the past, and in the spiritual realm by the Word of God as recorded in Holy Scripture."

form makes so strong an appeal to great masses of people in many parts of the world." Before we begin to ask *why* something is so we need to assure ourselves that it really *is* so. Is it really the case that Communism does appeal to great masses of people? Undeniably it is true that Communist rule is installed over populous countries, and every system of rule ever known must rest on the consent of a significant number of people. But where have "great masses of people" in free elections installed a Communist or any other form of totalitarian rule? Not in Russia. Not in China. Not in Czechoslovakia, nor in Hungary. "Great masses of people in many parts of the world" do live under Communist totalitarian dictatorship, but this is not because Communism "makes so strong an appeal" to them. Communism does, however, have an intense appeal for a dedicated and fanatic minority, and we agree that Christians should try to understand the reason why.

The Commission goes on to answer its deceptively loaded question. Much of Communism's strength derives from "the revolt of the multitudes against injustice," in which revolt Christians "should recognize the hand of God." These are indeed revolutionary times. There is a revolt of the masses, as Ortega made us see a generation ago, but what is it a revolt against? We can gauge the answer to this question by trying to figure out what the revolt is for. If we could discern a worldwide revolt *toward* justice we'd be correct in inferring that it was *away from* injustice. Justice consists of giving every man his due; it is Adam Smith's "liberal system of liberty, equality and justice"; it is constitutionalism, the rule of law. The Communist revolt is not in this direction; it heads in the opposite direction, toward a deceptively rationalized, more tightly organized, and therefore deadlier form of injustice. If it is a fact, as the report affirms, that "for many young men and women, communism seems to stand for a vision of human equality and universal brotherhood for which they were prepared by Christian influences," then it is not enough to mutely accept this fact; every concerned person should sound the alarm and point to those so misled that they are on the road to disaster. Men inspired by visions of equality and brotherhood are not to be denied their vision, any more than a man perishing from want of food is to be told that he is not hungry. But if the hungry man is about to gorge himself on food loaded with cyanide the least we could do is warn him that he is about to poison himself, and then we might offer him some proper food. Totalitarian dictatorship is no sort of answer to the vision of a more equitable, just, and fair social order; it is the murder of that vision.

"Christians who are beneficiaries of capitalism should try to see the world as it appears to many who know themselves excluded from its privileges and who see in Communism a means of deliverance from poverty and insecurity." Those in countries like Russia, China, India, or Ghana who are excluded from the benefits of capitalism are prevented from enjoying these benefits by their own rulers—not by any capitalist! No businessman anywhere in the world has the power—as a businessman—to set up a form of political organization which is incompatible with the free market economy. The conditions for maximizing economic production are known, and this knowledge is not the exclusive possession of Americans or Englishmen or of any other nation. It is no one's monopoly possession but is freely available for all who wish to help themselves to it. Beyond this, many are eager to impart it; technological know-how is available to implement it, and capital is seeking investment opportunities to get it into high gear at once. Nothing more is needed than the proper social conditions in the lands where people want to share the fruits of capitalist production. If the government of Rubarbaria maintains peace and order within its boundaries and provides assurance that there won't be confiscations of property, foreign or domestic, these relatively simple social requirements will generate, almost as if by magic, the very benefits which the people of that and other countries now think are being denied them by that grossly misunderstood thing labeled "capitalism."

After its somewhat fatuous appraisal of the nature of Communism, with its alleged appeal to the masses, the Commission report lists five criticisms: (1) Communism promises redemption within history; (2) it attributes messianic qualities to the proletariat; (3) it is materialistic and deterministic; (4) it is ruthless toward opponents; and (5) it makes an idolatrous religion out of party loyalty. Also, it is acknowledged that Communism "engenders new forms of injustice and oppression." But this criticism is, in the context, to praise with faint damns.

Having enlightened us as to the nature of Communism and the

why of its appeal to the modern world, the Commission now turns
to an elucidation of the other half of the equation, capitalism. The
first thing we need to know is that capitalism does not square with
Christianity: "The church should make clear that there are conflicts between Christianity and capitalism," even capitalism at its
best. The report goes on to say: "The developments of capitalism
vary from country to country and often the exploitation of the
workers that was characteristic of early capitalism has been corrected in considerable measure by the influence of trade unions,
social legislation, and responsible management."

To say that early capitalism—presumably during the initial
phases of the Industrial Revolution, or even during the entire
nineteenth century—exploited the workers, is to pass judgment on
a period of history. Historical judgments rest, mainly, on matters
of fact, which means marshaling the evidence in an effort to determine what actually happened in England during the first three
decades of the nineteenth century—or whatever period is in question. Myths about the Industrial Revolution have been assiduously
cultivated for decades, but historians of late have been sifting the
evidence anew and historical judgments are in the process of revi-
sion.

This is one half of the matter, the historical; but there is another,
the theoretical. All too often we think we are discussing capitalism, or the philosophy of the free market, when in fact we are only
describing certain features of the nineteenth century, some unpleasant and others pleasant. This distinction between theory and
history has been well put by Wilhelm Roepke: "We must make a
sharp distinction between the principle of a market economy as
such—bound as it is to no historical period but representing rather
one of the permanent elements out of which an historical economic order can be put together—and the actual development
which during the nineteenth and twentieth centuries has led to the
historical form of market economy. One is a philosophical category, the other an historical individuality; one is a simple structural element, the other an historical and therefore unique, a
non-recurrent compound of economic, social, legal, political,
moral, and cultural elements, a compound which, in this highly
complicated mixture of ingredients, never occurred before and
will never recur hereafter."[3]

3. *Civitas Humana,* pp. 6–7.

Once we have come to some understanding of what early capitalism was, and why, we can consider the impact on it of trade unions, "social legislation," and "responsible management." These considerations deserve separate chapters. In any event, the thing the Commission says the church must reject, along with Communism, has four earmarks: "(1) Capitalism tends to subordinate what should be the primary task of any economy—the meeting of human needs—to the economic advantages of those who have most power over its institutions; (2) it tends to produce serious inequalities; (3) it has developed a practical form of materialism in Western nations in spite of their Christian backgrounds, for it has placed the greatest emphasis upon success in making money; (4) it has also kept the people of capitalist countries subject to a kind of fate which has taken the form of such social catastrophes as mass unemployment."

In the course of the present book we shall be recurring again and again to the monumental misunderstanding represented by these four statements, but some brief comment on each is now in order. No economic order can meet every need of man, but how well has the economic order of the West met the economic needs of Western man? In the first place, he is better off than his counterparts in Africa and Asia. He is better off precisely because his economic and political arrangements are freer and, because of this freedom, man in Europe and America has more and better tools and machines at his disposal than do the peoples of the Orient. Because the Occidental is better equipped he is more productive, even though he expends less energy than a Chinese laborer or a Hindu coolie. As a result, he has more food in richer variety, he is better housed, better clothed, better educated, healthier, falls prey to fewer epidemics, and no longer faces the prospect of recurring famines. The market economy, in short, has actually catered better to human needs than have its alternatives, and continues to do so.

If a rebuttal is attempted in the form of an argument that Africa and Asia have suffered in the past from European colonialism, the answer is that economics or the market economy has nothing to do with the procedures by which an alien government establishes hegemony over the people of another country, and is, in fact, antithetical to any such arrangement. This is to establish a type of political control by one set of people over another, by which the ruling group advantages itself. This is the essence of colonialism and the antithesis of capitalism or the market economy, economically, as well as in other ways. All deviations from market economy–limited government structures in a given country set up a political arrangement within which some people are prevented from enjoying the full fruits of their labors in order to benefit the privileged group—those who rule plus their hangers-on. The planned economy might be termed "colonialism within one country"; more precisely, political planning of economic life is the manifestation of the same species of social organization applied internally which, when applied by some people of one country to the people of another nation is labeled "colonialism" or "imperialism." Modern collectivists profess to abhor this arrangement when conducted on an international basis; but when one group within a nation fastens itself on the rest for the same purpose—to acquire their labor products and control portions of their lives—this anticapitalistic arrangement is applauded.

The freer the economy, in other words, the better it meets the economic needs of people. An economy will be free, automatically, if the society properly structures its political agency; for men will produce the goods or render the services in the jobs they believe themselves best fitted for, and for the highest rewards they can obtain—in terms of their private value scales—and they will trade and exchange with whomsoever they will. This is a truism; it says no more than that people will work at the jobs of their choice and exchange with whomever they please unless they are prevented from doing so. If private parties interfere and go on interfering with men's peaceful choices in the economic sector or anywhere else, this means that government is falling down on its job and not doing what it should do, namely, redressing private injury; and if it is government that interferes, government itself is the transgressor, victimizing some citizens for its own benefit or at the behest of a private predatory group.

When the economy is free, each contributor will be weighed in the private scales of his peers; they will judge the value of his offering of goods and services and reward him accordingly. This is the market in operation, and the market holds a mirror up to society, reflecting the values and tastes of the masses. If a singer or an actor or a spellbinding promoter of "youth cream" or a glib salesman of mouthwash is rewarded more lavishly than a hardworking teacher or preacher or craftsman, this means that the masses appreciate the former more than the latter. The market does not assess the real worth of a man nor intend to convey the impression that a millionaire is a finer human being than a poor laborer. The market merely records the fact that the masses of people spend their money on whatever engages their interest, and, by their spending, create the millionaire; when they refrain from buying, the result is the man who is poor by comparison. The market is a continuous process of balloting with nickels, dimes, and dollars by people seeking to maximize their economic satisfactions. The man whom the people of the year 2069 will recognize as the great philosophic genius of the 1960s—or the great artist, poet, novelist, or what have you—goes unrecognized during his lifetime, which is why the people of the 1960s do not patronize him. They use their money to buy what pleases them, or what they think will please them; and often this is not what pleases the man of refined sensibilities and cultivated intellect. But this disparity is in the nature of things; it is a small price to pay for freedom. In the free society, the genius who is out of step with his contemporaries is, at worst, ignored. He is not burned at the stake or sent to Siberia.

The free society maximizes the scope of individual free choice; out of all possible choosings it forbids and penalizes just two. The free society does not permit a man to choose to live without working or without putting his money to work; nor does it permit a man to choose to live off his fellows by predation. Men being what they are—creatures who tend to satisfy their desires with a minimum of effort—every society will be the victim of some predation and will, therefore, need to devise means of protecting itself against predators. "Robbery," Lewis Mumford has written, "is perhaps the oldest of labor-saving devices, and war vies with magic in its efforts to get something for nothing—to obtain women without possessing personal charm, to achieve power without possessing intelligence, and to enjoy the rewards of consecutive and tedious labor without having lifted a finger in work or learnt a single useful skill. Lured by these possibilities, the hunter as civilization advances turns himself to systematic conquest: he seeks slaves, loot, power, and he founds the political state in order to ensure and regulate the annual tribute—enforcing, in return, a necessary modicum of order."[4] The police apparatus has evolved to deal with those who operate outside the law by thievery, blackmail, assault, racketeering, and the like; but this is only half the story. A subtle kind of predation operating within the law and inside the mores takes a toll on every kind of society, but only the free society acknowledges this internal threat to human liberty and wellbeing and tries to divest its legal structure of every kind of statutory privilege—legislative interference that distributes economic advantage to some at the expense of others.

Work is divinely ordained if anything is. The way things are on this planet we cannot consume or use them directly; we must expend effort on raw materials in order to get them into useful form. Work is a corollary of life itself; if we don't work we perish —unless, that is, we can devise a way to live off the fruit of some one else's labor. This is predation, and it is the job of the police power to prevent or deter it. When the police power, or government, properly performs its job, the society is free. Within this legal framework each man has the opportunity to exercise the normal human need and desire to perform useful work. Now, a different set of problems may arise because of the lame, the halt, and the blind. The helpless have, as a matter of record, a better chance of being helped in a free society than in any other, simply because a free society is that much more productive than any other. The free society makes more goods available for everyone precisely because it is hooked up and wired for productivity, not philanthropy. Philanthropy does not bring food, clothing, and shelter into existence; only productive work does that. Opportunity to satisfy one's charitable impulses occurs only after goods have been produced beyond the subsistence level. It is proper and necessary that organizations within the free society be designed to meet human needs apart from the market, but the free society presupposes that the overwhelming majority of men are reasonably sound of wind and limb and are in possession of their mental faculties. It gives each man an unmatched opportunity to meet his own needs and better his economic circumstances by correctly estimating the kind of goods and services that other people want and need, and which it is within his competence to supply. Should a man rebel against the necessity for this sort of interaction with

4. *Technics and Civilization*, p. 83.

other people and act upon his rebellion, he has to retreat into parasitism or predation. The free society, however, allows no place for either predation or parasitism, and the man who chooses either course will bring punishment upon himself. If he attempts predation his aggressions will be resisted, in the last resort, by force. If he attempts parasitism, he may survive by mendicancy. But confronted starkly by the alternatives of punishment or starvation, the sense of reality in a healthy individual will reassert itself and he will return to the economic processes of work and exchange.

It is a blunt fact, sad to the romanticist but old hat to those who have accepted the Christian idea of sin or the Greek idea of *hubris*, that men—by and large—are no better than they have to be. Men are in rebellion, covert rebellion for the most part, against the human condition and the requirements it imposes; they long to shed their creaturehood. Work is a condition imposed by the planet; division of labor and the exchange of surpluses—which means that each man must sensitively cater to the needs of other people while simultaneously serving his own—is a labor-saving device; and reward is meted out to each man in terms of what other people judge his effort to be worth to them. This is the market system in its bare bones, and men rebel against it because they resent their dependence on an impalpable and intricate organization whose workings they do not fully understand. They would prefer to be at the mercy of a patron like Lorenzo de' Medici, or his modern political counterpart, who may be arbitrary and unpredictable, but who might be worked on—to one's own advantage—if you approach him right. But when one's economic fate is at the mercy of the impersonal consumer, that's different. The consumer speaks *ex cathedra*, and from his pronouncements there is no appeal. This is the dreadful psychological barrier in capitalism as we have known it historically, but historical capitalism has coincided with the swift rise of secularism that has eroded the security man should know in his eternal nature. This is a need the economic order cannot, of course, meet; only religion can speak to the needs of the soul and it has too often spoken in tongues the modern man cannot understand and apply to himself. When there is a religious recovery giving men the confidence that the nature of things is on their side and can be trusted, then they will accept the way things are and must be in the economic sector.

Capitalism does meet the economic needs of men better than any conceivable alternative. But is it also true, as charged by the Commission, that at the same time it subordinates "the meeting of human needs to the economic advantages of those who have most power over its institutions"?

What are "its institutions"? Strictly speaking, economic institutions are such things as the division of labor, capital goods, money, deferred exchanges, and the like—the market, in short. The Commission does not say what it has in mind when it refers to the institutions of capitalism, but presumably it means factories, stores, banks, public utilities, and the transportation industries. The persons who have "power" over these "institutions" are, of course, their owners—managers and stockholders. This oblique way of viewing the matter has been characteristic of socialist parties everywhere who have long advocated what they call "public ownership of the means of production." "The public" is the society as a whole, which cannot own anything *en masse;* what the socialists mean, then, is that the society's enforcement agency, government, should own the banks, the factories, the power industries, and the transportation facilities. Taken together, these constitute the musculature of the social body, the part by which the whole is moved. The socialists view this takeover as merely transferring power from one set of owners to another; from the power of private owners to the power of government officials. It is, however, a mistake to identify private ownership as a power relationship; calling ownership power does not make it so. Bertrand Russell gives us a perfect example of this confusion: "Apart from the economic power of labor, all other economic power, in its ultimate analysis, consists in being able to decide, by the use of armed force if necessary, who shall be allowed to stand upon a given piece of land and to put things into it and take things out of it. . . . The power of the industrialist is of the same sort; it rests in the last analysis, upon the lock-out, that is to say, upon the fact that the owner of a factory can call upon the forces of the State to prevent unauthorized persons from entering it."[5]

Russell speaks of "power" when he should be using the word "freedom." If a man uses the piece of earth that is his to build a house on, and plants it with grass, wheat, potatoes, and if he lives

5. *Power,* pp. 120–121.

peacefully in his own home and reaps the harvest he has sown, he is a free man. He is not coercing anyone.

Likewise, the owner of a factory. The owner of any kind of property, may—if he is a free man—use it in any peaceful way he chooses. He is within his rights to lay down the conditions under which another man may be permitted to enjoy that which is his: his factory, his money, his automobile, or anything else that belongs to him. X has an automobile which he refuses to let Y borrow; it is fantastic to conclude that X has established a power relationship over Y by his act of refusal. This is, to the contrary, an act of freedom; if X has no right to refuse the loan of his vehicle to another, the vehicle is not really his, and if Y has the means of overriding X's refusal, it is Y who has established a power relationship over X, and X is no longer a free man.

The phrase "economic power" is a tricky one. If it means no more than ownership, it is misleading and clumsy. If it is used, as is customary, to convey the implication that ownership gives the designated person some sort of power over others, it is dishonest. Strictly speaking, there is only one power structure in a society, and that is its government; all other usages of the word power in a sociological context are metaphorical. This point will arise and be elaborated upon at several points, later in this volume.

In every civilized society known to history there has emerged a class of men who live by force or fraud off other men's production. Every theory of society except one—that of the free society —is elastic enough to accommodate this class. These theories differ among themselves on questions such as: Who shall exercise power? How shall rulers be chosen? Who shall benefit and who shall be victimized? And who shall be rich and who poor? The political concern of the free society is to establish private sectors of immunity against invasions by government, and the powers of government are circumscribed by limiting their exercise to the curbing and punishment of aggression. The theory of the free society thus seeks to establish a peaceful framework of law, a set of rules within which citizens seek to realize their private goals in a system of social cooperation.

The free society does not presuppose a race of heroes or a race of saints. It posits that people are still full of the same old human juices, but capable—in a system with a built-in set of rewards and punishments—of carrying each his own load, with some high-capacity men and women able to help along the stragglers. Because the free society is designed so as not to impede but facilitate the proliferation of goods and services, it is at the furthest possible remove from a subsistence society; it is the most productive arrangement possible for a given set of environmental conditions. The impulse to charity can hardly find expression in a subsistence society; philanthropy is made increasingly possible as the general level of wages and wellbeing rises, but it is a function of love or charity, whatever the social and political arrangement.

The distinction between those who perform useful work or render desirable service and those who get by without working is clear to most people. But what about the *rentier* class, which seems to occupy a gray zone between those who work and those who don't? The *rentier* class, that bugaboo of the Marxians, is composed of members who live on income from their property. Here is a couple in their seventies who have worked hard all their lives. They have saved and invested their lifetime earnings—now that they have retired—in a two-family house. They occupy one half of the dwelling rent free and derive an income from hiring out the other half, and this, plus a savings account and insurance, enables them to get by. It is obvious in cases of this kind, which might be multiplied by countless instances, that these people are living on the fruits of their own labor. The food they ate this past week is the economic equivalent of the vacation trip they did not take twenty years ago; every dollar of their savings represents some earlier satisfaction foregone. This class has been despoiled by inflation, which continues its silent erosion of their savings, and by every political intervention which causes a rise in the price of the things they buy with their depreciated dollars. But there is no direct attack on the small *rentier*. Even as he has been made the unwitting victim of much of the social legislation of the past generation, he has also received the solicitous attention of welfarists. The plight of this category of our citizens will be dealt with in fuller detail in later parts of this volume. Of all the victims of our slide into collectivism, they are the hardest hit.

The blow which lands on the small *rentier* is ostensibly intended for "the idle rich," the millionaire who has a large income from a bulky portfolio of investments in all kinds of enterprises, the member of the international set. We may retain a sneaking admiration for the man who made it the hard way, who came up from rags to riches and now looks about on his yacht; our rage is saved for wastrels who have been deprived of that invaluable discipline —the necessity for earning a living by meeting consumer demands —who never did a lick of useful work in their lives, on whom the mere accident of birth conferred luxury. Envy and covetousness are as old as man. These unlovely features of the spirit have been condemned by religion and by most codes of ethics, and their worst manifestations curbed thereby. But is something more at issue here than mere envy and covetousness? Should our sense of justice be outraged by the spectacle of the high-living heir of a family fortune when some honest, hardworking citizens are barely able to scrape together enough to live on? The free society has no place for the predator and parasite, and it holds that the proper end of government is justice. How, then, should the free society treat the wastrel who does not work, but consumes his inherited wealth in idle pleasures? Answer: the wastrel should be treated just like everyone else. He is obviously not a predator, nor is he a parasite in the technical sense of the term as here used. He has been given no legal advantage over his fellows, nor is he profiting from legal privileges. The law should not single out anyone for special treatment; it should treat all men alike, and should mete out like punishments for similar infractions. The rich wastrel may offend against good taste and good morals, but unless he breaks the law, the law should not act against him. And if the law is kept to its proper sphere he cannot unduly influence legislators, or with his money secure any special favors for himself or his kind.

The law should protect the wastrel's life and property as meticulously as it protects the life and property of everyone else. This is simple justice. Beyond this, there is an important distinction between the role played by the man of wealth in the precapitalistic ages and his counterpart today: today's wealth is largely in the form of productive capital, that is to say in machines and tools that increase the efficiency of labor, making more goods available at a cheaper cost. Thus, even the most outrageous wastrel profligate, whether he knows it or not, even against his will, contributes to raising the general level of economic wellbeing. He could do more if he had more sense and sensibility, but he cannot avoid doing something.

In the precapitalistic ages men of wealth lavished money and other perquisites on a corps of retainers, held extravagant banquets, built baronial castles, and otherwise indulged in ostentatious consumption. They used up their current wealth for their own pleasure and for that of their friends, relying on their position in the state to replenish the coffers for themselves and their descendants. Under capitalism, on the other hand, there is no other way for a family fortune to be retained except to invest it in capital equipment for the enhancement of productive efficiency. It used to be that a fortune was kept intact by virtue of a man's position in the political structure—it was a function of his share in rule. Now, unless a fortune is invested in enterprises that produce goods approved by consumers it is quickly dissipated. The eminent economist, Ludwig von Mises, puts the point as follows:

> The capital goods are for the owner a dead fund, a liability rather than an asset, if not used in production for the best possible and cheapest provision of the people with the goods and services they are asking for most urgently. In the market economy the owners of capital goods are forced to employ their property as if it were entrusted to them by the consumers under the stipulation to invest it in those lines in which it best serves those consumers. Virtually, the capitalists are mandatories of the consumers, bound to comply with their wishes.
>
> In order to attend to the orders received from the consumers, their real bosses, the capitalists must either themselves proceed to investment and the conduct of business or, if they are not prepared for such entrepreneurial activity or distrust their own abilities, hand over their funds to men whom they consider as better fitted for such a function. Whatever alternative they may choose, the supremacy of the consumers remains intact. No matter what the financial structure of the firm or company may be, the entrepreneur who operates with other peoples' money depends no less on the market, that is, the consumers, than the entrepreneur who fully owns his own outfit.[5]

5. Ludwig von Mises, "The Economic Role of Saving and Capital Goods," *The Freeman*, August, 1963.

Museums in every country, filled with paintings, pieces of sculpture, exquisite tapestries, elegant furniture, and objects of art, culled from past civilizations on every continent and from many different ages, testify to an economic fact of transcendent importance: Every culture has produced luxury items for the wealthy. These items from our past inspire the art collector and the connoisseur of antiques in the present. The rich in our society are still catered to in a variety of ways by men and women of talent— architects, cabinet makers, tailors, jewelers, bakers, yachtmakers, painters, and so on. But the distinctive feature of a free market society, in contrast to the precapitalistic ages, is large-scale production that lowers the unit cost of items which are distributed by the millions. Mass production is designed for the purpose of mass consumption. Most of us have never owned a tailor-made suit or a pair of handmade shoes; were shoes and suits not mass produced we'd be poorly clothed and poorly shod. The few wealthy who have the means to be outfitted by craftsmen are no better clothed today than they were in Elizabethan times, or during many other periods in the past. But the masses dress better. In order to better understand this aspect of the past, reflect on India of the present. In India during World War II an ordinary American G.I. could afford to have a pair of boots handcrafted just for him, but under this romantic system of individual craftsmen most Indian peasants go barefoot and most Indians are peasants. Reflections along these lines might be extended, and they render meaningless the second point in the Commission's indictment of the thing it calls "capitalism": "It tends to produce serious inequalities."

There are wealth differentials in every society, past and present; and it is inconceivable that any future society could exist on the basis of equality of income. The degree of political inequality needed to enforce an arbitrary dead level of economic equality would be intolerable; and inevitably, the class invested with that degree of political power needed to fasten a program of economic leveling on the rest of society would use their power to enrich themselves above that level.

Every society has its rich and poor, relatively speaking, but in every society except one, wealth and poverty are associated with political power or the lack of power. A man who stands high in the political hierarchy derives his wealth from an exercise of his power; and the poor are locked into their poverty because they occupy the lower rungs on the political ladder. Only in the free society is a man's income related to the measure in which he pleases consumers. It is a man's peers who decide whether he will be rich or poor, but that decision is one they make only indirectly. Their direct choice is to buy this or that good or service and in such and such a quantity; an indirect result of these consumer choices is to reward one manufacturer while giving another a clue that he should move into some other line of business.

In a free society the consumer is king. The manufacturer who wishes to get rich caters to the masses; he machine-produces shoes for the multitude although he might be able to produce better footwear at a much higher price per pair for the carriage trade. The consumer is the man in the street. In the democratic liturgy of our time, the common man is credited with superior political wisdom and virtue, but at the same time the ideologues regard him as an economic imbecile. They picture him as possessing, en masse, an inexhaustible skill when it comes to untangling political issues. But at the same time he is incompetent to select his own toothpaste; he buys things he does not need at prices he cannot afford to pay —all because manufacturers of unneeded luxuries team up with advertisers to dazzle and tempt him beyond his capacity to resist.

There are wealth differentials in a free society; some men are richer than others, and some are poorer than the average. But two points need to be underscored: first, these wealth differentials are not as sharp as they are in alternative social arrangements; and second, a man's economic status is a reflection of his skill at pleasing consumers—barring force and fraud. The marketplace is crowded with goods that reflect the taste of the masses. If this offends the sensibilities of those with educated tastes they should think a second thought and realize that this is a cheap price indeed to pay for freedom, especially when this same free market provides all sorts of nooks and crannies where the most exacting tastes in literature, art, music, drama, craftsmanship, and technique may be satisfied.

Is it not unfair, we hear it said, that the members of a singing group whose sole qualification is lack of musical talent should be millionaires many times over, whereas most people have to work harder and longer for a fraction of the reward? The market, it must be emphasized, is merely a reflection of popular choice; it does not assess the ultimate worth of a man, but leaves this task to the Almighty. The market merely records the intensity with which a man's peers appreciate his offerings of goods and services. No one coerces youngsters to buy the raucous records of the Beatles or the Dave Clark Five. This incredibly sensitive democracy, which is the market, records every penny spent as a vote in favor of some desired item and against its alternatives. It happens to be a fact of life that more people put a higher valuation on certain kinds of entertainment than on the services rendered by most teachers, preachers, shoemakers, butchers, bakers, and the like. The market is not an omnicompetent device for resolving every problem in human affairs, but it is the only way of handling the problem of economic calculation, that is to say, coming to a decision of how to use scarce resources most efficiently for the satisfaction of human wants and needs, as these are determined by the people involved. This is freedom in actual performance at the economic level, and freedom does cost. Freedom cannot long endure among a people unwilling to pay its price. But the personal and social damage of forcibly suppressing free choice exacts a toll that is intolerably higher.

The fourth indictment leveled by the Commission report charges that capitalism has "kept the people of capitalist countries subject to a kind of fate which has taken the form of such social catastrophes as mass unemployment."

A survey of the causes of the business cycle and of industrial depressions will occupy us in a later chapter, but a few preliminary observations on this fourth charge are pertinent here. If we ask about the nature of economic activity, the basic answer is pretty simple: Economic activity is someone manufacturing, growing, or transporting a good valued by himself or another. The three classic factors of economic production are Land, Labor, and Capital which combine to produce Wealth. In other words, human beings engaged in productive action, employ tools and machines, in order to operate more efficiently on and with raw materials to produce consumable goods. In the ingenious formulation of Clark and Rimanoczy, The Law of Production runs as follows: MMW   NR

HE x T, which, "when 'spelled out' to embrace all production, reads: Man's Material Welfare equals Natural Resources plus Human Energy multiplied by Tools."[6] Social cooperation under the division of labor constitutes the marketplace, one of the fundamental institutions of human society. The human community does not flower except as men are able to exchange their surplus energies and products freely as goods, services, and ideas. If individual persons were self-sufficient entities society would be unnecessary —if not inconceivable. A society is impossible unless there is some exchange, and it is rich and complex to the degree that exchanges multiply; and on every level of activity—from the provision of our creaturely needs for food, clothing, and shelter, to the level of our spiritual needs for education, art, and religion—exchanges multiply naturally unless they are sabotaged by the intrusion of nonpeaceful, noneconomic factors.

Human desires are not constant but recurring. A person eats to the point of satiety, but soon he will be hungry again. He builds a shelter, but after every storm it needs fixing. Periodically he outgrows his clothing or else it wears out and he needs new clothing. In brief, there are moments when the economic urge ebbs, and in those moments it is natural for land, labor, and capital to lie idle. But shortly, the self-starting cycle gets under way again naturally as satiety wears off and recurring wants and needs reach a certain urgency. This urgency overcomes the natural desire to loaf and take one's ease, and man goes back to work. That is to say, he picks up his tools and starts to dig.

In more sophisticated societies he has a wider variety of choices. Economic activities are immensely varied, but they are all interrelated. And they are an almost automatic response to the nagging demand of human wants which cannot be satisfied except by the fruits of human labor.

On occasion, a paralysis seems to settle on the market. Exchanges diminish in number, and production, in consequence, dries up. Idle men, idle factories and machines, idle fields and mines betoken an economic depression. The major feature of a depression, as it strikes the public eye, is mass unemployment. Factories are closed, business stagnates, and millions who want jobs can't find them at their price. As the depression lengthens or deepens, human suffering increases. Unmet human wants and

6. Fred G. Clark and Richard S. Rimanoczy, *How We Live*, rev. ed., 1960, Van Nostrand, Princeton, New Jersey, p. 49.

needs intensify, but a sort of paralysis seems to prevent these wants and needs from being met in the only way they can be met —by economic activity. Economic activity is, basically, the application of human energy to the natural opportunities, aided by tools, i.e., capital. To say that there is mass unemployment is only another way of saying that the three primary factors of production —land, labor, and capital—are not getting together despite their powerful affinity for each other. What's keeping them apart?

Unless land, labor, and capital *can* get together, there is no production. Economic activity, in which these three factors are joined, is a consequence of human wants, needs, and desires which cannot be satisfied except out of production. These wants and needs are, normally, the stimuli that drive a man into productive activity. If man were a creature without wants, or if his wants could be satisfied by wishing, he would not work, and economic activity would decline toward zero. But this is not the problem posed by a depression. In such a depression as this country suffered between 1929 to 1939, economic activity underwent a steep decline in spite of pressing human needs. The urgent unmet needs and wants which are the natural initiators of the productive process by which they can be met, somehow failed to get production going. Land, labor, and capital stayed apart even though urgent human needs exerted their strong pressures to bring these factors together. Something must have counteracted these pressures.

The three factors of production normally join forces in response to human needs. If there are obvious economic needs and no production results from them, the clear inference is that some force is at work to keep the three factors apart. There is a monkey wrench in the machinery; if we could identify and remove it, perhaps the machinery would start up again. This monkey wrench is not to be found among economic forces or factors. Thus we are forced to ask again: Is it not the intrusion of a noneconomic element which tends to paralyze the productive process?

Peaceful economic activity presupposes the general observance of certain ethical guidelines by the citizenry, boiling down to a general agreement to refrain from violence, theft, and fraud, and to stand by the principles of probity, honesty, and good faith. A framework of law emerges from these principles and, ideally, acts to preserve them and thus maintain the peace of the society against predators from within and aggressors from without. Government so conceived does not interfere positively with the peaceful and productive activities of the citizens and it deters them from interfering with one another. In practice, sad to say, governments often behave quite otherwise, interfering with the economic activities of some of the citizens for the assumed benefit of other citizens, according to the formula: Votes and taxes for all, subsidies for us and our friends. Thus there is nearly always an alien element in the marketplace; besides the native economic factors, there is a political factor. The role this plays in the business cycle and in depressions will be examined in some detail.

It should be somewhat simpler now to deal with a second question: Precisely what was it that collapsed in the United States in October, 1929? Was it the free market economy, or was it a politically rigged economy? Even a casual inspection reveals that the U.S. economy in the 1920s did not conform to the classical free market pattern. It was a politically rigged economy which crashed, and a politically straitjacketed economy which was prevented from rising during the decade of the 1930s.

The 1920s witnessed massive farm support programs, wage and hour legislation, extension of the tariff, private operation of the railroads yielding to stiff regulation and the Railway Labor Act, increased regulation of the utilities and other industries, and the cartelization of certain industries under an energetic Secretary of Commerce. There was the steeply progressive income tax to penalize the successful, there was Prohibition and the zest for political regulation of private affairs which undergirded it. Most damaging of all, perhaps, was the existence of a politically controlled central banking system, the Fed, which became the instrumentality of inflation. The Federal Reserve Board's cheap money policy during the 1920s encouraged speculation and unsound investments. These are some of the ingredients of the boom or bust. The cause of depressions must be sought in a disentangling of the elements which comprise this rigged economic system. No fair-minded person can possibly conclude after examination that the thing which came to a grinding halt in 1929 was the free, private enterprise system; it was not the market economy, or "capitalism," which collapsed.

What are the elements of economic action? What is their bearing on the ideal of freedom in human affairs, and their relationship to the political dimension? Is our Judeo-Christian heritage a relevant concern for those who cherish political and economic liberty, or may a society be at the same time wholly secular and also free? In the course of the ensuing pages I shall argue that the progress of secularism must be at the expense of freedom; that, in other words, the free society can be grounded only in a religious reading of man and his place in the total scheme of things.

But now, let's have a look at the actions of this creature called Economic Man.

CHAPTER 3

Why Economics?

MAN DOES NOT BEGIN TO THINK, ROUSSEAU ASSERTED, UNTIL something prevents him from acting. All thinking is in the form of problem solving or question answering; and it is obvious that, in the absence of problems and questions there would be little or no incentive to work out solutions or seek for answers. When things are running smoothly, we act; when they break down, we take thought. It is the set of problems posed by the fact that things men want on this planet are scarce—relative to human needs and demands for them—that has given rise to the discipline of economics. Economics, in other words, is the discipline emerging from men's efforts to cope with a fact of nature, the fact that the things people want are in short supply. This is one of the universe's built-in frustrations.

The pioneer Hungarian psychoanalyst S. Ferenczi wrote a famous essay shortly after World War I entitled, "Stages in the Development of the Sense of Reality."[1] The individual life cycle begins prenatally in a state of "unconditional omnipotence," Ferenczi maintains. We spend nine months in the womb as a beloved parasite, in an environment where our every need and desire is met even before we become aware of such inner urgencies. There are no unmet demands, no unfulfilled longings. "For what is omnipotence?" writes Ferenczi. "The feeling that one has all one wants, and that one has nothing left to wish for."

1. *Outline of Psycho-analysis*, ed. J. S. Van Tesslar, p. 112.

This blissful state is rudely interrupted by the traumatic experience of birth. Each of us is thrust out into a new environment whose most obtrusive feature is the discrepancy between excess of demands on the one hand, and paucity of means for satisfying them on the other. This is a planet on which things are scantily provided, where men's burgeoning needs and desires forever outrun the planet's capacity to satisfy them. Faulty organization of society exacerbates the problem, but not even the finest conceivable organization of human relationships will eliminate it. You can't pour a gallon of water into a quart jug, no matter how much you might improve the shape of the vessel, and regardless of whether it is a clay pot or a museum piece of fine gold. It is the capacity that counts. The discrepancy between demands and goods is one aspect of the way things are, and human nature is such that men will rebel against the several ineluctable conditions of their existence. Whether Ferenczi's intriguing thesis be accepted, or some simpler explanation be adopted, the plain truth is that men find it difficult to accept the fact that human life is contingent upon factors that human beings did not invent and cannot control. It affronts human pride to acknowledge that man is a dependent being who must yield to the way things are, but it is one facet of man's creaturehood that he is fated to bear the burden of a bundle of unsated wants as a condition imposed by human existence itself. No matter how he contrives he will not get out from under; conditions of human life on this planet decree that there will never be enough. Men have lived with this fact ever since man first appeared, but they have never gotten used to it and probably never will.

At this point economics comes onto the scene. It has no magic wand to eliminate the fact of scarcity; quite the contrary. Were it not for the fact of scarcity there would be no science of economics, for the problem faced by economics is to help people make what little there is go furthest by satisfying men's needs in the order of their urgency. Economics is concerned with the rationing and allocating of scarce goods, an activity forced upon us by the human situation itself.

The human organism after conception and before birth solves his ecological problem, as it might be termed, by being a parasite. The economic problem, properly so called, does not arise until man encounters and tries to resolve the problem of shortages. The womb creature is isolated, insofar as creatures on his own level are concerned. But the fact of scarcity in the human realm makes society necessary. Society is at the very least a labor-saving device, and therefore it is needed by creatures who must economize by conserving scarce goods. Society is thus rooted in the primordial fact of scarcity, but the fruits of human relationships are something else again; they are not limited by this initial stricture.

But if man cannot survive alone, neither is he wholly gregarious; he is a creature who maintains and furthers his identity as a person while living his life in communities. Elaborate theories have been concocted to explain the fact of social cohesion, but most of them overlook the fact that human beings are held together—at the basic level—because they sense that their very survival depends on it. With a part of his being man is an economic animal, a creature who must grade his own needs in terms of the limited means available for satisfying them. Unable to satisfy his every need, he must rank needs in the order of their importance to him, settling for substitutions in some cases, schooling himself to eliminate other demands entirely. In terms of his value system a man decides that a year at college would be more valuable to him than a trip around the world, not being able to enjoy both—or not in the same year, at any rate. Every person has to give up many things, those which rank lower on his value scale, in order to enjoy the things which rank higher.

Man, as a biological organism, cannot survive unless he can meet his creaturely needs from the products of human labor—his own or some other man's. When these needs are temporarily assuaged man becomes something more than a mere biological organism, and another set of needs comes into play. These orient man toward another dimension than the economic. In his effort to satisfy these new demands, man engages in the disinterested pursuit of truth, in the quest for beauty, and in worship. These activities are normal to civilized man, but they are not economic activities.

Economic activity in a healthy society is in the realm of means, being somewhat analogous to digestion in a healthy individual. A person has aims for his life which transcend the processes by which his body is maintained; but if these processes begin to falter and work badly, his attention is drawn away from his life's goals and begins to focus on the machinery of digestion instead. He becomes a hypochondriac. Given other circumstances he may become a glutton. In any event, he has idolatrously erected means into ends, to the detriment of both ends and means.

Economic activity, too, may become an end in itself for a person whose life lacks more worthwhile goals. And a society whose value system is scrambled may subordinate every other good to the pursuit of material success. It is up to a society's religious institutions to keep its value system in good repair; and if they fail to respond with new duties to meet new occasions, it is inevitable that the false gods will try to take over. Then we may have a society whose idol is "economism," a word used by Albert Jay Nock for the doctrine that the whole of life consists in the production, exchange, and consumption of things. This perversion has nothing to do with economics, as such.

Man is set off from nature and other creatures in several ways, and a consideration of his economic activities offers a telling instance of his uniqueness. All creatures take the world pretty much as they find it, except man. Man alone has a time-binding sense; only he can entertain an idea and then transform his environment in accordance with it. Man is equipped with needs that the world as it is cannot satisfy. Thus he is compelled by inner imperatives to alter and rearrange the natural order by employing his energy on raw materials so as to put them into consumable form. Before men can do much of anything else, he must manufacture, grow, and transport. Man shares most of his creaturely needs with the animals, but he alone employs economic means to satisfy them. Only he uses capital, and it is only his time-binding sense that permits him to produce for other than immediate consumption; he produces capital goods which he does not want for themselves, in order to produce more efficiently the consumer goods he does want. This is an enormous leap upward, for by being a capital user man becomes so efficient at satisfying his body hungers that he gains a measure of independence from them, thus exposing himself to the tug of a set of hungers no animal ever feels: for truth, for beauty, for meaning, for God. Man's mastery of his material environment confronts him with a new and different set of problems.

Whatever may be man's capacities in the upper reaches of his nature—to think, dream, pray, create—it is certain that he will attain to none of these unless he survives. And he cannot survive for long unless he engages in economic activities. Economic action at the lowest level merely achieves economic ends; food, clothing, and shelter. But when these matters are efficiently in hand, economic action is a means to all our ends, not only to more refined economic goods, but to the highest goods of the mind and spirit. Add flying buttress and spires to four walls and a roof, and a mere shelter for the body develops into a cathedral to engage the spirit of man.

It is difficult for some to reflect on economic matters without falling into error on one side or the other. On the one hand are the economic determinists, who argue as if man were merely a soulless appendage to his material needs. For them, the modes of production at any given time decree the nature of man's institutions, his philosophies, and even his religions. Economics, under this dispensation, will degenerate into a tool of the state. On the opposite side of the fence is a school of thought which appears to regard it as a cosmic calamity that each soul is sullied by its union with a body which must be fed and kept warm. Spiritual purity will not be attained until there is deliverance from this incubus, but until that happy day let us try to forget that man has creaturely needs which only the products of human labor can satisfy. Not much incentive is generated within this viewpoint to observe and reason out the rules for a functioning economy.

The mainstream of the Judeo-Christian tradition is characterized by a robust earthiness which makes it as alien to the materialism of the first of the above two alternatives as it is to the disembodied spiritualism of the second. The material universe is good, because it is the work of a good God; and a minimum meaning of the Incarnation is that the human body, chosen as a vehicle for the divine, is good. Attitudes of world and life denial are alien to the basic core of Christianity. In the outlook of this faith, properly understood, soul and body are not at war with one another, but are parts of our total human nature. And it is the whole man who needs to be saved, not just the soul. Creaturely needs are, therefore, legitimate; and being legitimate they sanction the economic activities by which alone they can be met.

Such an understanding of man and the human venture prepares

us to accept the idea that economics is a discipline in its own right, governed by its own natural laws. This tradition also makes it plain that economic action is in the realm of means, and thus properly subject to noneconomic criteria, which it is one function of man's religion to supply.

Men have always engaged in economic activities, but an understanding of the general rules underlying the seemingly separate actions of production, exchange, and consumption is less than two centuries old, dating back to the pioneering efforts of Adam Smith.

Men have reflected on production and exchange from earliest times, and attempted regulation of these activities occur and recur throughout history. The attempt to ban usury was common in the ancient world; medieval thinkers sought to establish a "just price" and a "just wage"—and finally found their answer in the market determination of prices and wages. Mercantilism during the seventeenth and eighteenth centuries sought to regulate and manage every facet of the economy. Not until *The Wealth of Nations* was anyone fully aware that market phenomena arising out of production and exchange were not mere haphazard events, but were instead delicately interlocked, exhibiting regularity and sequence in their operations. Economics, in short, is a new discipline in human affairs, and it occupies a strategic position in regard to every other human concern.

F. A. Hayek writes as follows: ". . . the economist can *not* claim special knowledge which qualifies him to co-ordinate the efforts of all the other specialists. What he may claim is that his professional occupation with the prevailing conflicts of aims has made him more aware than others of the fact that no human mind can comprehend all the knowledge which guides the actions of society and of the consequent need for an impersonal mechanism, not dependent on individual human judgments, which will co-ordinate the individual efforts. It is his concern with the impersonal processes of society in which more knowledge is utilized than any one individual or organized group of human beings can possess that puts the economists in constant opposition to the ambitions of other specialists who demand powers of control because they feel that their particular knowledge is not given sufficient consideration."[2]

2. Hayek, *The Constitution of Liberty*, p. 4.

If people do not understand how the market functions they will make impossible demands of it and then blame it for any disasters which may ensue. Or, people will demand economic remedies of government which it is not in the nature of the political agency to "supply". The repercussions of pressure group demands on government will be felt first at the economic level—political folly showing up as economic disaster. Economic ignorance will then dictate further political interventions in a vain effort to cure the evils caused by the initial interventions, and the disaster is compounded.

To sum up: Economics is a discipline called into being by the human need to conserve the earth's scarce goods. Were all goods free goods—as is the case with the outside air we breathe—our estate would be paradisal and there would be no such discipline as economics. But the planetary resources are, in fact, in short supply; this is no one's fault and no one can alter this fact. This is the way things are, and every person must come to terms with these conditions and cope with them as best he can, for time— including the life span allotted to each man—is itself a scarce resource. Time is short, which makes leisure an economic good. But a man cannot live on leisure; he needs an income—food, clothing, shelter, and all the rest. Therefore, he must make a choice: so much income balanced against so much leisure, each calibrated against his ever changing system of wants and demands. In short, he must economize. Because man is man and nature is what it is, each individual lives his life in the wake of a continuous series of decisions. The religious doctrine of free will is amply confirmed by the necessitous nature of economics.

The basics of the economic point of view have been well put by the distinguished theorist, Lionel Robbins:

> From the point of view of the economist, the conditions of human existence exhibit four fundamental characteristics. The ends are various. The time and the means for achieving these ends are limited and capable of alternative application. At the same time the ends have different importance. Here we are, sentient creatures with bundles of desires and aspirations, with masses of instinctive tendencies all urging us in different ways to action. But the time in which these tendencies can be

expressed is limited. The external world does not offer full opportunities for their complete achievement. Life is short. Nature is niggardly. Our fellows have other objectives. Yet we can use our lives for doing different things, our materials and the services of others for achieving different objectives.

The time at our disposal is limited. There are only twenty-four hours in the day. We have to choose between the different uses to which they may be put. The services which others put at our disposal are limited. The material means of achieving ends are limited. We have been turned out of Paradise. We have neither eternal life nor unlimited means of gratification. Everywhere we turn, if we choose one thing we must relinquish others which, in different circumstances, we would wish not to have relinquished. Scarcity of means to satisfy ends of varying importance is an almost ubiquitous condition of human behaviour.

Here, then, is the unity of subject of Economic Science, the forms assumed by human behaviour in disposing of scarce means. . . . Economics is the science which studies human behaviour as a relationship between ends and scarce means which have alternative uses.[3]

It is part of the argument of this book that a rigorous examination of economics reveals an aspect of its nature which tells us that economics by itself is incomplete. Economics is a science of means and, as such, presupposes an end or a hierarchy of ends which it serves. Analogously, an automobile is a means of transportation. Stepping up its power, speed, and efficiency does improve it as a vehicle, but an automobile does not serve its purpose unless those who use it have a destination. This is true even of a racer designed strictly for track use. The immediate purpose of the designers, engineers, and drivers of such a car is to win a particular race; the larger purpose is to learn from men and motors under stress how to improve the automobiles offered to the public for business and pleasure. The final purpose of the vehicle is to take the car owner where he wants to go with relative efficiency.

Economic theory in every department has been immensely refined and enriched since Adam Smith launched the new science. Putting this theory even partially into practice has made the pro-

3. *An Essay on the Significance of Economic Science,* pp. 12–13, 14, 15.

ductive efficiency of the American economy the marvel and envy
of the world. But it is the paradox of the modern world to have
advanced its means in potency and quantity in every department
of life while it has become increasingly uncertain as to what purposes these means should serve: improved means to unimproved
ends. The explosive charge gets bigger and more powerful while
the gun barrel's capacity to contain it becomes ever more questionable. The dilemma thus posed has not always come sharply to
the fore in the economic sector because here a premise has been
smuggled in, to the effect that whatever men may declare to the
contrary, the actual fact is that people everywhere act as if the real
goal of their lives is to maximize profits or accumulate material
possessions. This, therefore—productivity, prosperity—is the generally agreed upon human end for which economics is the
means.

If it be the case with man that his life cycle is aimed at material
accumulation as the overriding purpose of his existence, then it
must be added that he is of all the earth's creatures most
wretchedly adapted to his end. He is distracted by thoughts of
glory, hopes of heaven, dreams of power. He becomes enamored
of his past, he lives for some future; he pursues truth; he gets
hopelessly lost in poetry, music, drama, and art. He gives himself
up to pleasure, he stupefies himself on weird concoctions pulled
out of nature's vast pharmacopoeia, he kills and lets himself be
martyred for a broad spectrum of causes ranging from the most
noble to the utterly absurd. He achieves sanctity or philosophic
calm at one end of the scale, while at the other he goes berserk,
retreats into catatonia, or commits suicide.

Of this baffling creature it is not possible to say with certainty
precisely what his proper end is and gain universal assent to the
proposition, but it should be possible to assert dogmatically what
man's end is *not:* Man's end is not to maximize profits or to pile
up material possessions! No person who candidly consults the
human record can come up with any other conclusion. Material
possessions—like the science of economics itself—are in the realm
of means. Private property is a necessary means for the conservation of the planet's scarce resources, and a necessary institution if
we are to deal responsibly as individual persons with our material
environment. Profit is simply a token that scarce resources are

being used by some one whose custodial services meet with consumer approval; it is a reward for the creative act of combining resources so as to meet the needs consumers most urgently want satisfied.

When a man is starving or perishing from exposure, then the fight for survival becomes an end to be striven for, taking precedence over all other ends. But when pressures for mere survival ease, then he feels welling up within him urges of a uniquely human sort. Out of these urges are born his cultures, his arts, and his religion. It is with the last of these that we are especially concerned; that is to say with the conviction that finite human lives are lived against an infinity of background, that there is a transcendent dimension to the human situation, that men are involved in an order of events which is beyond society and beyond nature. There are things which are seen, touched, and tasted; but is it not obvious that men are also involved in something beyond the sensory order, in a realm of things intangible? The mind which would deny this is, presumably, a mind; and its denial is framed in an idea—the theories of materialism or naturalism. Now "mind" is not a tangible substance; it cannot be seen, nor can it be handled, weighed, or measured. It is intangible, and can hardly be invoked to deny intangibility. Similarly with an idea or a theory. Whatever these are, they are not material. A theory that only the material exists or that matter alone is real is thus a contradiction in terms.

Religion hinges on the reality of things not seen, on the reality of a divine or sacred order that transcends the earthly, natural world into which we are born and where we live out our three score years and ten. It is committed to the proposition that man is a creature of these two realms whether he acknowledges the fact or not, and a further proposition is implied, that men will not be able to order their economic and political affairs aright unless there is a consensus that these important sectors of human life are rightly regarded as neither unimportant, nor all-important, but as preparatory. Man is called to a destiny beyond society and beyond nature, so religion declares, and we need to test the validity of that claim. If it cannot be validated then there is no genuine end, aim, or goal for human life; there are only such transient targets as the pursuit of pleasure, fame, power, wealth, and the like.

The economic task is not one the individual can perform in isolation; in isolation he would die. Every person approaches the resolution of his economic problems as part of an organized network of relationships with his fellows. If John Doe chooses to live he has no choice but to involve himself with society and the market; man's life is contingent and this is one of the conditions. No human being can dictate the terms on which he will consent to reside on this planet; those terms—the rules for human survival —were etched into the nature of things by the Author of nature and they cannot be altered, amended, or repealed. The Unconditioned is God; all else exists on sufferance, and the minimum conditions for survival must be known and met or the organism ceases to be. This is as true now of man as it was then of the dinosaur. Freedom of the will is not mere indeterminacy nor a state of being unconditioned; an individual is free to terminate his own existence, but once having made his decision on behalf of life he has no choice but to meet its conditions, physical as well as social.

Most of the physical conditions for survival are obvious. Deprive a man of oxygen for a few minutes, of water for a few days, of food for a somewhat longer period, and he dies. If the temperature goes too high, he cooks; too low, he freezes. If atmospheric pressure is reduced beyond a certain point his blood literally boils. Internally, he cannot harbor certain microorganisms and live; without certain vitamins and hormones he sickens or perishes.

Social and psychic conditions for survival are not so obvious, but are no less real for all that.If a man derives no inner satisfactions, no psychic compensation, from his actions, he may survive, but he survives embittered, having lost the joy which gives living its savor. Then there are the social conditions that the individual must meet as he pursues his personal goals. The confrontation between the person and his society has been dramatically put by the late Benjamin M. Anderson:

> Objective, external, constraining and impelling forces, which are not physical, which are seemingly not the products of the will of other individuals with whom the individual holds converse, meet the individual on every hand. There is the Moral Law, sacred and majestic, which stands above him,

demanding the sacrifice of many of his impulses and desires. There is the Law, external to him and to his fellows, in seeming, failure to obey which may ruin his life. There is Public Opinion, which presents itself to him as an opaque, impersonal force, before which he must bow, and which he feels quite powerless to change. There are Economic Values ruling in the market place, directing industry in its changing from one sort of production to another, bringing prosperity to one individual and bankruptcy to another, not with the caprice of an individual will, but with the remorseless impersonality of wind and tide. He who conforms to them, who anticipates their mutations, gains great wealth—but no businessman dare set his personal values against them.There are great Institutions, Church and State and Courts and Professions and giant Corporations and Political Parties, and multitudinous other less formal or smaller institutions, which go on in continuous life, though the men who act within them pass and change. Their Life seems an independent life, and the individual who tries to change their course finds that his efforts mean little indeed, as a rule. There is a realm of Social Objectivity, a realm of organization, activity, purpose and power, not physical in character, not mechanical in nature, which is set in opposition to individual will, purpose, power, and activity.[4]

There are also wages and prices, which seem equally objective and external in the eyes of any given consumer. The price of a 1970 Cadillac is not set by the manufacturer, or by legislative fiat, or by any one customer: it is the resultant of an incalculable number of contributory elements which have gone into the pricing of the innumerable factors of production which fan out in all directions from the Cadillac as it now stands to the host of raw materials from which its thousands of components derive. At each step along the way over these countless routes from the earth to the finished product, consumer decisions to buy or do without, based on the shifting value scales of millions of people, issue in a temporarily fixed figure, a price expressed in so many dollars and cents. Before this figure appeared no one knew with certain knowledge what it would be; exactly what the price of a Cadillac is can be known only after the event, that is to say, after the exchange has been effected, and by that time it is history. And, as everyone

4. Benjamin Anderson, *The Value of Money*, pp. 19–20.

knows who has bought a car, the list price is a fiction; the real price takes account of the trade-in value of your old car plus all the "extras" on the new.

The magic of the computer has bemused some people into believing that the problem of economic production and pricing is the kind of enigma a computer can disentangle. Get all the data on last year's production in the United States, including prices and wages, feed it into the computer and we'd know how much of each commodity to produce next year and, knowing the prices of the factors of production we would know what price tag to put on each finished item. Such confident optimism rests on a complete misreading of the economic picture.

In the first place, no finite mind can comprehend "all the data on last year's production." Who can trace out the millions of decisions to buy this product rather than that, or what vague impulse prompted this sale? Poll individual purchasers and even they have difficulty in saying precisely why they bought this item rather than that. In the second place, economic production is global. No country is completely autonomous, and so long as international trade is not prevented by governmental action there will be exchanges across borders. If something is being produced in Outer Barbaria at last year's costs and offered to this year's consumers at last year's prices, there is no guarantee of sales. This year's consumers may buy, or their tastes may have switched to something else, or a producer in the next country may have discovered a way to cut costs so that he can sell the same item for half of the domestic producer's price.

But even if we could accomplish the impossible twice—feed *all* the data of last year's production into the computer, and secure worldwide cooperation—we'd still not have the information we want. The information we would get from the computer would be the history of what several billion consumers wanted, produced, and exchanged last year; and the information we need relates to what these billions will want and work for next year. The computer gives us a chunk of history; it does not provide us with prophecy, and accurate prophecy concerning millions of pieces of data, plus knowledge of innovations to be made in technological, managerial, and marketing areas, plus an accurate profile of constantly shifting tastes, desires, impulses, and actions of consumers is a minimum requirement in order to draw up a firm set of plans for world production. Such an expectation is wholly out of touch with reality; it is in the realm of fantasy. The future is not known to men; tomorrow is uncertain, next year more so. The only recourse available to human beings facing the future's uncertainties is in the protection that comes from spreading the risks, and this means encouraging entrepreneurial decisions on the part of everyone willing to stick his neck out.

Prices on the free market are a result of the buying habits of consumers, and anyone who has attended auctions has witnessed, in miniature, price formation in action. If many people want to acquire that battered, antique chest of drawers, the price of it goes up beyond what everyone but one person is willing to pay. He gets it, being willing to part with his fifty dollars because he wants the chest more than he wants his money. This transaction telegraphs a message to producers of battered, antique chests of drawers: "A chest that we can produce for seventeen and a quarter sold last week at the Shadyside Auction for fifty dollars." With the result that several chests are on display for the next go-round. If the supply increases and the demand continues, the price is going to be driven down to the price which clears the market. The market price is one which the consumer is willing to pay, and a price at which the producer and seller can make at least the going rate of profit and the going wage.

Anyone, of course, can put a price tag on his product, but the price of his product is what it will sell for, and no producer can control that. A man is, of course, within his rights to decide that he will not go on producing a gizmo if the prices of gizmos sink below a certain level; but if he wants to stay in business he has to yield to the whims of consumers, make some product they want, and offer it at a price they are willing to pay.

And just as no manufacturer can set prices, neither can he set wages. The market performs both of these tasks for him. "It is a proposition of elementary economics," writes the noted economist, Frank R. Knight, "that ideal market competition will force entrepreneurs to pay every productive agent employed what his cooperation adds to the total, the difference between what it can be with him and what it would be without him. This is his own product in the only meaning the word can have where persons or

their resources act jointly."[5] In short, each person will get his fair
share, defined as what others will voluntarily offer for his goods
and services—provided there is general freedom.

Each person, at any selected time, lives out his role within a
social pattern that appears to be simply given: as external and
objective as his physical environment. Neither he nor anyone else
invented, designed, or imposed it. The social order is not perceiv-
able by the senses, but can be grasped only by the intellect and
imagination, and it is spontaneous in the sense that it arises naturally as a by-product of individual human action over a period of
time pursuing a multitude of other ends. "Something greater than
men's individual mind may grow from man's fumbling efforts,"
writes Hayek, and then he quotes Adam Ferguson, contemporary
of Adam Smith, who marveled "how nations stumbled upon estab-
lishments which are indeed the result of human action but not the
execution of human design." The social order, therefore, is fully
comprehensible only to omniscience, and as soon as this point
sinks in there arises the understanding that a "planned society" is
a contradiction in terms. "The case for individual freedom,"
continues Hayek, "rests chiefly on the recognition of the
inevitable ignorance of all of us concerning a great many of the
factors on which the achievement of our ends and welfare depends."[6]

We have moved some distance from the simple pioneer or the
Robinson Crusoe who bends every effort of nerve and muscle
merely to survive. His effort is the mainly physical one of expend-
ing his energy, augmented by the tools he has accumulated, to
transform the raw materials at his disposal into consumable form.
We never lose touch with this basic equation, but in developed
economic action a great many new factors enter the picture. When
mere survival is not a critical factor and after large amounts of
capital in the form of complex tools and machines have been
accumulated, the entrepreneur plays a vital role in economic action. Available human energy, natural resources, and tools can be
combined in a variety of ways to accomplish a myriad of ends, but
not all ends at once. The decision to combine economic factors in
this way rather than that is an entrepreneurial decision, and it is

5. Knight, *Goals of Economic Life*, p. 222.
6.Hayek, *The Constitution of Liberty*, pp. 29, 57, and 59.

a creative act just as surely as the act of writing a poem or composing a symphony.

Manufacturing things, growing them, and transporting them from here to there, are all properly regarded as productive activities. After an entrepreneurial decision has been made as to what shall be manufactured, grown, and transported, the problems are technological; they are in the engineer's province. The engineer serves a vital function in production, but it is to be distinguished sharply from that of the entrepreneur. Production at the engineering level ". . . is not an act of creation," writes Ludwig von Mises, "it does not bring about something that did not exist before." He continues:

> It is a transformation of given elements through arrangement and combination. The producer is not a creator, man is creative only in thinking and in the realm of imagination. In the world of external phenomena he is only a transformer."[7]

The entrepreneur makes the difference, supplying the creative mind.

> Only the human mind that directs action and production is creative. The mind too appertains to the universe and to nature; it is a part of the given and existing world. To call the mind creative is not to indulge in any metaphysical speculations. We call it creative because we are at a loss to trace the changes brought about by human action farther back than to the point at which we are faced with the intervention of reason directing human activities. Production is not something physical, natural, and external; it is a spiritual and intellectual phenomenon. Its essential requisites are not human labor and external natural forces and things, but the decision of the mind to use these factors as means for the attainment of ends. . . . The materialist metaphysics of the Marxians misconstrues these things entirely. The "productive forces" are not material. Production is a spiritual, intellectual, and ideological phenomenon. It is the method that man, directed by reason, employs for the best possible removal of uneasiness. What distinguishes our conditions from those of our

7. Mises, *Human Action*, p. 140.

ancestors who lived one thousand or twenty thousand years
ago is not something material, but something spiritual. The
material changes are the outcome of the spiritual changes.[8]

Mindful of the spiritual and cultural factors that set off human
beings from other organisms, and within a given society with its
own traditions and history, the individual finds his place in the
economic order in a niche called a job. A job is not precisely the
same as work. In order to work a man needs only to be free to
scratch the earth, pick its fruit, catch its game, or lure its fish out
of their watery habitat. Many primitives still eke out a meagre
existence at this level, being without any capital except the sim-
plest tools. The overwhelming majority of men and women who
have ever lived on this earth have lived in abject poverty and as
the victims of hunger and disease; such is the lot of most men and
women alive today. The teeming populations of Africa and the
Orient are poor today because they lack capital. There is nothing
like an instinct in man, nor any overwhelming drive, which urges
him on to continuously improve his material circumstances. It
may be granted that the fellahin and the coolies who make up the
masses in the East do want to survive and do not consciously
waste their resources; but the urge to break out of their poverty
routine is a weak one. Granted also that their energies are sapped
by endemic malaria and other diseases, and by parasites of various
kinds—this is more of an effect than a cause. They live at the
starvation level because there is so little capital per worker; their
tools are too few and too poor to fully augment human energies.
They have too little capital because the layer of wealth is too thin,
and too little of the wealth is turned to capital use, which is the
only way to increase the production of wealth. Wealth is not
accumulated, because material possessions are discouraged by the
prevailing taboos, and private property is not safe because it is not
sacred—according to the same taboos. Wealth and property are
scorned because they are material, and the material world is evil.
If the world is evil, why seek to improve our position in it? And
over the whole hangs a paralyzing fatalism, leading to a placid
acceptance of poverty, starvation, and disease as the natural lot of
mankind.

8. *Ibid.*, p. 141.

The progressive attitude of Western man as it has exhibited itself periodically ever since the Age of Pericles is not a characteristic of man per se. It is a cultural trait, religiously inspired. If the religious philosophy posits the world as the creation of a good God, Who gives man a soul and makes him responsible for its proper ordering, puts him on earth as a sort of junior partner with dominion over it and with the admonition to be fruitful and multiply, commands him to work, makes him a steward of the earth's resources, holds him accountable for their economic use, and makes theft wrong because property is right—when this outlook comes to prevail then the groundwork is laid for a free and prosperous commonwealth. This is the world view of Biblical religion, taught to the West by Christianity which incorporated Hebraic, Greek, and Roman elements to lay the foundations of Christendom. The alternative Oriental world view does not breed the kind of mentality which sets out heartily to improve human circumstances.

The world has an infinite amount of work to be done; there will never be a shortage of work, which is why the economists call work a dis-utility. Work is what we try to save ourselves from because we are really after the products of work. To secure this end result, consumable products, it is a job we want—a context in which work is performed augmented by anywhere up to one hundred and ten thousand dollars worth of tools and machines, usually belonging to some one other than the user. The average amount of capital invested per worker in the United States is somewhere between seventeen and twenty thousand dollars. In the petroleum industry, the average, according to a recent Department of Commerce estimate, is $110,700. American productivity is higher than that of any other country, and wages here are higher in consequence; and the reason is not that we are smarter, soberer, more industrious, or work longer hours. We have more and better tools and machines; that is to say, there is far more capital invested per worker here than in any other country, and our prosperity follows naturally. In the hundred-year period beginning just before the Civil War, our population has increased sevenfold and our work force eightfold. Available goods and services during this period have multiplied more than thirty-three times (3300%), while at the same time hours of work have decreased by 40%.

There is no route to Paradise in this direction, but these figures do represent an undeniable achievement. If our achievements have been less spectacular in other directions—in the arts, for example, as some critics tell us—then the reply is that there is no conceivable way a nation can improve its culture by destroying its economy. This can only lead to a general impoverishment when our professed aim is to move in the other direction.

Poverty in a society is overcome by productivity, and in no other way. There is no political alchemy which can transmute diminished production into increased consumption. Government interventions into economic life can redistribute goods by taxing everyone and subsidizing a few, taking money out of the pockets of some and putting it into the pockets of others. But obviously no such scheme can elevate the *general* welfare. The economic welfare of all can be raised only by removing artificial (usually political) impediments from wealth production. More can be consumed only if more is produced.

Men have been freer to produce up to individual capacity in American society, historically, than in any other society, and our affluence, as a result, is the envy of the world. Hindsight tells us that we might have done even better if our statutes had permitted as much economic freedom as we said we believed in. Actually there has been much antieconomic legislation since 1789, but it was not till a generation ago that we began cutting our economic throat on principle.

When the spiritual, cultural, political, and social conditions are right, the economy spontaneously forms a complex order out of the separate actions of men seeking economic betterment. This order comes into focus for the individual in his job. In this context he receives the wages he later transforms into the variety of things he wants; he is provided with a means for gaining satisfaction out of measurable accomplishments; he has an economic base as a buttress to personal independence and integrity. Freedom is important here, because if it is lacking in the context of a man's work it can hardly survive elsewhere, as we shall see in the next chapter.

CHAPTER 4

The Market: Its Strength
and Limitations

THE MARKET ECONOMY IS WIDELY IGNORED AS A SUBJECT OF study by men otherwise well read; it is wildly misrepresented, and wantonly attacked. On the other hand, it has exceedingly able supporters, superior to their opposition in the battle of ideas, but badly outnumbered. Compared to the army of detractors, the defenders of the market are a tiny Gideon's band. Given this situation, with its attendant frustrations, it is to be expected that some champions of the market should be seized by a sense of mission which sometimes leads them to overstate their case. Government comprises the coercive, political sector of society; the market is in the noncoercive sector. What takes place there? Production of material goods, creation of artistic and spiritual goods, but in addition, everything stupid, ignorant, evil, mean, and vulgar— except coercion itself.

The market is not an omnicompetent contrivance; it is not a kind of magic mill through which all sorts of problems may be run for instant solutions, or all sorts of questions for perfect answers. It is not a superhuman thing at all. The inherent frailties and shortcomings of the market follow from a definition of it: The market consists of people in free, voluntary exchange of goods, services, and ideas. It is nothing but that and people are fallible. People are fallible, not only when they have shaken off the delusion that coercion is a fruitful source of social good, but always. They are fallible when they are neither being coerced nor coercing;

even when they are acting peacefully, with the best will in the world, and on the fullest information available, they fall into error. It follows, therefore, that the market will exhibit every shortcoming men exhibit in their thinking and peaceful acting, for—in the broadest sense—it is nothing else but that. The market is a magnificent tool for operating on the economic problem—which is the problem of allocating the planet's scarce resources efficiently and without waste. It is, in fact, the only tool available to men in this area of life. But the market is not a universal tool; it is not the appropriate tool for every human problem, and the effort to so use it results in a loss of focus which distracts from the market's economic competence.

Catalog human shortcomings and you have compiled a list of the weaknesses and limitations of the market. Operating in the private sector, entirely apart from government, men have concocted the weirdest sorts of notions which they have then teased into the semblance of a system. Some have set themselves up as the grand panjandrum of a cult, and followers come out of the woodwork. Think of the offbeat money cranks; the oddballs and fanatics in metaphysics; the faddists in diet and medicine; the people who claim contact with creatures from outer space, and so on and so on. There is always a ready market for nonsense. On a more serious level there is the example of Karl Marx. He lived, worked, and wrote as a scrounger, but not off any government. He spent part of his life on the other side of the law, as *persona non grata* with the governments of Germany and France, ignored by the government of England. He wrote, organized, and intrigued. He acquired followers and launched a movement which has gained fateful power in today's world; but long before the Communists gained political power Marx's ideas had become convictions in the minds and wills of thousands of people by the only means open to the penetration of ideas—by peaceful, voluntary, willing acceptance and exchange. Broadly speaking, this traffic and barter of ideas is the market, and all the market tells us about ideas and ideologies is that they have won acceptance in the minds of the multitude. This fact—the mass acceptance of a philosophy or of a single idea—says nothing about the merit of the ideas themselves; it merely acknowledges their popular appeal.

Ideas are generated, accepted, exchanged, developed, and

propagated only under conditions of voluntary and willing exchange—free market conditions—because this is their nature. A
government may step into the picture at some late date to put its
coercive power behind some idea or ideology, now inflated into a
received orthodoxy—but only after the ideology has first won
widespread acceptance among a significant number of people, who
at the same time are convinced that their ideology is so important
that doubters and heretics are properly punishable by law. A set
of ideas has to capture the market; that is, win the allegiance of
the masses, before government gets into the picture at all.

When a person affirms that he believes in a free market of ideas,
he may be uttering a mere truism—for ideas operate only under
conditions of free and willing exchange—or he may be saying—
along the lines of Milton and Jefferson—that government should
be nonideological. A society should have freedom of worship,
press, and the academy, so that truth and error might slug it out
in the forum; truth needs no authority other than itself, and error
should have none. The classical liberals were unanimous in contending that true ideas needed their help; they did not believe in
merely sitting back to wait for "the free market in ideas" to sort
out truths from falsehoods. Truth needs champions willing to go
to the mat for it, willing to expose entrenched error in full and free
discussion, willing to expound truth attractively, until the old
falsehoods finally slink away. The fact that certain ideas have, at
a given time, gained "majority acceptance" is only another way of
saying that "the masses have an ideology." This fact tells us nothing as to the merits of the ideology the masses have accepted, by
comparison with those they have rejected. Widespread public acceptance of an idea is no valid test of the idea. A philosophical
judgment is not passed merely by a show of hands, pro and con.
Nor is man's intellectual stature measured by the results of a
popularity poll.

Imagine a poll to be taken among the professors of economics
in our colleges, asking them to rate living economists on a scale
from one to a hundred. Where would Mises stand on this list—
assuming he would even make it! Ask the professors of political
science to do the same for their profession. Would Hayek make
it? There is, in today's world, a very weak market demand for free
market exponents. What then? Either we fall into step with the

herd and make the mass judgment our own, or we deny that this kind of test has any validity whatsoever. The free market is an incompetent instrument in the realm of ideas; it is merely a way of saying that the majority or the masses or the public has willingly embraced this ideology rather than that. The merits of this idea compared to that idea poses a question that cannot be resolved by counting noses, but only on the basis of reason and by weighing the relative evidence.

Unsound and phony ideas and philosophies are produced, exchanged, and traded just as freely and willingly as worthier products of the intellect—or more so. It has been argued persuasively by H. L. Mencken, among others, that the average man has a positive libido for expansive buncombe, coupled with a definite aversion to realities which restrict. The masses today embrace disastrous notions of political and social organization, while sound ideas go begging, or find lodgment in a few minds only. Given this situation, the market in candidates for political office will present us with a choice between Tweedle-dum and Tweedle-dee. Once in office, a politician is part of the apparatus of coercion; but up to and through election day he is the product of a willing exchange of ideas, actions, and promises.

The public taste which runs to collectivism in social theory is not likely to exhibit elevated tastes in the arts. The most popular novelists, playwrights, poets, and musicians of our day run true to form—or, rather, formlessness. The current market in the arts is on the same level as the current market in economic and political theory, and that level is pretty low.

Economic fallacies, even when embraced by the masses, do not cease being fallacies; and the fallacies should be resisted with economic truths even though all men but one embraced them. The test of whether a doctrine is true or false has nothing to do with the numbers lined up on one side or the other. The same considerations apply to every other intellectual question. Likewise, moral questions. Ethical norms are not established by mass or majroity; the validity of a moral judgment is not affected by the number of people who register an opinion for or against. Likewise, esthetic judgments. Ian Fleming is outselling Shakespeare; the Beatles are more popular than Beethoven and Bach combined. But mass taste is not the touchstone of artistic merit.

There is an area of life, however, where intellectual, ethical, and esthetic considerations are either very weakly implicated or absent altogether. It is a matter of intellectual and moral indifference whether John Doe chooses a green or black Chevrolet, and how much chrome is wrapped around it, and whether it has tail fins or not. Tastes vary in these matters, and because mass produced goods must appeal to the masses, many an individual may not be able to find an automobile whose every specification suits him. The public likes gaudy wagons with white sidewalls and lots of chrome, and the manufacturers have no choice but to cater to the public taste. If a manufacturer tries to impose his taste on the public he'll go out of business. It is amusing to recall a top official of one of the major automobile companies who bought one of his company's finest cars and proceeded to paint out the chrome and replace the white sidewalls with black tires.

The capitalist may not share the tastes of the buying public, but nevertheless he must cater to popular taste if he would stay in business. So long as no moral violations are involved, this is perfectly proper.

The economic problem is posed by the inevitable tension which exists between the facts of nature and the facts of human nature. On one side of the economic equation is man, a creature with insatiable wants and needs. On the other side is nature, where the things by which man's wants and needs may be satisfied are located. The equation is out of balance, by definition. The resources of the planet are limited, whereas every human want fulfilled breeds new wants. Everything which man needs, wants, and desires from nature is a "good" because he wants it, and because his wants are unlimited, all goods are scarce.

To qualify as an economic good a thing must be both wanted and scarce relative to the demand generated by the want. Air is not an economic good, because it exists in sufficient quantity and is so universally available that everyone can have all he wants merely for the taking, and there is lots left over. But conditioned air *is* an economic good. It is scarce; therefore, those who want it must want it badly enough to be willing to give up something in order to get it. They exchange something they value a little less for the conditioned air, which obviously ranks higher on their value scale than the item they have exchanged for it.

We have seen that the area open to the voluntary and willing exchange of goods, services, and ideas is vast, and that within this area there are relevant intellectual, ethical, and esthetic criteria which must be brought to bear upon certain problems. Mass commitment to an idea is no guarantee of its truth; an idea is tested for truth by other criteria than its victory in a popularity contest. Likewise goodness and beauty. But there is an area of life where these values are not at stake, and where there is no other criterion of what the public should be given than what the public wants. This is the area of political economy. If the public buys Brand X in preference to Brand Y, it is exercising its rightful power of choice, and its free choice here has enormous implications for the way in which society is to be organized. Free choice exercised here, in the economic area—the realm of means for provisioning our material and creaturely needs—produces the seedbed for a free society. Whereas the organized effort to stifle free choice at this point must result in the closed society, some form of collectivism.

In the opening pages of his mighty work, *Human Action*, Ludwig von Mises observes that "In the course of social events there prevails a regularity of phenomena to which man must adjust his action if he wishes to succeed." This is but another way of saying that the ancient concept of the natural law extends to the activities by which men produce and exchange goods, and earn a living.

We live in an age of group-think. Some forms of group-think wave enough red flags to warn off the wary, but other forms sneak up on us. One variety of group-think may, if we are not careful, stem from the method of science. Science deals with the laws which govern the behavior of things; it is not concerned with particular things except insofar as these exemplify a general rule. A freely falling body moves at a constant rate of acceleration, whether it be an apple falling on Newton's head, a weight dropped by Galileo from the Leaning Tower of Pisa, or a bomb falling on Dresden. Analyze the falling object scientifically and another general rule emerges which the apple, or the weight, or the bomb exemplify. The uniqueness of this particular apple, weight, or bomb eludes the method employed by the scientist. The scientist, however, may step out of his professional role and—for instance —acting as a concerned citizen, condemn the bombing of defenseless cities.

Economics is, in some respects, a science. It asserts that every human being's every deliberate action aims at improvement in the acting agent's condition. But at the same time it stresses the impossibility of predicting just what action John Doe will take at a given time and place in order to better his circumstances. Its terms are all general and abstract. "Human being" is a concept generalized from experience with particular John Does and Jane Roes. Particular persons exist in time and space, but "human beings" and "individuals" are merely useful ideas. "Human action" is a purely formal term for describing whatever alters future conditions; inaction thus is a variety of action. Nor does the economist, as such, try to tell John Doe what standards he ought to employ to help him decide whether his changed circumstance is really for the better or the worse. Satisfactions are not merely quantitative; they are of differing qualities. Perhaps there are some satisfactions that are more appropriate to our nature and the fulfilling of our destiny than others; and some satisfactions we ought to shun altogether. Mere feelings, at this point, are not a reliable guide. A painkilling and euphoric drug may give us that "feel better feeling fast." Relying on this drug to upgrade our feeling states, we pass the point of no return with a cancer which, if we had accepted the warning pain earlier, would have been operable. The sadist maximizes his satisfactions by hurting others; the masochist by being hurt. The misanthrope functions optimally in the presence of other folk's misery; the man of good will raises the level of his own satisfactions by spreading happiness among his friends. "Satisfactions," in other words, is a purely formal term, an abstraction; content and meaning have to be supplied. It is not science's role to fill in the specific and the concrete, for it deals with the general and the abstract.

Economics can lay down the general rules which a nation or society must follow if it wishes to attain maximum prosperity and material wellbeing. If John Doe wants to learn how his nation or society can prosper, economics can tell him. But if John Doe asks a radically different question, namely, "How can I make the most money with the least effort?" he will not find his answer in economic science—although certain men with economic and other skills might be able to help him by correctly calling the turn on business trends and the like. But economic science per se cannot predict, so when it comes to forecasting it can offer no more than educated guesses, at best.

Economic science can provide John Doe with a prescription for making his nation or society prosperous, but it cannot tell him that he ought to obey that set of rules. If he, being of a predatory or parasitic disposition, concludes after much study that he can best enrich himself by judicious predation and/or parasitism, the economist steps out of character and assumes the role of moralist if he criticizes John's conduct. John Doe may know the laws of economics making for national wellbeing, and encourage their adoption in his society—knowing that the more prosperous the society the more successful will be his predation and parasitism. Very few nonproducers can live off a society at the subsistence level, but a wealthy society can support a great many. A predatory class needs a society with a high standard of living if it is to operate successfully; which means that the society must, for the most part, obey economic laws, even if the predators don't. Further, it is to the self-interest of predators to see that it does. The market, if it is to function optimally, needs the protection of a framework pieced together from spiritual, ethical, and legal components. Thus the need for government.

Government is the coercive sector of society. We have government because of the notorious fact that cooperation sometimes breaks down. Not all private human action is voluntary, some is coerced; some people threaten other people, use violence on them, aggress against them, invade their privacy. This is criminal action, and society has a legal agency of coercion with a sufficiency of counterforce to deter aggression; or, when the aggressor is not deterred, to punish him. Now there are borderline cases in all fields of human inquiry. Of certain organisms we cannot say for certain whether they are animal or vegetable, dead or alive. The tobacco virus exists in a border zone between organisms and matter. We can distinguish between an oak and an acorn, but there is not a stage in the development of this seed when we are able to say, "At this particular moment it has ceased being an acorn and is now a tree." Likewise, we may be in doubt about certain actions as to whether they are aggressive and criminal on the one hand, or defensive and peaceful on the other. But there can be no disputing the fact that the concepts "defensive" and "aggressive" exist and are theoretically intelliglble, and that we do readily distinguish between some acts of aggression and some acts of defense. Government is the instrument for settling disputes of this kind, being the repository of the rules by which the people of a given society have chosen to live, and possessing in its legal apparatus for interpretation and enforcement the means for countering criminal actions. Government, like the market, is composed of people and is, therefore, fallible.

The market, to repeat, is but a name for people in peaceful, voluntary, willing exchange. When Mr. A aggresses against Mr. B or coerces him in any way, the market has been eliminated from this situation; it ceases to exist. Mr. B may decide to ignore the aggression, or the two men may iron out their dispute in some way. But if the aggression continues so that Mr. B's rights and prerogatives are constantly transgressed, and transgressed on principle, then this violation constitutes a moral evil and calls for the lesser evil of counterforce to eliminate it. Society's legal agency of coercion, government, goes to work.

Peaceful, willing exchange between Mr. A and Mr. B breaks down, really breaks down, when Mr. A refuses to abide by the rules governing it and willfully aggresses against Mr. B. The market is now nonoperative in this situation. The necessary counterforce and legal coercion required to break this impasse will compel Mr. A to desist from actions that he cannot be persuaded to desist from. Force is used on Mr. A to recover the peace that was broken by his unpeaceful action. A human arrangement utterly unlike the market must be invoked when the market—the peaceful, voluntary way—is breached and driven out by acts of violence. The market, by its very nature, cannot traffic and barter in acts of coercion; market coercion is a contradiction in terms, like peaceful force. The life of social cooperation under the division of labor, with the resulting exchange of specializations, requires another and different kind of social institution to protect its operations. The market, in other words, needs government, not—it must be insisted—to make it work, but to protect it from those who will not permit it to work.

CHAPTER 5

The Philosophical Framework of the
Free Economy

NEARLY EVERYONE HAS A STAKE IN A PROSPEROUS SOCIETY.
General prosperity and an abundance of material goods provide
the optimum conditions under which every peaceful citizen can
achieve his own life goals with an economy of effort. If his goal is
to make a million dollars, the average man's chances are better in
New York or Wichita than in some remote village in Africa or
Asia. If his goal is scientific research, a prosperous society has
more and better laboratories—other things being equal—than a
poor society. If he wants to be a classical scholar, a prosperous
society opens up greater possibilities for the average boy to acquire
an education, and provides him with great universities and librar-
ies. Even the man who renounces the world and takes a vow of
poverty can pursue his life's goal better in a prosperous society
than in a society at the subsistence level; and more people, relatively speaking, have this opportunity when production is efficient.

So much for the plus side; now for the debit side. There is the
famous line of Oliver Goldsmith, "Where wealth accumulates and
men decay." Case histories in support of this dictum occur to
every one of us; of families ruined by riches, and nations as well.
Youngsters who have had everything handed to them on a silver
platter by indulgent parents face life terrifically handicapped. A
nation which has forgotten the meaning of hard work goes soft,
and is easy prey for nations with no fat around the middle. Share-
the-wealth schemes do not arise seriously in nations which have

no wealth to share; socialism is strictly a disease of prosperous societies. Finally, every crook, con man, predator, and parasite has a stake in a rising level of general prosperity. The petty thief exists in every society, but racketeering and thievery on the grand scale operate most successfully in a wealthy society.

The economist gets into this picture by prescribing the rules for a prosperous society. The science of economics does not tell people what to prefer or what to produce; it abstains from value judgments. Economics operates in the realm of means. Once people decide what they want in the way of the good things of life, economics can tell them the most efficient means for attaining their ends—the fullest satisfaction of their wants.

I would stress the importance of lining up question and answer; they must be on the same plane; they must be congruent. If we think we are answering question A when actually the matter before the house is question B, we are in trouble. Economic science faces the question: How can society or the nation attain maximum prosperity? And it answers: A society or nation will use its scarce goods most efficiently and attain maximum material wellbeing if the market is permitted to operate freely, without hampering restraints or controls from outside. Economic science deals with general rules and principles; it does not deal with the specific application of those rules by John Doe or Richard Roe. John Doe asks himself the question: Why should I conform my conduct to the recipe for national prosperity? The set of answers given by economics is for a different question, though a related one. A true answer for the economic question is not necessarily the right answer for a moral question. In order to get from the general recipe for a prosperous society offered by economics to an answer congruous with the question asked by John Doe we have to move into another discipline, the discipline of ethics. When John Doe asks what he *ought* to do, he has moved from the vocabulary of economics into the vocabulary of ethics. It is only a sense of moral obligation that can get us from the recipe for general prosperity to a sense of individual responsibility for the personal practice of the rules which make for freedom in exchange.

Two things, wrote Immanuel Kant, filled him with awe: the starry heavens without and the moral law within. The moral law is sometimes referred to as the natural law, or the moral order; it boils down to the conviction that there are objective standards for human conduct to which all men are properly subject. Human beings have some difficulty deciding what things are right and what things are wrong, but they are virtually unanimous in believing that some things are right and others wrong. Few persons have not at some point experienced the pull of moral obligation, or a sense of duty. There may be persons who lack a conscience, just as there are colorblind people, or people with tone deafness. But a person without a moral sense is deficient in one of the essential ingredients in the makeup of a human being. Every man who has ever said to himself: "I'd like to do this, but I ought to do that," has felt the influence of moral obligation. This is why we resist those who try to reduce morality to legality, or to custom, or to majority decision, or to tribal ways, or to the will of the stronger, or to any nonethical base whatsoever.

Belief in a moral order in the universe is no guarantee that disputes between men will not arise—or, once having arisen will be settled automatically. All a common ethical code can promise is that when disputes do occur—and disputes are a built-in feature of human action—the parties to them can have recourse to a method by which they *may* be settled by men of good will. The alternative is that all disputes be fought out, which is to abandon right for might.

The idea of a moral order is indeed a restraint on the individual; it curbs many actions he might want to take by condemning them as wrong or unjust. Some persons with a spurious idea of individualism reject the moral law precisely because every man, in their view, is or should be a law unto himself. This view results in situations where might or guile substitutes for right, and if we're all in the clear about this we can take care of such persons. Obviously, it is impossible to have a free society on such terms; a free society needs rules.

There is another school of thought among libertarians which is reluctant to admit the fact of moral obligation because it thinks such an admission commits it to the welfare state. Christian charity is the obligation to play the role of Good Samaritan when the occasion indicates. This is a voluntary act, where a man gives of himself, his own money, his own time, his own resources. This is diametrically opposed to the welfare state or socialistic idea, in which the apparatus of compulsion first deprives everyone of a portion of his resources, then impersonally redistributes this booty according to political expediency. This has no resemblance whatsoever to genuine charity. To suggest that the Good Samaritan kind of moral obligation commits one to socialism or the welfare state is utter nonsense! The opposite is true; one feeder of the socialistic idea is the weakening or the denial of moral obligation.

The idea of a moral law superior to tribal mores or national folkways is one of the leading spiritual principles of the West, according to New York University historian, H. Bamford Parkes. The other main principles are the idea of ethical monotheism—belief in a God of righteousness—and the idea of the Christian kingdom of heaven. With these two items we move out of the realm of ethics into that of religion.

What is the relevance of ethical monotheism to the idea of a free society? In order to answer this question let us compare our situation with that of the ancient world. It was the belief in the Egypt of old that God himself, in the person of the Pharaoh, had taken charge of human affairs. There is a name for this idea of government; it is Oriental Despotism, a characteristic political form in Asia. We are so familiar with the distinction between "sacred" and "secular" that it is only with difficulty that we can imagine living under conditions where the sacred and the social are coterminous. Oriental Despotism presides over a sacred society in which individuality is submerged. The situation was somewhat better in ancient Greece, but nothing like our idea of limited government is to be found in the writings of Plato and Aristotle. Man, Aristotle said, is a political animal. Aristotle was not merely calling attention to the obvious fact that men live in social organizations as their natural habitat; by calling man a political animal Aristotle was saying that man is the kind of creature who might find complete fulfillment within the Greek city-state. The Greek *polis* was church and state in one; its politics, one might say, was salvational. Our idea of relegating the state to the modest role of umpire, keeping the peace by merely enforcing the agreed upon rules, would have been largely incomprehensible to men of the ancient world. The head of the ancient state was also its religious leader; Julius Caesar, you recall, was also Pontifex Maximus, the chief priest. The individual, in this kind of setup, was really locked into society—body and soul.

Then, along came a new religion which transformed the ancient world by teaching that only part of man is social, that man's essence belongs to God. The individual within society now has a leverage on something beyond and above society. Politics no longer has an absolute value; something more important has a claim on man.

This idea is part of our heritage from the Old Testament, with its stress on God's transcendence. The common opinion in the ancient world was that a god was useful to have around to sanction social practices, to guarantee prosperity, and to insure victory in war. If a tribe lost a battle, this would be accepted as signifying the superiority of the god or gods of the victors; if a crop failed, the particular god who fouled up that situation was sacked. Some such idea of god is still widely held by our contemporaries. The Victorian novelist Samuel Butler satirized this notion when he said: "To love God is to have good health, good looks, good luck, and a fair balance of cash in the bank." This is the god of magic; not the God of religion. The ancient Israelites, although they lapsed now and again, discarded the notion of a god kept on tap to bestow prosperity and victory. They believed in a God of righteousness and truth, and they saw the workings of God even in their own poverty and defeat. The God of religion is not to be used as it suits the whim of man; he is the Absolute to which men must conform their lives—if they would really live.

The God of religion transcends human affairs. No longer is it possible to believe that the social and sacred orders coincide; the sacred or divine order overarches the social order; it is the larger category which includes society within it. Man's destiny, then, is not simply to be a creature of society or the state; this is the beehive or anthill conception of life. Each man has an individual destiny which enables him to emerge out of society and propels him beyond it; he has a soul, for whose proper ordering he is responsible to his Creator.

This idea became part of Christian doctrine and it made a big difference to the politics of the West; it undercut the totalitarian idea which ruled the ancient world. Here is the way a British political scientist, J. B. Morrall, states the new political development which occurred after the fall of Rome: "Medieval Europe offers for the first time in history the somewhat paradoxical spectacle of a society trying to organize itself politically on the basis of a spiritual framework (which gives to political life merely a relative value). By so doing western European thought about politics was propelled along lines which were to be sharply different from those of any other human society."[1]

Political theory in our tradition is based on the assumption that men must be free in society because each person has a destiny beyond society which he can work out only under conditions of liberty. In other words, the inner and spiritual liberty of man proclaimed in the Gospels implies the outer and social freedom needed for its completion. Loyal to these premises, the peoples of the West began their long and painful ascent toward the ideal of political liberty.

The Declaration of Independence declares that all men are created equal and derive certain rights from the Creator. It would be more accurate to say that if there is a God, we derive not simply our rights from Him, but our entire nature—which includes responsibilities as well as rights. The writers of the Declaration dealt with what, to them, were self-evident truths; among them the idea of God-given rights. Today, neither the idea of God nor that of inherent rights is self-evident; both have to be argued for. Some libertarians think the idea of God is not necessary, but they want to retain the idea of rights. They think we can have the idea of rights all by itself without going into the question of where men get their rights. Let's treat the idea of individual rights merely as a working hypothesis, they say; it's an "as if" proposition.

Now if a group of men can come to an agreement that each person shall be treated *as if* he possessed inherent rights—regardless of whether or not he actually has them—then conflict will be reduced and things will work out better than they would in the absence of this hypothesis. But at this point, three comments are in order. First, if a formula produces the desired results, that is, works out in practice, it is because the formula is true, in accord with the facts, in harmony with the way the universe wants us to act. The directions you have for driving to Boston will get you there only if they correspond to the highways leading to Boston.

1. Morrall, *Political Thought in Medieval Times*, p. 10.

The directions work because they are a verbal formulation of the way things are. Similarly, the idea of individual rights works out in practice because the universe, so to speak, wants it that way; the idea of rights is derived from something more fundamental—from the nature of things. Secondly, we are faced with a problem of the same nature as that of the rules for national prosperity and a given person's moral obligation to practice them. If every person but one in a society respects individual rights, that one person can get a good thing going for himself by taking advantage of other people's trust. If we say that everyone, including this man, *ought* to respect the idea of inherent rights we have moved again into the field of ethics. Third, the idea that every person in society has the right to be treated just like every other person is a fragment of the much larger idea of the mystery and sacredness of persons. If the realm of nature—the world we can see and touch and taste and measure and weigh—plus society within nature, is all there is, the whole extent of our experience, then human beings are simply fragments of nature. They are in the same category as any other fact of nature. The same natural forces which produced the contours of the earth, the vegetation and the animal life, produced man— *unless* man somehow participates in another dimension of existence, a realm of being other than the merely natural world. Most people agree that man possesses some unique mental attributes, and that his mind links him to a reality which transcends him, to the mind of his Maker. If these are the facts of the matter, if this describes what man is, then the idea of individual rights in society is a requirement to be met before man can have the opportunity to realize his potentials. In short, the idea of equal rights for all men within society implies convictions about the sacredness of persons, and the idea of the sacred implies some convictions about the relevance of the idea of God to the life of man.

The gift of life is precious to most people, who will bend every effort to stay alive. But there are some unhappy individuals who find that life is too much for them. They commit suicide, which now ranks ninth among fatal illnesses in America. Hostility to life is manifested in other ways as well; people occasionally go berserk and take out their rage against life by going on a killing spree. Now, just as some are hostile to biological life, there are people who are hostile to social life. They do not want society. Their rebellion against society may not assume overt form; it may disclose itself merely as a refusal to meet the conditions on which a given society depends for its existence.

Suppose you and I agree to play a game of chess.But as we sit down I say: "Let's not play according to chess rules, and let's use dominoes." Is it not evident that despite the fact that I *say* I want to play chess my real intentions are quite different? One cannot really will any end without simultaneously willing the means by which that end is achieved. There are requirements which must be met before a society is achieved or maintained, and a refusal to meet the requirements is equivalent to not wanting society. The antisocial individual may take out his aversion in rebellion, or he may live as a predator or parasite. In any case, he is not giving value for value received.

Every individual, unable to survive and propagate by himself needs the fellowship of his own kind; he needs society. Consideration of the minimum conditions for biological survival confronts us inescapably with the question of the rules which undergird social life. Every society has a set of minimum rules which its citizens must practice, a set of conditions which—if not met— must result in social decay. As Albert Jay Nock puts it, there must be "the 'substratum of right-thinking and well-doing' . . . because no kind of collective life can possibly go on without it. . . . The mass man," he continues, "is one who has neither the force of intellect to apprehend the principles issuing in what we know as the humane life, nor the force of character to adhere to those principles steadily and strictly as laws of conduct." Intellect and character are both at issue here, and this brings us again face to face with the moral order, or the idea of the moral law, which we have already touched upon, but it also brings us to the last of the three major spiritual principles which have guided Western civilization: the first two are ethical monotheism and the natural law; the third is the Christian kingdom of heaven.

It was Aristotle's notion that man was the kind of creature who might find complete fulfillment in such a society as the Greek city-state. This idea is denied by the Christian analysis of man which views him as a creature whose destiny transcends any conceivable great society or good society which human effort might construct. A huge draft horse, a Percheron, say, is overbuilt for the job of pulling a pony cart. Man, likewise—to borrow from the vocabulary of the space scientists—has "redundancy built into him." He has potentialities that can never be realized within any social order. Utopia is out! The idea of the kingdom of heaven is premised on this belief; it regards every human society as, at best, a launching platform for the individual soul. This idea, like every other idea, can be perverted and abused. It can be used as a sordid excuse by the powerful for denying freedom and justice to the weak on the grounds that pie in the sky will come later. But if we discarded every idea which might be caricatured we'd have little left.

The idea of the kingdom of heaven fell to earth with a thud in the eighteenth century, and every scribbler peddled some utopian scheme or other. The historian, Carl Becker, writes about these people in his book, *The Heavenly City of the Eighteenth-Century Philosophers*. "The celestial heaven was to be dismantled in order to be rebuilt on earth . . . since it was an article of philosophical faith that the end of life was life itself, the perfected temporal life of man." Man is now the architect of his own fate; scientific know-how, coupled with democratic political processes, will usher in the earthly paradise. Utopia, the perfect society, is within reach, it will arrive just as soon as government is the maker of every decision and men are robotized. This is the major utopian strain of modern times; a minor one is the expectation that utopia will arrive when political government is no more. Both views are alike in making government—which is but an offshoot of human nature —the determiner of human destiny; to fulfill it in the first instance, to frustrate it in the second. The socialistic view anticipates a perfect society as soon as government takes over; the anarchistic view anticipates a perfect society as soon as government gets out of the way. Both ignore the fact that government is nothing more than a projection of human imperfections, and that these imperfections or imperfections like them, are here to stay as long as man is man. What the situation would be if men were angels, I haven't the faintest idea.

I stress the fact of human imperfection and the consequent frustration that must dog man's earthly career because of its relevance to the science of economics. You can never match men's unlimited wants against the planet's limited resources and come out even. In human life there will never be enough; there will always be a demand for more. These demands for more are not, of course, always on the same plane. Human life is lived on several levels; biological, social, esthetic, spiritual. Satisfied demands on one level give rise to new demands on higher levels, but at no point in life is there complete fulfillment of every desire.

This is not a difficult point to grasp with the intellect, but the human race has found it virtually impossible to really feel this thing in its very bones. It is a fact of nature that a creature with unlimited wants will be forever unsatisfied on a planet that has only limited resources for satisfying them; despite which—or perhaps because of it—utopia has exerted a tremendous appeal on millions of men in the West. Utopia, a perfect society, a kingdom of heaven on earth, is based upon the false premise that scarcity is an artificial condition. The assumption is that there *is* a sufficiency of all the good things of life which men want, so that each man might help himself to all he likes and yet there would be enough left over for everyone else. How do utopians account for the fact of scarcity under actual conditions in society? By bad institutions. "Man is born free," said Rousseau, "but is everywhere in chains." Civilization is at fault, according to the author of *The Social Contract*. Life in every society we have known is artificial, and these artificial conditions have kept man in a straitjacket. Free man from his institutions and he will be free indeed! Half a century later, Marx and Engels were to write that all history up to that time had been the history of class struggle. The class struggle would end, however, as the natural outcome of the dictatorship of the proletariat. In the classless society, men would be as gods.

Human life, as seen by those who have the utopian vision, might be compared to one of the old-fashioned arithmetic books. As you struggled to solve the problems posed by the author of the text you knew that there was a correct answer to each problem which you could no doubt work out if you gave the matter sufficient time and thought. Furthermore, you knew that all the correct answers could be found in the back of the book, so that if you got stumped you had only to turn to the proper page for a solution. But real life is not like this. Life is not merely a problem to be solved; it is a reality to be lived. And one of the fundamental facts of this reality is scarcity; yesterday, today, and forever. Scarcity is a built-in fea-

ture of the human condition. Now if we have lived with the idea
of the kingdom of heaven long enough so that we know what it
means, we can take the fact of scarcity in stride. Frustrations
within the natural and social orders are precisely what we would
expect; so we brush them off. But if we make unrealistic demands
of life the frustrations of the world drive us to despair. We wreck
society after society, trying to achieve the impossible—a heaven
on earth.

Each one of us is related to the other people comprising society
in thousands of subtle ways, in ways that defy enumeration, in
ways that cannot possibly be planned by any economic czar, planning commission, or bureau. Individual survival depends on social
cooperation and the willing exchange of specializations, but life at
this level does not satisfy any of us for long. Man wants to live,
but he also wants to live well. And so he proceeds to civilize
himself by specializing beyond his material needs—in ideas, music, poetry, science, and religion. The tools he uses in this civilizing
process are artifacts he finds at his elbow; no writer today has to
invent the English language; composers avail themselves of musical notation; the scientific method is available for today's physicists; athletes already have the training program for running a mile
in four minutes, and so on. We lucky ones do not start from
scratch; we can bankroll our projects today from the huge capital
fund of our heritage.

Scarcity leads to society, and society makes possible the humane life for individuals. Nobody got together and invented our
society, or manufactured it, or conjured it into existence; we are
the heirs of countless generations of aspiration and struggle on the
part of our ancestors. Lacking this background we'd be nothing
more than a bunch of pretty smart anthropoids.

No one has dramatized this point better than Graham Wallas,
writing in the early years of this century. "If the earth were struck
by one of Mr. Wells' comets," he wrote, "and if, in consequence,
every human being now alive were to lose all the knowledge and
habits which he had acquired from preceding generations (though
retaining unchanged all his own powers of invention and memory
and habituation) nine-tenths of the inhabitants of London or New
York would be dead in a month, and 99 per cent of the remaining
tenth would be dead in six months. They would have no language

to express their thoughts, and no thoughts but vague reverie. They could not read notices, or drive motors or horses. They would wander about, led by the inarticulate cries of a few naturally dominant individuals, drowning themselves, as thirst came on, in hundreds of riverside watering places, looting those shops where the smell of decaying food attracted them, and perhaps at the end stumbling on the expedient of cannibalism. Even in the country districts men could not invent, in time to preserve their lives, methods of growing food, or taming animals, or making fire, or so clothing themselves as to endure a northern climate."

This brings us full circle. We are now back to the proposition with which this chapter opened—that everyone has a stake in a prosperous society. Human society is an achievement, and a society both good and free is an immense accomplishment. An anthill or beehive, by contrast, is a mere fact of nature; if there are ants or bees, a hill or hive follows automatically. Insect communities are formed and kept going by instinct; but the human community is sustained only by the proper beliefs and convictions, by a correct understanding of human nature and destiny and by an appreciation of the economic and political instrumentalities necessary for a free society.

The free society rarely comes in for explicit attack or even criticism. Freedom today has what might be called a good press; everyone speaks well of freedom. It is in the same category as motherhood, sunshine, and pure water. Nobody will admit that he is against freedom. In modern times there has been a booming market for the Four Freedoms, and for Freedom Now. There is a vocal Free Speech Movement on college campuses. We celebrate freedom of the press and condemn censorship; we cherish religious liberty and hail academic freedom. The mood of our time is favorably disposed toward every freedom except one, and that outcast freedom is Freedom of Economic Enterprise, i.e. market freedom or capitalism.

Economic freedom suffers attrition from within and attacks from without. Individual businessmen often seek to evade market mandates, and intellectuals do not want people to have complete latitude for their peaceful economic transactions. This is how Professor Milton Friedman views the problem: "It has often seemed to me that the two greatest enemies of the free market are

businessmen and intellectuals, for opposite reasons. The businessman is always in favor of free enterprise—for everybody else; he
is always opposed to it for himself. The intellectual is quite different; he is always in favor of free enterprise for himself, always
opposed to it for everybody else. The businessman wants his special tariff or his special governmental commission to interfere with
free enterprise, in the name, of course, of free enterprise. The
intellectual, too, wants such commissions to control the rapacious
man. But he is against the idea of any interference with his academic freedom, or his freedom to teach what he wants and direct
his research as he wants—which is simply free enterprise as applied to him."[2]

It is self-evident to most intellectuals that liberties of the mind
are valuable. No man whose business it is to think and write, no
man who deals in ideas, wants his efforts along these lines to be
hamstrung. He wants to be free to think daring thoughts and come
up with novel ideas that challenge the prevailing orthodoxy. And
he is right. Mankind has no way of advancing *en masse;* every step
forward out of primitivism has been accomplished first by some
innovator who moved out beyond the herd and then drew the rest
of us painfully forward. There is a sort of gravitational pull that
operates on the human enterprise, which makes our normal condition one of stagnation. We get on dead center and most of us are
content to stay there. Then, along comes some inventor with a new
idea which counteracts the pull of gravity, and we move off dead
center. Thus, over the millenia, have people climbed the stiff ascent of civilization—only to slide down over the other side when
they neglect the intellectual and spiritual heritage which spurred
their climb.

Liberties of the mind are not under serious attack today. Nearly
everyone favors the freedom to think, write, teach, preach, and
publish. But it seems to many scholars and intellectuals that the
grubby concerns of the marketplace are beneath them. They have
little concern with what takes place in factories, stores, and banks
because, after all, this is the material side of life and the intellectuals are concerned with higher things, with things of the mind. And
so it happens that many believers in freedom in general attack

2. Milton Friedman, "Why Does the Free Market Have Such a Bad Press?," *Farmand*
II:46, December, 1966.

economic freedom in particular. In this they are not only wrong, they are disastrously wrong; there is an economic base supporting every one of the intellectual and spiritual freedoms these people cherish. And if this economic base is not free, if authoritarian controls are wrapped around this economic base, the controls will inevitably and eventually extend to the superstructure. Liberties of the mind and spirit do not and cannot exist in a vacuum; they form, in connection with economic liberty, a package, and this package cannot be picked apart without being destroyed. The arguments which support the right of a man to spend his energies in any peaceful way he chooses—in the editorial office, the classroom, or the pulpit—likewise support his right to the free exercise of those energies in his store or factory. Or, to put it the other way round, every argument for controlling the peaceful exercise of a man's energy in his workshop is an equally valid argument for controlling him in his study or classroom. Freedom is all of a piece; philosophizing is not the same as digging a ditch, but socialize the ditchdigger and the philosopher begins to lose some of *his* freedom. Freedom in the marketplace and liberties of the mind go together.

If we could look at this planet with fresh eyes it might seem to us that the most unlikely things are hooked up with each other. What do pigs and chickens have in common to suggest that eggs need ham? Gilbert and Sullivan couldn't stand each other, but they teamed up and now most of Sullivan's music is unthinkable without Gilbert's words, and vice versa. Mind and body, matter and spirit, are polar opposites, but each one of us is a precarious union of the two. No one has ever been able to explain just how the mind and body interact and get along with each other. Philosophers have been trying, without much success, for more than two thousand years, but the mind-body problem, as it is called, is still a moot point in philosophy. Despite the disagreement among philosophers, each of us gets along reasonably well with himself. He knows that his mind influences his body because he can worry himself into an ulcer; a toothache, on the other hand, can effectively prevent a man from philosophizing, and poor digestion can so monopolize a man's attention that he has no mind left for anything else.

George Santayana reflected sadly that the things that matter

most in life are at the mercy of the things that matter least. A
bullet, a tiny fragment of common lead, can snuff out the life of
a great man; a few grains of thyroxin one way or the other can
upset the endocrine balance and alter the personality, and so on.
But the more we think about this situation and the more instances
of this sort we cite, the more obvious it becomes that the things
Santayana declared matter least, actually matter a great deal. They
are tied in with the things which matter most and the things which
matter most depend on them. In precisely the same way, economic
liberty matters a great deal because every liberty of the mind is
connected with freedom of the market, economic freedom.
There's an old proverb to the effect that whoever controls a man's
subsistence has acquired a leverage over the man himself, which
impairs his freedom of thought, speech, and worship.

F. A. Hayek put it this way: "Economic control is not merely
a control of a sector of human life which can be separated from
the rest; it is the control of the means for all our ends."[3]

The government of a totalitarian country like Russia or China
acts as a planning board to direct the production and distribution
of goods. In practice, there is bound to be a lot of leakage—as
witness the inevitable black market. But to whatever extent the
state does control the economic life of a people it directs every
other aspect of life as well.

The masses of people everywhere and at all times are content
to drift along with the trend; they pose no problem for the planner.
But what happens to the rebels in a planned economy? a man who
wants to publish an opposition newspaper in a place like Russia or
China would have to obtain presses, paper, and a building from the
state—to attack the state. He would have to find workmen willing
to risk their necks to work for him; ditto, people to distribute;
ditto, people willing to be caught buying or reading the paper. Or
take the orator who wanted to protest. Where could he find a
platform in a country in which the state owns every stump, street
corner, and soap box—not to mention every building? Suppose
you didn't like your job, where could you go and what could you
do? Your job is pretty bad, but it is one notch better than Siberia
or starvation, and these are the alternatives. Strike? This is treason
against the state, and you'll be shot.

3. Hayek, *The Road to Serfdom*, p. 92.

Under primitive economic conditions a man has to be a jack-of-all-trades, able to turn his hand to a variety of occupations. If a pioneer family wants shelter it builds a sod house or a log cabin; if it wants clothing it weaves the cloth and fashions the garments; if it wants potatoes it raises them; if it wants meat it shoots a deer; and so on. But we live in a division-of-labor society where individuals specialize in production and then exchange their surpluses for the surpluses of other people until each person gets what he wants. Most of us work for wages; we produce our specialty, and in return we acquire a pocketful of dollar bills. The dollars are neutral, and thus we can use them to achieve a variety of purposes. We use some of them to satisfy our needs for food, clothing, and shelter; we give some to charity; we take a trip; we pay taxes; we go to the theater, and so on. Our money is a means we use to satisfy our various ends.

Economic action by itself does not generate a world view, although Marx believed it did. Economics has often been called a science of means. The economist, speaking as an economist, does not try to instruct people as to the nature and destiny of man, nor does he try to guide them toward the proper human goals. The ends or goals people strive for are, for the economist, part of his given data, and his business is merely to set forth the means by which people may attain their preferences most efficiently and economically.

When people are free to spend their money as they please they will often spend it foolishly. As consumers they will demand—and producers will obediently supply—goods that glitter but are shoddy; styles that are tasteless; entertainment that bores; and music that drives us nutty. Nobody ever went broke, H. L. Mencken used to say, by underestimating the taste of the American public. But this, of course, is only half the story. The quality product is available in every line for those who seek it out, and many do. The choices men make in the economic sector will be based upon their scales of values; the market is simply a faithful mirror of ourselves and our choices.

Now, man does not live by bread alone, and no matter how much we increase the quantity of available material goods, nearly everyone will acknowledge that there is more to life than this. Individual human life has a meaning and purpose which transcend the social order; man is a creature of destiny.

As soon as we begin talking in these terms, of human nature and destiny, we move into the field of religion—the realm of ends. And a science of means, like economics, needs to be hitched up with a science of ends. The more abundant life is not to be had in terms of more automobiles, more bathtubs, more telephones, and the like. The truly human life operates in a dimension other than the realm of things and means; this other dimension is the domain of religion—using the term in its generic sense.

If we as a people are squared away in this sector of life, we'll be able to take economic and political problems in our stride. On the other hand, if there is widespread confusion about what it means to be a human being, so that people are at sixes and sevens in this matter of the proper end of human life—some seeking power, others wealth, fame, publicity, or pleasure—then our economic and political problems overwhelm us. If economics is a science of means, that is, a tool, we need some discipline to help us decide how to use that tool. The ancient promise is that if we put first things first, by giving top priority to the search for the Kingdom of God, our actions will then conform to the law of our being and we'll get the other things we want as a sort of bonus. You may rephrase this idea, if you wish, to put it into a contemporary idiom; but the truth of it is hardly contestable.

I have spoken of economics as a science of means. What is the distinguishing feature of a science, and in what sense is economics a science? Adam Smith entitled his great work *The Wealth of Nations* (1776); one of Mises's books is entitled *The Free and Prosperous Commonwealth* (1927). It is clearly evident that these works deal with national prosperity, with the overall well-being of a society, with upgrading the general welfare. These are works of economic science, insofar as they lay down the general rules which a society must follow if it would be prosperous.

The distinguishing feature of a science, any science, is that it deals with the general laws governing the behavior of particular things, often reducing these laws to mathematical relationships. Science is not concerned with particular things, except insofar as some particular thing exemplifies a general principle. When we concentrate on a particular flower, like Tennyson's "flower in the crannied wall," we move into the realm of art and poetry. Should we want the laws of growth for this species of flower, we consult the science of botany. These books by Smith and Mises lay down the rules a society wishing to be prosperous must follow. They do not tell you as an individual how to make a million in real estate, or a killing in the stock market. This is another subject.

The subject is the economic inquiry: "How shall we organize the productive activities of men so that society shall attain maximum prosperity?" And the answer given by economic science is: "Remove every impediment that hampers the market and all the obstructions which prevent it from functioning freely. Turn the market loose and the *nation's* wealth will be maximized." The economist, in short, establishes the rules which must be followed if we want *society* to be prosperous; but no conceivable elaboration of these rules tells John Doe that he *ought* to follow them. There's a big IF here. If John Doe wants to know how to maximize the general well-being, the economist can tell him which rules to follow. But this might not be the only question we are asking. What John Doe may want to know is, "How can I make a million with no sweat?" Of course he wants society to prosper because he knows that it will be easier for him to make a million in a rich society than in a poor one, but his interest in the rules for national prosperity are secondary to his interest in lining his own pocket. He may understand the case for the free market, but nevertheless decide that he can do better for himself by getting in on a racket. Economic science can prescribe for general prosperity, but it cannot tell John Doe that he ought to obey that prescription. That job can be performed, if at all, by the moralist. The problem here is to bridge the gap between the economist's prescription for national prosperity and John Doe's adoption of that prescription as a guide for his personal conduct. Only a sense of moral obligation—and not additional economic arguments—can persuade John to close this gap.

Enter the moralist. If you want to persuade John Doe to follow the rules of economics for maximizing the general prosperity you must argue that he has a moral obligation to conform his actions to certain norms already established in his society by the traditional ethical code. He should deal justly and fairly with his fellows, he should injure no man, he should not steal, and so on. Practice the ethical code and the rules for national prosperity can be taken in stride; but in the absence of an ethical code which John Doe tries to live up to, there's no reason for him to feel any moral obligation for national prosperity when his own enrichment is a much more immediate concern.

If we want a free market and a free society we need a genuine ethic. This genuine ethic is available to us in the traditional moral code of our culture, which extols justice, forbids murder, theft, and covetousness, and culminates in love for God and neighbor. This is old stuff, you say; true, but it's good stuff.

The market is not something which comes out of nothing. It emerges naturally whenever the conditions are right, and those right conditions provide a framework for the market to keep it functioning smoothly. In other words, there is a realm of life outside the realm of economic calculation, on which the market depends. Let me cite Ludwig von Mises again, from his great work, *Socialism*. Mises speaks of beauty, health, and honor, calling them moral goods. Then he writes: "For all such moral goods are goods of the first order. We can value them directly; and therefore have no difficulty in taking them into account, even though they lie outside the sphere of monetary computation."[4] In other words, the market is generated and sustained within a larger framework consisting of, among other things, the proper ethical ingredients. There are also political and legal elements in this framework, and a theological dimension as well.

As well as being a science of means, economics is also a science of scarcity. As we have seen, goods which are not scarce, such as air, are not economic goods. Economics deals with things which are in short supply, relative to human demands for them. Our situation on this planet is an unbalanced equation with man and his wants on one side, and the world of raw materials on the other. The human being is a creature of insatiable wants, needs, and desires; but he is placed in an environment where the means of satisfying those wants, needs, and desires are scarce. Unlimited wants on one side of the equation; limited means for satisfying them on the other. Now, of course, it is true that no man, nor the human race itself, has an unlimited capacity for food, clothing, shelter, or any other item singly or in combination. But human nature is such that if one want is satisfied the ground is prepared

4. Ludwig von Mises, *Socialism*, p. 116.

for two others to come forward with their demands. A settled condition of satiety is inconceivable, short of death itself. Even if a condition of repletion and satiety can be imagined, this condition itself begets a want—the desire to be left alone for rest and relaxation. Rest and leisure, however, are breeding grounds for a renewed set of wants and demands.

This creature who demands more, whose wants are insatiable, is placed in an environment where there is not, and can never be, enough. Almost everything is scarce. In the first place, the planet is crowded; there is not enough elbow room in the pleasant places of the earth to accommodate everyone. Second, resources, the raw material which we must by our labor transform into consumable goods, are limited in quantity. Third, our individual supply of energy is limited; we get tired, and so we have to economize our strength with labor-saving devices. Fourth, time is always running out on us, and time is valuable. Finally, the planet's physical energy is scarce, nor will the common use of atomic power alter this fact; not even an atomic reactor is a perpetual motion machine.

What does this all mean? The upshot of all this is that the economic equation will never come out right. It's insoluble. There's no way of taking a creature with unlimited wants and satisfying him by any organization or reorganization of limited resources. Something's got to give, and economic calculation is the human effort to achieve the maximum fulfillment of our needs while avoiding waste.

Economics is the science of scarcity, but the scarcity we are talking about in this context is a relative thing. Whenever we drive in city traffic, or look vainly for a place to park, we are hardly in a mood to accept the economic truism that automobiles are scarce. But of course they are, relative to our wants. Who would not want to replace his present car or cars with a Rolls Royce for Sundays and holidays, plus an Aston Martin for running around?

These simple facts make hash of the oft-repeated remark that "we have solved the problem of production, and now if we could just distribute our abundance more equitably—which of course is a problem that only government can solve . . . ," and so on. Economic production does involve engineering and technology, in that men, money, and machines are linked to turn out airplanes, or automobiles, or tractors, or typewriters, or what not. But resources are limited, and the men, money, and machines we employ to turn out airplanes are not available for the production of automobiles, or tractors, or anything else. The dollar you spend for a package of cigars is no longer available to buy a movie ticket. With the resources available to us we might produce a number of different commodities, but obviously we could not produce as much of every commodity as everyone would want. The problem of deciding to use our resources to produce the gizmo rather than the thing-a-ma-jig is an entrepreneurial decision; but no matter who makes the decision, something has to be sacrificed when we commit our resources to a thing rather than to one of the other possibilities.

As John Kenneth Galbraith said in *The Affluent Society*, we do have an economic abundance that would astonish Adam Smith, but this merely confirms the free market economics that Smith expounded. There is not, as Galbraith claims, a new economics of abundance which outmodes the old economics of scarcity, for however abundant commodities become they will still be scarce relative to human wants and desires.

The economic equation can never be solved; to the end of time there will be scarce goods and unfulfilled wants. There will never be a moment when everyone will have all he wants. The candid economist is a man who comes before his fellows with the bad news that the human race will never have enough. Organize and reorganize society from now till doomsday and we'll still be trying to cope with scarcity. But the modern mind takes the dogma of inevitable progress for granted. Most of our contemporaries assume that day by day, in every way, we are getting better and better, until some day the human race will achieve perfection. The modern mind is passionately utopian, confident that some piece of social machinery, some ideological gadgetry is about to solve the human equation. Minds fixed in such a cast of thought, minds with this outlook on life, are utterly immune to the truths of economics. The conclusions of economics, in their full significance, are incompatible with the facile notions of automatic human progress which are part of the mental baggage of modern man, including many economists.

There is genuine progress in certain limited areas of our experience. This year's color television set certainly gives a better picture than the first set you bought in, say, 1950. The jet planes of today deliver you more rapidly and in better shape than did the old prop jobs. Automobiles have improved, we have more conveniences around the house, we are better equipped against illness. There has been true progress in certain branches of science, technology, and mechanics. But are the television programs improving year by year? Are the novels of this year so much better than the novels of last year, and last century? Are the playwrights whose offerings we have seen on Broadway this season *that* much better than Shakespeare? Has the contemporary outpouring of poetry rendered Homer, Dante, Keats, and Browning obsolete? Is the latest book on the "new morality" superior to Aristotle's *Ethics?* Are the prevailing economic doctrines of today, reflecting the Samuelson text, sounder than those of a generation ago, nourished on Fairchild, Furness, and Buck? Are today's prevailing political doctrines sounder than those which elected a Grover Cleveland? Henry Adams in his *Education* remarked that the succession of presidents from Washington, Adams, and Jefferson down to Ulysses Grant was enough to disprove the theory of progressive evolution. What would he say if he were able to observe the recent past?

The dogma of inevitable progress does not hold water. Perfect anthills may be within the realm of possibility; but a perfect human society, never. Man is the kind of creature for whom complete fulfillment is not possible within history; unlike other organisms, he has a destiny in eternity which takes him beyond biological and social life. This is the world outlook of serious religion, and the conclusions of economics are just what a person of this cast of mind would expect. Economic truths are as acceptable to this world view as they are unacceptable to the world view premised on automatic progress into an earthly paradise. If there is another dimension of being which transcends the natural order—the natural order being comprised of the things we can see and touch, weigh and measure—and if man is truly a creature of both orders and at home in both, then he has an excellent chance of establishing his priorities in the right sequence. He will not put impossible demands on the economic order, nor will he strive for perfection in the political order. He'll leave heaven where it belongs, beyond the grave. Man's recent efforts to build a new-fangled heaven on earth have come to resemble, in the totalitarian countries, an old-fashioned hell. Let us strive for a more moderate goal, a tolerable society, and we may achieve it.

Man is the kind of creature who seeks to economize scarce goods, and so he invents labor-saving devices. The primordial labor-saving device is the market, which enables men to freely exchange the results of their specialization for items they prefer. In a typical economic transaction you walk into a book store and stumble upon a volume which you need to complete a set; it is in good condition and the price of two dollars is right, so you buy it. You are delighted to exchange your two dollars for the book, and the proprietor who had been anxious to sell it is happy to have your money. Satisfactions on both sides of this exchange have been enhanced.

But there are other kinds of action in society where goods and services are not exchanged for goods and services to the benefit of both parties; there is theft, and predation, and violence. The same human drives which issue in economic action; namely, the need to economize on scarce means, might drive a man into theft for, as has been observed, robbery is a labor-saving device. There is only one way by which wealth comes into being, and that is by production; but there are two ways by which wealth may be acquired: first, by producing it, and secondly, by helping yourself to the fruits of someone else's production.

Contingencies of this sort in society create a demand for the protection of the peaceful and productive activities of men, that is to say for government. The market is simply a name for the peaceful and voluntary exchanges of goods and services occurring constantly between people who trade the results of their specializations. It is the organization of peaceful means. Policing, by contrast, is the regulated use of force against peacebreakers for the protection of peaceful people; it is the organization of coercive means. When a policeman overtakes a thief and forces him to disgorge the items he has stolen, he may use something stronger than persuasion; he may use a club or a gun. In any event, the policing transaction, in contrast to the economic exchange, does not enhance the general level of well-being of both parties to the exchange. Policing, in other words, cannot be organized as a market transaction; although policing costs money it is not within the domain of economics.

Carry the argument through one more stage: Two men differ in wealth today because their market place offerings of goods and services yesterday and the day before met with varying receptions. Because the buying public appreciates the man who sings like a Beatle more than the man who philosophizes like a Socrates, the former is rich, the latter poor—relatively speaking. The former buys three Cadillacs while the latter must content himself with a 1958 Chevrolet. When we understand the reasons for wealth differentials of this sort, we realize that such disparities are in the nature of things. Our sense of justice and fair play is not offended, however much our good taste may suffer. But if the singer commits a crime and, because of his wealth, is able to buy himself out of jeopardy, we know in our bones that an additional evil has compounded the original crime. Legal justice is not a marketable commodity; justice which becomes an item of merchandise ceases to be justice. Justice is not for sale, and the market cannot allocate things which—by their very nature—are not salable. It is right that people acting voluntarily in the marketplace should decide that one man be given three times as many cars as another; but any voluntary action which metes out to one man only a third as much justice as it accords to another is on the order of mob rule, lynch law, violence, and is a moral evil.

Things human tend to get out of hand, and government is the prime example of this tendency. Time and again throughout history, government has become a cancer-like growth detrimental to social health and individual well-being. Seeking to curb this tendency, those in the old-fashioned Whig and classical liberal tradition sought to keep government out of the productive and creative areas of society.

Once we grasp the point that government is a society's legal agency of coercion and not a mere committee we will seek to limit governmental action to the things which can be accomplished by coercion. The overwhelming majority of citizens are peaceful and productive men and women; but there are also predatory men, and society, therefore, needs to be policed. If government be limited to curbing aggression, fraud, and violence then peaceful people are free to go about their daily tasks. This is as it should be.

CHAPTER 6

Conflicting Viewpoints on Man

IT IS THE CONTENTION OF THIS BOOK THAT THE MOST APPROPRI-
ate way of organizing economic life, granted a Biblical outlook, is
the free market way. Christianity is geared to human nature and
the free economy accords with the nature of things, so this is a
natural pairing off.

But influential spokesmen from both sides enter a vigorous dissent. Some sound economists regard religious beliefs as an impediment; and some theologians regard socialism as a mandate of
Christian ethics. And, because the language in this area has been
fouled, the communication is less than perfect. Many churchmen,
as we have seen, would describe "capitalism" in such invidious
terms that any sane man would reject it. Many social scientists, on
the other hand, criticize a thing they call "religion," but that to
which they object turns out to be what many churchmen and
philosophers themselves reject: "magic" or "superstition."

There are, of course, irreconcilable differences between atheism
and theism, between those who believe that man is a chance occurrence in a meaningless universe, a waif produced purposelessly by
natural forces and condemned to a pointless existence; and those
who sense a Conscious Self behind phenomena, soliciting the cooperation of men in working out His mighty purposes. Merely to
pose these alternatives is to posit a mind or consciousness capable
of awareness and choice; and genuine atheism forces us to believe
that the meaningless dance of atoms issued, at some point, in the

human mind. The human mind is not adequately accredited in this account of its origin. It would take a miracle not inferior to the act of creation itself, to bridge the gap between material particles in motion on the one side and, on the other, life, awareness, meaning, and purpose.

The typical agnostic position implies that human reason is so inferior an instrument that it is incapable of grappling with the issues which separate atheism from theism; unable to make a choice, it would suspend judgment on ultimates. As a practical matter, a man's real creed consists of the premises—often unsuspected or unacknowledged—on which he habitually acts; and as a practical matter it is impossible not to act *as if* the universe were meaningful or *as if* life were purposeless. Practically, a man is either an atheist or a theist, that is to say, he inclines toward one position or the other.

The genuine religionist is keenly aware of his own ignorance of the divine mysteries. He is instructed by his religious heritage that every picture or conception he dares frame of God falls short of the reality, or grossly misses the mark. "My ways are not your ways," his Bible tells him. The Old Testament drove home this point by forbidding any graven images, lest any get the mistaken notion that God's Being and a thing's existence are in some way alike; Israelites were not permitted even to pronounce the secret name, let alone spell it out. "God is a Spirit," we read in the Gospels, implying that we cannot form a visual image of Him— much in the same vein as today we try to divest ourselves of all visual images of the atom and the planetary system "within" the atom. "Now we see through a glass, darkly," wrote Paul. Augustine, writing in fifth-century Rome, said: "We can know what God is not, but we cannot know what He is." And the Englishman, Hooker, living in sixteenth-century England, wrote: "Our soundest knowledge is to know that we know Him not as indeed He is, neither can [we] know Him; and our safest eloquence concerning Him is our silence, when we confess without confession that His Glory is inexplicable."

Most thinking is limited by the verbal symbols we are forced to use, and most words are labels attached to items which populate the sensory world; rocks, trees, houses, books, chairs, and so on. Thinking about things is not easy, and the difficulties are compounded when we try to think about abstractions such as liberty, love, justice, and the like. And if there is an order which transcends the realm of sense and the realm of qualities alike, it follows that the human mind must pause at that boundary and acknowledge its necessary limitations. The sacred order provokes a reaction of awe; if a man feels under pressure to invent pat formulas to encompass this order, we can surmise that he has not truly encountered it.

In short, no conception of God is adequate, but some concepts are surely more inadequate than others; to think of God in terms of creative will and purpose is surely less inadequate than to picture Him as nine feet tall wearing gleaming white robes and adorned with a flowing beard. If, however, we refuse to acknowledge our human limitations and insist on the absolute accuracy of our representations of the divine, then, in effect, we are commanding God to conform to our limited understanding of things or be dismissed from His universe! This egotistic idolatry may be several degrees worse than ordinary atheism. Contemporary atheism may, in fact, be regarded as a reaction to such an idolatry, which it mistakes for religion.

Differences at the level of theology will manifest themselves in contrasting attitudes toward the problems of social organization. The atheist, one who believes that nothing humanly significant exists beyond the social and natural orders, will think of society as an autonomous human creation, explicable in its own terms, serving no purposes beyond those defined from within, closed to possible wider meanings from outside. The theist, on the other hand, will attempt to assign the social order to its place in the total scheme of things in which the personal is sacred and central. God is more like a conscious self than anything else, and God is personal in this sense. For the theist, man is created in God's image as a conscious self, and it follows that human personality is to be cherished because God values persons. Jacques Maritain refers to "the indirect ordainment of political life toward the life of souls and immortality."[1] Political and economic life, therefore, make their authentic demands on us as necessary social means to personal ends. Earthly society cannot be an end in itself, for nothing

1. *The Social and Political Philosophy of Jacques Maritain* ed. Evans and Ward, p. 285.

temporal extends over the full range of the life of persons. Societies come and go, civilizations rise and fall, but if the Christian hope is to be trusted, the person is forever.

Differences in ethical theory will follow from these conflicting theologies. For the theist, God's will as made known to man conveys mandates for his personal and social life. The universe itself, in some mysterious way, is ultimately against theft and murder and false witness; it is on the side of justice, mercy and love. True, the moral law is put into words by men; but even so have chemists constructed the table of the elements. The elements were there before any man acknowledged them, and back of the moral law as men have formulated it lies something that just is. Men did not invent this ultimate reality, any more than the human action which assigned the atomic weight of seven to nitrogen created the atom itself. Such queries as: "Who's to say what's right?" or "Who decides what is just?" really beg the question. Back of such queries lies the dubious assumption that moral norms and standards do not really exist as objective factors in the universe, that "right" and "just" are merely subjective, merely some one's say-so and the only question is whose? The upshot of such an approach is that all moral questions are up for grabs; all ethical imperatives are merely human contrivances which might just as well be the reverse of traditional ethics: "Evil be thou my good," as Milton's Satan put it.

The rules of the games we play are conventional. Most games have a history and their rules have evolved and been elaborated to the point where they are now standardized, semipermanently, "according to Hoyle." But the dimensions of a baseball field are not written into the nature of things. Conceivably the game could use ten players on a side, third base could be made into first so that the runners would move clockwise, and so on. The game of basketball has been made over within the memory of many of us, and football of the flying wedge era is just a memory. Canadian football plays three periods instead of four quarters, and what goes by the name of football in other countries is a different game.

There are some who would have us believe that ethics is of a nature similar to the rules of the playing field: invented by men, having no cosmic significance, alterable at will, strictly relative to a given society. "It's all a matter of taste." Men of a former time and under radically different social conditions, it is suggested, got together and proscribed theft merely because they thought that salutary consequences might follow such a restraint; people in this new day are working toward the proscription of property because to social planners the results seem promising, or even amusing. Murder, too, can be fun, if we are to believe a contemporary school of novelists. One of them, an essayist as well, expresses his infatuation with psychopaths, men who cannot be helped by psychiatry because they are "more complex, more experienced, or more adventurous than the analyst himself." Such personalities "are an elite with the potential ruthlessness of an elite." If such a person wants to be cured he must go "backward along the road of the homosexual, the orgiast, the drug-addict, the rapist, the robber and the murderer . . . the decision is to encourage the psychopath in oneself. . . ." Relativists who profess to judge conduct in terms of its consequences here come a cropper; an act of murder is now recommended as a way to maximize the agent's sense of well-being. The judgment that murder is evil per se invokes a standard that runs tangential to the act and its consequences, and such a standard exists prior to the deed or not at all.

If an act cannot be judged right or wrong until it has been committed and its consequences assessed, then we can never pass judgment, for we become entrapped in an infinite regression. We cannot assess these consequences except in terms of *their* results, because our ideology will not permit us to pass a moral verdict on an act as such. But consequences follow consequences *ad infinitum*, so that we'd have to be omniscient before we could know the full ramifications of a single act of murder, and then we'd have to forgo the verdict because in the first round we abandoned norms or standards which are the only tool we have to pass judgment with. If murder is not wrong prior to a given act of murder, it cannot be deemed wrong at any subsequent stage as its consequences work themselves out.

The present deterioration in ethics would shock the good nineteenth-century atheist who hoped only, by jettisoning superfluous theological and ecclesiastical baggage, to encourage a nobler morality and a higher standard of humanitarianism. It has hardly worked out that way, and thus "there is a special need today, which perhaps only a reborn philosophy can wisely meet," writes

Professor E. A. Burtt in a book which sums up a lifetime of productive thinking. "One of the most salutary discoveries and at the same time one of the most malignant diseases of our century goes by the name of 'moral relativism.' So far as such a view indicates an expanded awareness of the great variety of moral values that have somewhere and some time been accepted, and of the degree of success· commitment to each set has won, it has brought an illuminating perspective; so far as it has led to the idea that one pattern of cultural life is as good as another, and that intelligent discrimination between values can fill no positive role, it is one of the saddest superstitions that have found currency among educated people."[2]

Relativism as a philosophical position is self-defeating. According to this creed, every person has his own private notion of what is right and wrong, or good and bad. Relativism opposes the idea that there are ethical norms or standards which somehow occupy a ground common to all men and are thus morally binding on all. As this theory views the ethical problem, men have a moral obligation to yield to these absolutes, identified by some as the commands of God, and by others as parts of an impersonal moral order. There is a danger in a setup of this kind, relativists point out, that a shrewd class of people will appoint themselves sole guardians and interpreters of these absolutes, to the detriment of the masses. Furthermore, studies of peoples around the world have revealed great differences of custom and convention, and because these things in most cultures do acquire the sanction of ethics, the dubious implication has been drawn by relativists that the concepts of right and wrong are a function of latitude; what's right at one spot on the globe is wrong at another spot or at another time. Unfortunately for relativism, further anthropological studies have corrected this superficial view, and it is now generally acknowledged that each of the great cultures is indissolubly linked to a religion and that each of these great world religions has a common core of similar moral principles. But it is the dubious implications drawn from the earlier view which have seeped into the modern mentality to generate the idea that there are no universal standards, and that everything, therefore, is relative.

Relative to what? we ask. If every person is entitled to his own

2. Burtt, *In Search of Philosophic Understanding*, p. xi.

idea of what's right and what's wrong, what is the nature of that which he has an idea of? How could anyone have an idea of Gibraltar unless the rock actually existed? If there is no objective right and wrong how is it possible for every person to have an idea of right and wrong? There were, in the fable, six blind men of Hindustan. Each in turn walked up to an elephant and each felt a different part; tusk, trunk, ear, leg, flank, and tail. The six blind men, then, entertained six different ideas as to what an elephant is like; it is like a spear, a snake, a fan, a tree, a wall, a rope. And this, the relativist might say, is something like the situation in the realm of ethics; just as every person has merely his own idea of what an elephant is like, so each person has merely his own idea of the right. Yes, but in the fable there really was an elephant! None of the six blind men would have even his mistaken notion of an elephant if the real elephant did not exist in the first place. A mirror does not give back the reflection of a vacuum, nor does a mind have an idea which is not an idea of something. Now what is the nature of the something, which a man's private idea of right and wrong reflects? As soon as we face up to the challenge of a question like this we are back in the main stream of ethical inquiry. No sensible ethicist, no matter how categorical his imperative, has denied his own and all other men's limitations. Our human finiteness limits our grasp of all truths, and not just the truths of ethics. The whole truth is beyond human ken; the truth we have come into possession of is relative to our aptitude for it. But relativism in its commonly used sense is surely an untenable position.

Those who begin their philosophizing with a premise which limits reality to the social and natural orders and denies the reality of an order which transcends them, must necessarily seek to root ethical theory in either nature or society. Man, according to this view, is nothing but a biological and social organism, gifted in certain directions beyond all other organisms but a mere part of nature nonetheless. Put the ethical question to nature and what does she reply? Many have answered on nature's behalf, and some of the phrases have entered the vocabulary: "red in tooth and claw," "struggle for existence," "survival of the fittest," "law of the jungle," and the like. The chain of life in nature is also a chain of death; eat or be eaten is the rule. Arthur Schopenhauer observed that every animal is the graveyard of thousands of others, and if you think that pleasure outweighs pain in nature, he continued, contrast the pleasure of the eater with the pain of the animal being devoured. Each slayer slays, and in turn is slain. It is possible to overdraw this picture, for nature has her merciful aspects as well. Animals live in the eternal now; the rabbit which the hawk has just missed goes back to feeding, its instant of terror forgotten. Also, there is social life among organisms; there is helpfulness and mutual aid.

This last phrase suggests Kropotkin's great study, entitled *Mutual Aid*, written originally as a corrective to certain viewpoints championed by T. H. Huxley and published as a series of articles in *The Nineteenth Century* between 1890 and 1896, appearing as a book in 1902. Kropotkin had no intention of denying the mutual struggle in nature, as the following quotation proves; he merely wished to point out that this is not the whole story.

> Rousseau had committed the error of excluding the beak-and-claw fight from his thoughts; and Huxley committed the opposite error; but neither Rousseau's optimism nor Huxley's pessimism can be accepted as an impartial interpretation of nature.
>
> As soon as we study animals—not in laboratories and museums only, but in the forest and the prairie, in the steppe and the mountains—we at once perceive that though there is an immense amount of warfare and extermination going on amidst various species, and especially amidst various classes of animals, there is, at the same time, as much, or perhaps even more, of mutual support, mutual aid, and mutual defense amidst animals belonging to the same species or, at least, to the same society. Sociability is as much a law of nature as mutual struggle.[3]

The mutual struggle part of the story, it is usually contended, affords little or no ethical guidance for human beings. Every organism seeks something beyond mere survival; it seeks supremacy; it acts as if it and its species might rightfully take over the planet, overpowering other life forms en route. Friedrich Nietzsche, however, sought to extract an ethical imperative from this aspect of the behavior of organisms. "Life itself is essentially assimilation, in-

3. Kropotkin, *Mutual Aid*, p. 5.

jury, violation of the foreign and the weaker, suppression, hardness, the forcing of one's own forms upon something else, ingestion and—at least in its mildest form—exploitation. But why should we always use such words which were coined from time immemorial to reveal a calumniatory intention? Even that body to which we referred, the body within which individuals may treat each other with equality (and it is so in any healthy aristocracy) —even this body itself, if it is alive and not dying off, must do to other bodies all the things from which its members refrain; it will have to be the will to power incarnate; it will have to want to grow, to branch out, to draw others into itself, to gain supremacy. And not because it is moral or immoral in any sense but because it is *alive*, and because life simply *is* will to power."[4]

There are idyllic aspects of nature, but there is a dark side as well —even as in human nature. Man cannot deny his kinship with all life, and he is forced to admit that some of his behavior patterns stem from his relationship to nature; he is a mammal and exhibits many of the earmarks of mammalian behavior. The religionist agrees, but he goes on to affirm that after man's natural and biological components have been exhaustively analyzed, there is something left over which is not reducible to nature; not to speak of the mind which does the analyzing. In the second place, the religionist, while not denying that some of man's behavior patterns are rooted in nature, affirms that the norms for truly human conduct are not contained within nature, but derive from a source beyond nature. We can observe the behavior of other organisms in nature as predator, parasite, victim, or host. But, however much we multiply our observations of lives in nature, the facts we have gathered cannot be bent into the shape of a moral imperative. We observe predation in nature, but such an observation does not tell us that men ought to be predators. Some organisms are parasites, but a

---

4. Nietzsche, *Beyond Good and Evil*, No. 259.
A grim sidelight is thrown on nature when we encounter situations where the predator and his victim have come to need each other. Gerald Heard describes one such relationship: "The ungulates, those whose hands have become blunted into hoofs have now a dreadful need of the unguiculates—those whose hands have become twisted into claws to satisfy *their* horrid need for the flesh of their fellows. For if the deer are not stimulated by the constant uneasiness that an enemy prowler may be near they become so slack without the adrenaline in their blood that they suffer from disease through lowered general resistance. While many of the sheep, if they are not constantly roused will, to graze the easier, go down on the knees and so walk till the foot rots off at the joint." (*Is God Evident?*, p. 29.)

recital of this fact does not suggest parasitism as an ideal to which men should aspire. The facts of nature derived from observation and experiment are facts of nature and nothing more; they do not, of themselves alone, generate a moral imperative. The naturalist can perhaps describe for us the facts of nature and explain something of how they came to be; but he cannot, as a naturalist, select certain of nature's facts and tell the rest of us that they exemplify the pattern to which human conduct ought to correspond. The difficulty here is explained by W. P. Sorley. Theories of this kind, he writes, "all pass from propositions about reality of what 'is' to propositions about goodness or what 'ought to be'. They make a transition to a new predicate; and the difficulty for them lies in justifying this transition."[5] However emphatically we utter "This is," the sound refuses to come out as "This do!"

The moral imperative which some think to find in nature is one that has been surreptitiously smuggled into nature. From whence? From society, obviously, if we start from the premise that the natural and social orders alone are real. "Society is the repository of all values, the ultimate arbiter of truth, beauty and goodness," writes V. Gordon Childe, the eminent British explorer of the human past. "Nature is alien to the idea of right and wrong," we read in *Human Action.* "It is . . . the social system which determines what should be deemed right and what wrong. There is neither right nor wrong outside the social nexus."[6]

From the time of *Wealth of Nations* down to the present, economics has been recommended by its practitioners as the means of promoting and maximizing the general happiness of mankind. Utilitarian and pragmatic theories of ethics and the teachings of free market economics have been regarded as implying and reinforcing each other, with no reference to anything beyond the acting agents. This outlook probably derives mainly from Jeremy Bentham, for Smith himself, in his earlier work, *The Theory of Moral Sentiments* (1759) ascribed the fountainhead of moral values to a source beyond society and beyond nature. Smith entitles Chapter V of Part III, "Of the Influence and Authority of the General Rules of Morality, and that they are justly regarded as the Laws of the Deity."

5. Sorley, *Moral Values and the Idea of God,* pp. 9–10.
6. Mises, *op. cit.,* pp. 716–17.

The happiness of mankind, as well as of all other rational creatures, seems to have been the original purpose intended by the Author of Nature when he brought them into existence. No other end seems worthy of that supreme wisdom and divine benignity which we necessarily ascribe to him; and this opinion, which we are led to by the abstract consideration of his infinite perfections, is still more confirmed by the examination of the works of Nature, which seem all intended to promote happiness, and to guard against misery. But by acting according to the dictates of our moral faculties, we necessarily pursue the most effectual means for promoting the happiness of mankind, and may therefore be said, in some sense, to co-operate with the Deity, and to advance, as far as in our power, the plan of providence.

Smith goes on to say:

That our regard to the will of the Deity ought to be the supreme rule of our conduct, can be doubted of by nobody who believes his existence. The very thought of disobedience appears to involve in it the most shocking impropriety. How vain, how absurd would it be for man, either to oppose or to neglect the commands that were laid upon him by infinite wisdom and infinite power! How unnatural, how impiously ungrateful not to reverence the precepts that were prescribed to him by the infinite goodness of his Creator, even though no punishment was to follow their violation! The sense of propriety, too, is here well supported by the strongest motives of self-interest. The idea that, however we may escape the observation of man or be placed above the reach of human punishment, yet we are always acting under the eye and exposed to the punishment of God, the great avenger of injustice, is a motive capable of restraining the most headstrong passions, with those at least who, by constant reflection, have rendered it familiar to them.[7]

Jeremy Bentham was a younger contemporary of Adam Smith and sought to lay down a new basis for morals and legislation, dispensing with any need to invoke the deity. He found this in the

7. Smith, *The Theory of Moral Sentiments*, pp. 235, 241.

greatest happiness principle: "Priestly was the first (unless it was Beccaria) who taught my lips to pronounce the sacred truth—that the greatest happiness of the greatest number is the foundation of morals and legislation." "Greatest happiness for the greatest number" is a campaign slogan, and Bentham under fire revised the latter portion so that the increase of the happiness of the whole community became the aim. This slogan regards happiness in purely quantitative terms, viewing it as a thing which can be legislated or otherwise obtained by direct action. This position marks a departure from a tradition dating back at least to Aristotle: Happiness is not a thing-in-itself but invariably a quality of other things; it cannot, therefore, be gotten at directly, but only as a by-product of other things. It is in the nature of a bonus or dividend following upon the correct performance of certain actions.

Such high-flown talk was not for Bentham. "Morality," he wrote, "is the art of directing men's actions to the production of the greatest quantity of happiness, on the part of those whose interest is in view."[8] John Stuart Mill believed himself responsible for bringing the word Utilitarianism into use. His short treatise entitled *Utilitarianism* was compiled from previously written papers and published in 1861. Here is Mill's own description of what Utilitarianism is:

> The creed which accepts as the foundation of morals, Utility, or the Greatest Happiness Principle, holds that actions are right in proportion as they tend to promote happiness, wrong as they tend to produce the reverse of happiness. By happiness is intended pleasure, and the absence of pain; by unhappiness, pain, and the privation of pleasure. To give a clear view of the moral standard set up by the theory, much more requires to be said; in particular, what things it includes in the ideas of pain and pleasure; and to what extent this is left an open question. But these supplementary explanations do not affect the theory of life on which this theory of morality is grounded—namely, that pleasure, and freedom from pain, are the only things desirable as ends; and that all desirable things (which are as numerous in the utilitarian as in any other

8. Quoted by C. E. M. Joad, *Guide to the Philosophy of Politics and Morals*, pp. 325–6.

scheme) are desirable either for the pleasure inherent in themselves, or as means to the promotion of pleasure and the
prevention of pain.[9]

Utilitarianism, besides being a theory of morals, makes pronouncements in psychology as well. It declares man to be the kind
of creature who is drawn willy-nilly along the path he believes
conduces to his greater happiness, and then offers the superfluous
advice that man *ought* to pursue the course it has just told him he
cannot avoid. "Nature," writes Bentham, "has placed man under
the governance of two sovereign masters, pain and pleasure. It is
for them alone to point out what we ought to do, as well as
determine what we shall do. . . . We owe to them all of our ideas,
we refer to them all our judgments, and all the determinations of
our life. He who pretends to withdraw himself from this subjection
knows not what he says."[10] Mill writes in a similar vein, asserting
that "to desire anything, except in proportion as the idea of it is
pleasant, is a physical and metaphysical impossibility."[11]

Most economic thinking has come packaged in utilitarian theories of ethics and human motivation, but not all. Böhm-Bawerk
goes out of his way to insist that his theory of value be judged on
its own merits, because it is not merely an offshoot of utilitarianism. "I myself *abjure* any adherence to the tenets of hedonism,"
he writes, "and in the presentation of my theory of value I desire
to avoid any statements that could be interpreted as an expression
of such adherence."[12]

With noted exceptions, most free market economists have been
utilitarians; they have made utilitarianism an intrinsic part of their
explanation of how the economy works and should work, and they
profess to believe that the immense effort of philosophers, from
Plato on down, to establish an intuitionist ethic has been wasted.
("Never in history has more intellect and ingenuity been expended in defending an untenable position.") In effect, this dogmatic position acts to exclude all those who have come to embrace
a moral theory which acknowledges the objective reality of ethical
norms from the inner sanctum of the free market position. If

9. Mill, *Utilitarianism, Liberty, Representative Government*, p. 6.
10. Joad, *op. cit.*, p. 328.
11. Mill, *op. cit.*, p. 36.
12. Böhm-Bawerk, *Capital and Interest*, Vol. II, p. 184.

economics really implies utilitarianism, then those who reject utilitarianism on philosophical grounds must logically reject economics. The principle of inference, which lies at the heart of logic, states that "whatever is implied by a true proposition is true," and it applies here. Thus have many come to reject sound economics without having conducted an examination of economic reasoning, because they have been authoritatively told that, first, they must accept utilitarianism and only then may they embrace economics.

The plain truth of the matter seems to me quite the reverse of this: Utilitarianism is not a viable proposition and, in any event, it is not an ethical theory. However, if it be true or accepted as true, then it is a doctrine that harmonizes poorly with the free economy. The standard objections which philosophers have raised against utilitarianism may be found in any one of several treatises on ethical theory. I shall not rehearse these objections here, but shall limit myself to a criticism of the uses to which utilitarianism is put in the literature whose main purpose is to promote the free economy.

If the contents of the universe be seriously inventoried, say those who oppose the doctrine of the utilitarians, it will be found to contain, in addition to the things of the natural and social orders, ethical norms or standards. The theistic position goes something like this: The Being whose purposes we dimly discern being worked out in history has laid down a set of rules for human behavior—God's will for men. Men ought to seek to know and do God's will, for it is the prescription for optimum human functioning. God's commands are "out there" in the sense that they are actual ingredients of a salient dimension of reality, but they are also inscribed on man's innermost being, "nearer than breathing, closer than hands and feet." Thus, although ethical norms and standards are objective and external, they are not for all that, alien; to the contrary, they represent a mandate from man's deep self.

Those persons who have really explored the inner world and have, in consequence, some inkling of its depths and complexities —of the layer upon layer of consciousness that is within man— report a plurality of selves. The surface self, or ego, is a sort of home-made contrivance, pieced together out of the customary opinions, attractions, and aversions of the age. It tends to reflect what we think people think we are and what they expect of us, and thus tends to mask what we really are. It yearns to be one of the in-group and shudders at being outside. The ego tries to keep us in line with current trends and fashions as we pursue power, wealth, fame, pleasure, or mere distractions. It jams the signals coming from our essential self, the divine spark within, which is ours to know and then to nurture and mature during our three score years and ten to the point where it may be launched into another order of reality. The mandates of this deep self, insofar as finite men with limited intelligence can intercept and interpret them, are hammered out into the ethical code. Obey the code and we truly live from within, in harmony with ourselves and with the universe. The ethical code thus provides the laws of life for man, which he is free to follow or not. Instinct plays this role in animal life, aligning the organism with the forces of life, and no animal is free to disobey the laws of its nature. With man it is otherwise. The rest of creation is complete; we alone are unfinished. The Creator has given the animal world all the answers it needs, which answers are locked up in instinctual responses as old as time. But man has not been given the answers; before our eyes the Creator has posed a gigantic question mark. We are handed a series of questions and the answers are ours to give; the freedom and the capacity to respond is likewise ours.

Many moral philosophers accept the position that ethical norms are objective and real without committing themselves to any form of theism. They point out that nearly every person, and the people of virtually every culture on record, acknowledge the categories of right and wrong, or good and bad. People may differ on the question of what belongs in which category, but such disputes, far from denying the categories, assume them. The ethical categories are as fundamentally part of the human mind as the categories of causality and teleology.[3]

Francis Bacon commended natural science to his fellows by telling them that we cannot command nature except by obeying her. Atmospheric pressure will support a column of water thirty-two feet high, and men must take this fact and limitation into

---

3. "There are for man only two principles available for a mental grasp of reality, namely, those of teleology and causality. What cannot be brought under either of these categories is absolutely hidden to the human mind. An event not open to an interpretation by one of these two principle is for man inconceivable and mysterious. Change can be conceived as the outcome either of the operation of mechanistic causality or of purposeful behavior, for the human mind there is no third way available." (Mises, *Human Action*, p. 25.)

account when they want to raise water from a well. A pump will work only if nature's conditions are met; obey them if you want good results. The moral code is to be conceived in a somewhat similar fashion, say the ethicists: Obey the code and things will work out; happiness and satisfaction will be maximized as a consequence. But an effect cannot precede its causes; the end result we want cannot be achieved without submitting to the processes which are calculated to bring it about. Happiness is the end result of properly conducting human relationships according to the fundamental laws of our being. "For this alone can truly be called and esteemed the peace of reasonable creatures," writes Augustine in Book XIX of *The City of God*, "consisting as it does in the perfectly ordered and harmonious enjoyment of God and of one another in God." An abundant supply of water pumped out of the ground is a token that we are abiding by the laws of hydraulics; the successful performance of our duty attunes us to the pattern laid down in the nature of things and is a prelude to joy.

Every living organism seeks to maintain the internal balances necessary to the preservation of the conditions on which its health and growth depend. The coordination of the physiological processes toward maintaining the inner environment is called "homeostasis." Furthermore, the organism must be "in play" with its external environment. Let the balance be upset within or without and the resultant malaise sets the whole organism into action to recover equilibrium. Turn a turtle on its back and it makes frantic efforts to right itself. The unease it feels when disoriented leads to action designed to overcome the dis-ease and get itself into a position where it is somewhat less at the environment's mercy. The turtle acts to improve his material circumstances, to acquire a better mastery over his conditions or at least to avoid succumbing to them. All organisms react in this fashion, and the behavior of at least some plants may be so interpreted. The heliotropism of the common sunflower is a case in point; if the blossom were fastened facing north the plant would ingeniously attempt to overcome the uneasiness it feels in this unnatural position.

All living things are from the hand of the same Creator, so man is kin to all life and demonstrates this in his behavior. He, too, has his internal physiological balances to maintain as well as his necessary adjustments to the physical environment outside. Let the

equilibrium slip a peg or two and the malaise he feels spurs him
into action; internally, it may be that one of his endocrine glands
discharges a hormone into the blood; externally, his effort to maintain a favorable relationship to the world outside may cause him
to do a simple thing like opening a window or a complex thing like
designing a computer.

It is a common observation that all organic behavior may be
interpreted as a movement of the organism away from uneasiness
toward an optimum relationship with the environment which, humanly speaking, equates with happiness, pleasure, or satisfaction.
The utilitarians think to derive an ethical system from this observation of organic behavior and thus reduce all human action to the
manifestation of a simple prinicple.

It is asserted by the spokesmen for this general position that the
aim of every human action is to promote the pleasure, happiness,
or satisfaction of the acting agent; to which the following objections may be made. Words like pleasure, happiness, or satisfaction
are what might be called "container words." They are words need-
ing a content, like the word "assistant." When someone tells you
he is an assistant, you are told nothing about his actual job. All you
know is that he is not an executive. To make it specific, the job of
being an assistant needs some entity to hook up with. Similarly,
happiness or pleasure. There is no such entity as pleasure or happiness; these are mental states which may be associated with many
different things. Likewise satisfaction. Have you ever seen a satisfaction all by itself? What color was it? How long was it? Can you
fold it? Actually, pleasures or satisfactions are states of feeling that
attach themselves to all sorts of actions. The satisfaction obtained
by eating a steak is easily distinguished from the satisfaction a
good book gives. The object of human action is never pleasure or
satisfaction as such—it can't be, because there is no pleasure or
satisfaction per se. The aim of action must be something specific
and concrete. "Satisfactions" do not comprise a homogeneous
lump, as does a piece of chemically pure sulphur at fifty degrees
centigrade. In the vocabulary of today's semanticists, words like
happiness, pleasure, and satisfaction have no "referent."

Pleasure or satisfaction is neither the motivation nor the goal of
action; it is the by-product. Now, one man's meat is another man's
poison; acts that are pleasurable for one may be painful for

another. One may maximize his own satisfactions by minimizing the satisfactions of others. The sadist enjoys hurting people, the masochist enjoys being hurt. Satisfactions differ in quality as well as in quantity. Some satisfactions are more appropriate to our nature than other satisfactions, and such pleasure as some men get from torturing other men ought to be shunned altogether.

To illustrate: A man at the starvation level has a hunger for anything remotely resembling food, but normally the appetite is not nearly so generalized. No man walks into a restaurant and says: "One plate of food, please; over lightly." To the contrary, he decides first of all between such available choices as a chop house, a hamburger joint, a Chinese restaurant, a pizza parlor, or a place specializing in seafood. Once this decision is made, there are further choices as to the specific cut of meat, how it is to be cooked, what side dishes, and so on. Furthermore, the unease felt as the result of hunger is recognizably different from the unease felt as the result of thirst. There is no such thing as "unease" all by itself, but only individual urges, each looking toward its peculiar kind of fulfillment. Inventory every edible thing on the planet, and let X represent their number. There is not, in addition to X an additional item called "Food"; food is the category of things of which X is the number. There is not a single calorie in a category, nor any taste, and this would not be worth mentioning except for the fact that several centuries of rationalism have made what Whitehead calls "The Fallacy of Misplaced Concreteness" all but universal— to the great detriment of sound thinking. This might also be called "The X + 1 Fallacy." Ask the rationalist how many edibles there are and his reply is "X + 1"; X representing the number of different things we can eat, plus Food. Ask him how many people inhabit the globe and he replies "X + 1"; the census figure plus Man. His capital M Man exists on capital F Food and thus overcomes unease and multiplies satisfactions! Utilitarianism and related movements cannot be understood unless they are viewed in relation to rationalism, which lives and moves among categories, classes, and abstractions and only rarely touches a real thing.

The obvious ambiguity in the utilitarian position is due to the fact that the utilitarian thinks he is answering one question, whereas his response is to quite a different one. It is as if we were to ask the utilitarian, "What is the temperature of this room?" and he replied, "I feel chilly." Now this answer is not on the same wave length as the question. We didn't ask him how he felt. His actual answer has something to do with the question, in that the feeling state of being chilly might result from a low reading on the thermometer. But if we want to know what that reading is in degrees Fahrenheit, it is of little help to be told that our utilitarian is chilly. He might, in fact, be down with malaria, and then all bets are off. In ethics we want to know what actions are right, and why; the state of a man's feelings are important, but hardly relevant here. Utilitarianism is not an ethcal system, nor is it a substitute for one. It does not come up with ethical answers because it doesn't ask ethical questions.

One branch of this school asserts that all human action is selfish, or that everyone should aim at promoting his own self-interest, and again we are lost in ambiguity. The human self which acts is the subject of every action, obviously. Every action is selfish in this sense— that a self is the subject. But it is the freely chosen object of human action which sorts out the men from the boys, and these objects are to be measured against moral norms. In other words, there are two sides to every human action; there is the self which initiates the action, and there is the objective which the self seeks to accomplish by the action. And as to self-interest, it makes all the difference in the world whether a man promotes his seeming self-interest at the expense of other people, or promotes the genuine interests of the self by conforming his actions to the rules.

Then there's the pragmatic wing. The utilitarian claims that an action or a thing is all right if it spreads happiness and makes people feel good; the pragmatist says it's all right if it works. The pragmatist might return from a motor trip and say, "This proved to be a good road map."

"Why do you refer to this as a good map?" we ask.

"I used it driving to Boston and back and I didn't get lost," he replies. "It's good because it works."

"Why do you suppose that particular map worked?" you ask him.

"I can't be bothered with metaphysics," he replies, "It did work, and that's all I care about." So we have to explain to him that his map worked, that it served his purposes, because it was a map of New England, not of California, and the lines on it correspond to the terrain. A thing is not good or true because it works; it works because it is good or true.

Utilitarianism, as we have seen, states its principles in various ways, but invariably it emphasizes two cardinal points—maximum satisfaction and minimum effort. Man, in terms of this theory, acts only to maximize his happiness, pleasures, satisfactions, or comfort, and he seeks to do this with a minimum expenditure of energy. Utilitarianism has little or nothing to say about the spiritual, ethical, or cultural framework within which its "maximum economy—maximum satisfaction" principle operates. It minimizes or denies life's spiritual dimension, it uses the word "good" in a nonethical sense, i.e., equivalent to "happiness-producing," and it asserts that men are bound together in societies solely on the basis of a rational calculation of the private advantage to be gained by social cooperation under the division of labor.

Robbery, it has been observed, is the first labor-saving device. If a man accepts, without qualification, the precept "Get more for less" as his categorical imperative, what will he do when a combination of circumstances presents him with a relatively safe opportunity to steal? His ethical compunctions against theft have already been dulled, and the use of theft as a means of acquiring economic goods is one of the possible logical conclusions that may be drawn from the "greatest economy" principle. Theft is, of course, forbidden in most of the world's ethical codes, and conformity to these codes over the millenia has bred in most men a reluctance to steal. Thievery there has been aplenty despite the bans, but it has been accompanied by a guilty conscience. The "maximum economy" principle, when first accepted, is applied to productive labor within the framework of the code. But if "Get more for less" is a principle, why not apply it across the board? There are two impediments to a man's acquisition of economic goods: First, there is the effort required to produce them, and second, there is the prohibition against stealing them. The former is in the nature of things, but the latter comes to be regarded as merely a man-made rule. The "greatest economy" principle goes to work on the first impediment—productive effort—by inventing labor-saving devices; it goes to work on the second impediment— the moral code—by collectivizing it. It reduces the commandment against theft to a matter of social expediency. *Society* is admonished against theft on the grounds that a society in which property is not secure is a poor society. But this truism offers no guidance to the individual who finds himself in a situation where he can steal with relative impunity. To the extent that he is emancipated from "outmoded taboos" and follows the line of least resistance, he will steal whenever he thinks he can get away with it. And to make theft easier and safer he will even start writing a form of theft into his statutes: "Votes and taxes for all, subsidies for us." Utilitarianism, in short, has no logical stopping place short of collectivism. Utilitarian collectivism is not a contradiction in terms, although particular utilitarians, restrained by other principles, may stop short of collectivism.

Nineteenth-century utilitarianism spawned an aphorism: All men seek to achieve their ends with a minimum of effort. Men do in fact tend to economize on means, trying not to waste resources. They devise ways to save labor and to increase the unit of output per unit of input. Because the amount of capital per worker in America has increased beyond what is is in other countries, wages here are the highest in the world. And so on. Up to this point, focusing on means, the aphorism appears to fit the facts.

But the aphorism also mentions ends. Man is a goal-seeking creature; he chooses an ideal for his life and works toward it as best he can, with as much resolution and purposiveness as he can muster. It is not difficult to distinguish in thought between means and ends, between a goal and the route to the goal, between the road and the inn at the end of the road. But who would seriously maintain that we choose those ends, goals, and destinations that put minimum demands on us? Which is the way our aphorism is commonly and carelessly interpreted.

Men choose their life goals and tasks for reasons which may be obscure, but it is overwhelmingly obvious that this choice is based on something other than a simple desire to conserve energy. A man does not act in order to rest; he rests in order to act. The more of a man he is, the higher the level he seeks to energize himself on ; he wears himself out for his religion, his art, his science; he finds himself and his happiness by becoming absorbed in causes he deems noble.

Men choose the goals that strike deeply into their imaginations and their idealism; they do not choose to sink into an easy situation whose selling point is that only a minimum energy expenditure is required of them. Now, once having chosen a goal which challenges their capacities to the utmost, men realize that they can pursue it with vigor only if they conserve their resources, and it is at this point that they try to economize.

A conclusion such as this is implicit in the proposition that economics is a science of means. If economics is indeed a science of means it is self-evident that the choosing of ends proceeds along other lines. A man chooses his goals by one method, and very properly selects his means by another. The universe can count above two, H. G. Wells said somewhere, in commenting on the pathetic desire that seems to possess men in every age to reduce the variety and richness of life to a single, simple formula. The paradigm of this vain effort, ever since the Renaissance, has been Euclidean geometry. Here is a structure, so it seemed, in which every facet logically implicates every other, the whole being hooked up so that a rational man might start anywhere with a simple proposition and by a process of deduction arrive at the whole truth. This is rationalism, which has loomed large in economic inquiry and will be considered in the next chapter.

CHAPTER 7

Critique of Rationalism

FEW, IF ANY, ECONOMISTS ARE JUST THAT. ADAM SMITH WAS a professor of Moral Philosophy at Glasgow University, John Stuart Mill wrote extensively on ethics, and in the writings of contemporary economists are to be found sweeping pronouncements on philosophy, history, literature, psychology, ethics, religion, and other subjects. This all-too-human fault of pretended omniscience is more serious in the case of the free market economist than it would be in the case of the psychologist, say, or the historian. A fatuous psychologist makes some asinine pronouncements in the field of judicial procedure, for example. His auditors —assuming them to be reasonably well-educated men with some practical experience in human affairs—merely recognize that the psychologist's opinions in the field of law are those of a rank amateur. They dust him off and send him back to his own preserve. They do not, as a rule, use this faux pas as an excuse to pass an adverse judgment on psychology as a whole. But let an economist utter a dubious pronouncement in fields where he is an amateur and his listerners are likely to discount the soundness of his economics to the extent that they disagree with his pronouncements on other subjects.

Why is this so? The average well-read American has had a considerable exposure to history, psychology, literature, and the like. He has read Freud and Adler, or read enough about them, so that he does not turn his back on psychology merely because some psychologist is incompetent in other fields. But the average well-read American is woefully illiterate in the field of economics. One might say that he is negatively equipped to judge economics; what he understands by the term is derived from hostile sources, mainly Marxian, and he has to cut through this verbiage before he can even stand on neutral ground as a preliminary to forming an objective opinion on the merits of the Manchester and Austrian Schools of free market economics. So when an economist ventures into the field of literary criticism or religion and utters nonsense—or what strikes his hearers as nonsense—they dismiss his theories of literature or religion and turn their backs on his economics to boot!

It is a subtle matter of authority. A genuine expert in economics fails to convey authority in this subject if he puts his lack of expertise on exhibit in other fields. It happens to be a fact—for whatever reason or reasons—that the overwhelming majority of otherwise well-educated people do not know how the market economy operates. People who are proud of their smattering of technical jargon in several fields have never heard of such terms as marginal utility, or time preference, or Says' Law. Such great names in economics as Menger, Böhm-Bawerk, Jevons, Clark, and Wicksteed mean nothing to them. Furthermore, some terms in common use in two or more fields have in economic discourse a meaning quite distinct from their usage elsewhere. The phrase "subjective value" is a case in point. When an economist says that "values are subjective" he is saying: What a man will offer in exchange for a gizmo relates back to the intensity of his preference for the gizmo—its relative place in his hierarchy of values—over against alternatives, including doing without. When a philosopher declares that "values are subjective" he is proclaiming that the universe contains no dimension whose nature is such as to validate ethical and esthetic judgments; he is aligning himself with the ethical relativists or nihilists who assert that there are no norms or standards for man written into the very nature of things. Now an economist may, on grounds relevant to ethical or esthetic inquiry, conclude in favor of nihilism or relativism; but it is surely a bizarre situation to reach such a conclusion merely because of a failure to understand how words are being used.

An economist may be an expert in several fields beyond economics, and many have been. Smith was a moralist, Ricardo a stock broker, Mill a logician, Jevons a mathematician, Wicksteed a clergyman, and so on. But a question may be raised about the propriety of using the presumed authority of economics as the grounds for passing judgments on non-economic matters. Take, for example, the assertion that the case for the free market economy cannot be made except on the three-fold basis of rationalism, individualism, and utilitarianism. Such a statement might appeal to persons who are 100 percent sold on free market economics and not too well versed in philosophy, for there is much to be said in behalf of rationalism, individualism, and utilitarianism. But those who have rehearsed the several battles of the mind which have stirred men during the past two centuries are aware that some devastating objections have been and can be brought against each of these three positions.

It is a fact that free market practices have been successfully engaged in by people who reject each of these positions, and it is somewhat presumptuous to hinge the acceptance of free market theory on the requirement that debatable theories in the fields of ethics, psychology, and philosophy must be embraced first. The religionist, furthermore, will feel that these three preliminary requirements are aimed especially at him; rationalism, individualism (in the nineteenth-century sense), and utilitarianism do not square with Biblical theology and ethics.

Modern thought since the Enlightenment displays several characteristics: it has tended to be rationalistic, it has talked a great deal about The Individual, and its ethical tendency has been utilitarian and pragmatic. All men are, in some measure, creatures of their age, and it would be strange indeed if economists were immune to the influences of the prevailing thought currents. It has seemed to some leading economists that the ideology of the Enlightenment was made to order as an ideal carrier and base for economics, but by this same token many have been alienated needlessly from economics because of its alleged dependence on this ideology.

Economics is a relatively new discipline. The discovery of regularity and sequence in market events, and the working out of many of the implications of these regularities, were the achievements of Adam Smith. Those on the alert for new ideas in the century following Adam Smith would naturally take up with the new economic knowledge, and at the same time their eagerness for new ideas would make them susceptible to rationalism, individualism, utilitarianism, and other exciting notions. It is part of our purpose to demonstrate that another set of ideas will provide a surer framework for the free economy.

Liberalism became the prevailing social philosophy among intellectuals during the nineteenth century, and it was either indifferent to religion or—this is especially true of Continental liberalism—actively hostile. The dimension of the transcendent lost its significance in men's thinking during this period, while at the same time there was a great upsurge of humanitarian endeavor. Much of the religious fervor hitherto directed toward otherworldly objects reversed its direction and now was aimed at improving the material and social conditions of this life. An abundance of natural piety was displayed in reform movements and in the working out of political liberty and economic freedom. Religious interest moved away from God, immortality, and the Kingdom of Heaven to center on man, his mundane happiness, and the creation of an earthly paradise by scientific advancement under popular control in democratic societies. The mood and temper of the period in which these ideas settled and became domesticated was shaped in large measure by rationalism.

Webster's Unabridged defines rationalism as the "elaboration of theories by reasoning alone without testing them by experience, as in pure mathematics." It goes on to say, "The theory that philosophic knowledge may be arrived at by deductions from a priori concepts or necessary ideas." Turn now to the classic work on epistemology by William Pepperell Montague, *The Ways of Knowing*, where two chapters are devoted to a combined discussion of rationalism and empiricism. "Rationalism," says Montague, "is the method of proving propositions by appealing to abstract and universal principles; empiricism is the opposite method of proving propositions by appealing to concrete and particular occurrences. . . . The rationalist contends that our knowledge of universals is far superior to our knowledge of particular objects and in no sense derived from that knowledge. The empiricist, on the other hand, holds that universal concepts, in so far as they can be admitted as genuinely present to the mind, are derived from the concrete particulars of experience, and that their importance is secondary and instrumental."[1]

The word rationalism contains the Latin root "ratio" meaning a reckoning, account, computation, calculation; and the appeal of rationalism as a philosophy has always been in terms of the elegance and symmetry exhibited by mathematics. The word empiricism derives from the Greek stem "empeiros," a trial or experiment; which calls up the vision of the scientist experimenting in his laboratory or collating observations made in the field.

The world of the mathematician is not the familiar world of sense; it is the realm of ideas. A Euclidean point is a thing with no dimensions, that is to say it does not exist—except as a concept. Move the point along a plane and a line results, with no dimension but length; move the line and a plane is formed, having length and breadth, but no depth. Points, lines, and planes put little strain on our imagination, for we readily visualize something like them in real life—they are not far removed from the ordinary sensory world which we can see and touch. But the concepts of zero and negative numbers are out of this world altogether. They are pure idea. We use them easily in our mathematics, but it took several thousand years and many generations of mathematicians to conceive them. The great mathematician and philosopher Alfred North Whitehead writes: "The originality of mathematics consists in the fact that in mathematical science connections between things are exhibited which, apart from the agency of human reason, are extremely unobvious. Thus the ideas, now in the minds of contemporary mathematicians, lie very remote from any notions which can be immediately derived by perceptions through the senses: unless it be perception stimulated and guided by antecedent mathematical knowledge."[2]

The tidy world of mathematics—a realm where there is no disorder, no surprises, no items that cannot be catalogued, no wild facts, nothing absolutely unique, but where everything fits logically into everything else—makes a strong appeal to a certain type of mind. Bertrand Russell, in a personal memoir, speaks of "the restfulness of mathematical certainty." The passage reads:

1. Montague, *The Ways of Knowing*, pp. 69–70.
2. *The World of Mathematics* (Jas. Newman, Ed.), I, p. 402.

"Throughout the rest of my boyhood, mathematics absorbed a very large part of my interest. This interest was complex: partly mere pleasure in discovering that I possessed a kind of skill, partly delight in the power of deductive reasoning, partly the restfulness of mathematical certainty; but more than any of these (while I was still a boy) the belief that nature operates according to mathematical laws, and that human actions, like planetary motions, could be calculated if we had sufficient skill."[3] Russell, obviously, altered his outlook as he matured, but the temper which regards mathematical knowledge as the paradigm of all knowledge is deeply ingrained in the modern psyche, which finds here a safe anchorage against the storms and uncertainties of life. Much of this mood is derived from René Descartes, whose *Discourse on Method* appeared in 1637. He thought he could "grasp this sorry scheme of things entire" by "long chains of simple and easy reasoning." The entire passage reads as follows:

> The long chains of simple and easy reasonings by means of which geometers are accustomed to reach the conclusions of their most difficult demonstrations, had led me to imagine that all things, to the knowledge of which man is competent, are mutually connected in the same way, and that there is nothing so far removed from us as to be beyond our reach, or so hidden that we cannot discover it, provided only we abstain from accepting the false for the true, and always preserve in our thoughts the order necessary for the deduction of one truth from another. And I had little difficulty in determining the objects with which it was necessary to commence, for I was already persuaded that it must be with the simplest and easiest to know, and, considering that of all those who have hitherto sought truth in the sciences, the mathematicians alone have been able to find any demonstrations, that is, any certain and evident reasons, I did not doubt but that such must have been the rule of their investigations.[4]

Thomas Hobbes wrote duirng this same period, and was similarly bemused by "geometry, which is the only science that it hath pleased God hitherto to bestow on mankind. . . ."[5]

3. *Ibid.*, p. 384.
4. *Discourse on Method*, Everyman's Library, p. 16.
5. *Leviathan*, Part I, Ch. 4.

Early experimental science was crammed into the same mold.
E. A. Burtt writes,

> Galileo's exact study of velocities and accelerations forced
> him to devise a simple technique for the geometrical represen-
> tation of time, which was fairly adequate to the truths he
> sought to illustrate. With him, the physical world begins to be
> conceived as a perfect machine whose future happenings can
> be fully predicted and controlled by one who has full knowl-
> edge and control of the present motions. With man eliminated
> from the real world, the latter appeared bound by mechanical
> necessity. Thinking was started on that current which led
> nearly two centuries later to the famous remark of Laplace,
> that a superhuman intelligence acquainted with the position
> and motion of the atoms at any moment could predict the
> whole course of future events. To hypothesize such an intelli-
> gence in a world whose present is nothing but a moving math-
> ematical limit between past and future—in fact, the existence
> of any intelligence, reason, knowledge, or science in such a
> world—strikes one as something of an anomaly.[6]

Many nineteenth-century men of science were supremely confident that the universe had finally yielded up its last secret, that the
mind of man was competent to comprehend all and capable of
eventually bringing everything under its control. Such assurance
is exuded in the course of the 1874 presidential address delivered
to the British Association for the Advancement of Science by John
Tyndall, friend and colleague of Faraday. Tyndall predicted that
the future of science would enable us to survey the "ultimately

---

6. Burtt, *The Metaphysical Foundations of Modern Science*, p. 96. Laplace's full statement
is found in the Preface to his *Analytic Theory of Probabilities*, published in 1812: "We ought
to regard the present state of the universe as the effect of its antecedent state and as the
cause of the state that is to follow. An intelligence knowing all the forces acting in nature
at a given instant, as well as the momentary positions of all things in the universe, would
be able to comprehend in one single formula the motions of the largest bodies as well as
of the hightest atoms in the world, provided that its intellect were sufficiently powerful to
subject all data to analysis; to it nothing would be uncertain, the future as well as the past
would be present to its eyes. The perfection that the human mind has been able to give to
astronomy affords a feeble outline of such an intelligence. Discoveries in mechanics and
geometry, coupled with those in universal gravitation, have brought the mind within reach
of comprehending in the same analytical formula the past and the future state of the system
of the world."

natural and inevitable march of evolution from the atoms of the primeval nebula to the proceedings of the British Association for the Advancement of Science." Sir William Cecil Dampier in his standard *History of Science* summarizes the nineteenth-century outlook in these words: "Throughout the nineteenth century, most men of science, consciously or unconsciously, held the common-sense view: that matter, its primary properties and their relations, as revealed by science, are ultimate realities, and that human bodies are mechanisms, though perhaps occasionally controlled or influenced by minds. When they thought about ultimate scientific concepts, many physicists realized that these opinions, convenient as working assumptions, would not stand critical examination; but, in the laboratory as in practical life, there was no time for philosophic doubt."[7]

Dogmatic self-assurance is an occupational hazard that lingers on in some contemporary scientists, but it is no longer characteristic of the scientific outlook as it once was. A fair statement of the new mood in contemporary science is found in Warren Weaver's address before the American Association for the Advancement of Science upon his retirement from the presidency of that body:

> Science has impressively proved itself to be a powerful way of dealing with certain aspects of our experience. These are, in general, the logical and quantitative aspects, the method working superbly for linear and stable physical problems in two or three variables. . . . We simply do not know yet how far these methods, which have worked so well with physical nature, will be successful in the world of living things. . . . It is, incidentally, not at all necessary that the particular analytical techniques of the physical sciences be forced upon biological or social problems with the arrogant assumption that they can and should make unnecessary other types of insight and experience. . . .
>
> Science does not deserve the reputation it has so widely gained of being based on absolute fact (whatever that is supposed to mean), of being wholly objective, of being infinitely precise, of being unchangeably permanent, of being philosophically inescapable and unchallengeable. There seem still

---

7. Dampier, *History of Science,* p. 202.

to be persons who think that science deals with certainty, whereas it is of course the case that it deals with probabilities.

The development of western science, rather than constituting a uniquely inevitable pattern, has been influenced by the general nature of Greco-Judaic culture, including especially the standards, arising within that tradition, of what is interesting and important.[8]

This is an age of scientific popularizers and pseudo-science, and we should hardly expect it to be otherwise, for the ideas entertained by advanced thinkers of the past and now discarded by their counterparts of today have seeped into the popular consciousness. When it comes to ideas, the man in the street acquires by a sort of osmosis the leading opinions of several generations back; the things he takes for granted, his massive certainties, are the dogmatisms of last century.

Contemporary physicists explore a world which conforms to no common sense model. As A. d'Abro writes in the Preface to his *Rise of the New Physics*, "In the subatomic world mechanical representations and classical concepts are no longer of much avail, except as props to a bewildered imagination which is unable to feel at ease in its new surroundings."[9] One of the most brilliant of the modern physicists, Werner Heisenberg, has declared that to deal adequately with all his data he needs not one, but four mathematical systems, and that these four do not seem to be mutually consistent. Scientists declare that they deal with probabilities, not with certainties, and they entertain the possibility that "there are no mathematically exact laws in the physical world," to quote d'Abro again. Furthermore, contemporary scientists press against the limitations of language and are forced to communicate some of their truths by means of mathematical equations, and the rationalist's reliance on verbal formulations receives another blow.

Supreme confidence in man's ability to acquire certain knowledge of his total environment, and to wield control over it commensurate with his assured knowledge, once seemed to be sanctioned by both mathematics and the natural sciences. The natural sciences have withdrawn from this entangling alliance, and

8. *Science News Letter,* Jan. 14, 1956.
9. d'Abro, *Rise of the New Physics,* p. v.

the higher branches of mathematics no longer coincide with the simple Euclidean scheme.

What mathematicians call "Goedel's Proof" appeared in 1931 in a paper entitled "On Formally Undecidable Propositions of Principia Mathematica and Related Systems." The author was Kurt Goedel, a twenty-five-year-old mathematician at the University of Vienna, and his paper has been called a "milestone in the history of modern logic and mathematics." Its subject is hardly for the layman, but the account of it by James Newman and Ernest Nagel, found in Volume III of *The World of Mathematics* exposes the high spots. Mathematics, with its "chains of simple and easy reasonings," once supplied the model for rationalism's universe of consistently interlocking parts, but now it announces radical discontinuities within itself. Euclid "apparently selected his axioms so as to make it possible to deduce from them all geometric truths which were already established, as well as those still to be discovered," write Newman and Nagel. "Until recently, it was assumed as a matter of course that a complete set of axioms for any given branch of mathematics could always be specified. In particular, it seems to have been generally believed that the axioms proposed for arithmetic by nineteenth-century mathematicians were in fact complete, or at worst could be made complete by the addition of a finite number of further axioms. The discovery that this is not so, is one of Goedel's achievements. . . . Goedel's second main conclusion is even more surprising and revolutionary in its import, for it makes evident a fundamental limitation in the power of the axiomatic method. Goedel showed that *Principia*, or any other system within which arithmetic can be deveoped, is *essentially incomplete*. In other words, given *any* consistent set of arithmetical axioms, there are true arithmetical statements which are not derivable from the set."[10]

The specific disabilities of rationalism when it comes to social theory are set forth in Chapter IV, entitled "Freedom, Reason, and Tradition" of F. A. Hayek's monumental book, *The Constitution of Liberty*. We have "two different traditions in the theory of liberty," he writes, "one empirical and unsystematic, the other speculative and rationalistic," the former largely English, the latter mainly French. "It has been the rationalist, plausible, and

10. *Ibid.*, pp. 1684–5.

apparently logical arguments of the French tradition, with its flattering assumptions about the unlimited powers of human reason, that has progressively gained influence, while the less articulate and less explicit tradition of English freedom has been on the decline."[11] It goes without saying that the author of this book takes his stand with the tradition of English freedom, which "broadens down from precedent to precedent," as does Hayek. My analysis of rationalism is based on the assumption that rationalism renders it impossible to apply reason and experience to human affairs, and on the further assumption that rationalism is incompatible with human liberty. Rationalism offers a faulty map of the universe, one guaranteed to lead us astray—as the catastrophes of the twentieth century bear witness. It necessarily ignores or neglects important segments of reality. It generates the "Let's-take-charge-of-human-affairs" mentality.

The urge to play god is not exactly alien to human nature, if the record thus far is a clue, but the urge does not get out of hand among men who sense the overwhelming size, majesty, and mystery of the cosmos in contrast to their own finitude. Men who realize their own limitations freely admit that the universe contains levels or reaches which are not simply unknown to the present generation of men but are beyond human ken. Some of this mystery is within themselves, they recognize, and also within other people. When this attitude prevails, individual liberty has a chance. People may not frame elegant theories of liberty, but in practice they let each other alone.

The basic assumption of rationalism is the belief that all reality is hooked up logically, so that even without experience an intelligent man might, by ruminating on a self-evident premise, deduce all the truth and knowledge there is. Theoretically, he might do this without stirring from his study, and just by relying on his own reasoning. Today, of course, he would simply feed data into a computer. The corollary is that there is a one-to-one correspondence between verbal formulations or propositions and the totality of the universe. Rationalism tends to disparage the actual, the observed, the historical, the concrete, the particular, the individual; it is more at home with the abstract, the general, the theoretical, the elegant.

11. Hayek, *The Constitution of Liberty*, pp. 54–5.

One of the characters in C. S. Lewis's novel, *That Hideous Strength*, is a professor of sociology, of whom Lewis writes: "His education had had the curious effect of making things that he read and wrote more real to him than things he saw. Statistics about agricultural labourers were the substance; any real ditcher, plough-man, or farmer's boy, was the shadow. Though he had never noticed it himself, he had a great reluctance, in his work, ever to use such words as 'man' or 'woman.' He preferred to write about 'vocational groups,' 'elements,' 'classes' and 'populations': for, in his own way, he believed as firmly as any mystic in the superior reality of the things that are not seen."[12]

The realm of concepts and classes is outside time, so in addition to having attained to certain knowledge of the present, rationalism knows the future as well.

Free market economic theory is based on the premise that no man can predict the future. A famous outburst of a couple of generations ago had it that not even God Himself knows what it costs to ship a ton of steel from Pittsburgh to New York. God wills human freedom, and this, therefore, is a natural observation to make. Steel is an economic good, and no one can know with certainty how much steel the consuming public will actually want, nor with what intensity they want it—as measured by what they will give up in order to get it—nor can anyone correctly estimate in advance the costs of the various factors involved in shipping steel from here to there. After the transaction has been completed, prices are affixed to the numerous goods and services involved and then we can tote up costs; but not before.

But rationalism contains the implication that both the present and the future can be known with certainty, the only distinction being that the future isn't here yet. If this is so, collectivist eco-nomic planning in the computer age is possible. It is the central contention of economic theory that economic calculation is based on the market; no market, no calculation. It follows that sound economic theory has hard going in a rationalistic milieu; it is discounted because of the milieu rather than rebutted on its own grounds.

Let me expand on this point. Goods are scarce, scarcity in fact being one of the qualifications which makes a thing a "good."

12. Lewis, *That Hideous Strength*, p. 93.

Some means must be devised, therefore, for allocating goods so that they will satisfy the most urgent wants of people. It was the pious belief of the socialist movement until 1922 that the allocation of scarce resources was a simple matter of setting up a planning board empowered to tell the citizens what to produce, in what quantities, colors, sizes, and so on, where to produce it, transport it, and for what reward. Then, by fiat, the planning board would ration these goods and give each person what the board thought he needed or deserved. No socialist theoretician, in other words, had regarded economic calculation as a problem. It is easy to see why. In any society which is relatively free, people adapt their economic activities to their wants and needs as naturally and unconsciously as they breathe. We become aware of breathing as a problem only in the absence of air, and economic calculation becomes a problem when there are no market data; that is, when economic freedom is replaced by state planning. Ludwig von Mises tossed a bombshell into the socialist camp in 1922 with his book entitled *Socialism*, containing an extended demonstration that economic calculation has to use market data, and that under socialist planning which eliminated the market the bureaucracy would have no way of pricing the factors of production.

If rationalism be sound, the future is knowable and prediction is a simple matter of reasoning correctly from self-evident premises. A man, therefore, can know exactly what action consumers will take, and a socialist planning board can operate a society. The Mises position, on the other hand, is that no man can know in advance of their actual manifestation, the tastes, preferences, and consequent market demands of any individual or any collection of individuals. "The market" is the configuration precipitated by the public's actual buying or not buying and, obviously, such data cannot exist until after these events occur. Only after people have bought or refrained from buying does the entrepreneur have the market data without which he cannot possibly make his decisions. The entrepreneur's approach is that of the empiricist, not that of the rationalist; he reasons a posteriori, not a priori.

If rationalism were correct in its premises, a competent logician, reasoning from a few axioms, or a computer properly programmed, could deduce all the truths necessary to make economic calculation possible in the absence of a market. The fact that economic calculation is impossible if the market does not function demonstrates the deficiency of a priori reasoning at this point. Economic calculation takes place after the fact, a posteriori. If it were not thus, if all truth could be ascertained merely by accurately drawing out the inferences contained in a few axioms, then knowledge of that portion of "all truth" which is labeled market data could be gained a priori, and economic calculation could take place under socialism. The converse is equally true; if economic calculation is impossible in a socialist society, then the data on which calculation is based must be arrived at empirically. Rationalism, as a consistent theory, breaks down at this, as well as at other points.

Rationalism, in one of its aspects, is hostile to sound economic theory and practice; in several of its aspects it is hostile to all religion and to Christianity in particular. Man is only a tiny part of the total universe, his mind is only a part of man, and the top layer of the mind, which specializes in the framing of syllogisms, is only a part of the whole mind. This tiny fragment presumes to say that nothing is except what can be netted in the meshes of its verbal formulations as couched in one of the European languages. T. H. Huxley's lecture on a piece of chalk is a convincing demonstration that our idea of a simple, common object is a pretty thin slice of the total reality which is that object. How infinitely more true is this of even the most sophisticated idea men can frame of God! The reality is not only more than the idea, but is of a different order than the idea. Rationalism denies the transcendent but elevates capital M Man to the godhood.

God, for Aristotle, was the Prime Mover; He was a speculative necessity demanded by logic to cap off a line of reasoning. This approach is alien to the mentality of the people of the Bible. The God of the Bible is "encountered," He reveals Himself in history. He embodies His will in a person. The "faith" He demands is not mere belief in a set of propositions which might be held at arm's length, analyzed, and debated, and then formally accepted or rejected. The venture of faith commits a man's life to testing the belief that man did not invent himself nor write the laws of his being; it lives the premise that man is a creature whose creaturehood implies a Creator from Whom he has the gift of life and to Whom he is ultimately responsible. This is a belief which can be tested only in the living of it, and if we may credit the testimony of those who put it to the trial, there comes to them a sense of participation in and contribution to the divine purpose for man in which they find the meaning of individual life.

This faith is meaningful in a universe whose future is not determined. Men are free and their personal choices shape the future; their cumulative decisions cast the deciding vote.

CHAPTER 8

The Fact of Transcendence

IF WE CUT THROUGH TO THE HARD CORE OF RELIGION WE COME to the conviction that men and women are involved willy-nilly in a realm of being which transcends the social and natural orders; plus the implied corollary that human beings will function properly at every level only if they participate intelligently in this higher—or third—order.

The sensory world falls into two divisions: The first order is society; the second is nature. Human beings have seldom existed as solitaries, for language is an earmark of the human and speech could not have developed except out of social intercourse and the need to communicate with one's fellows. Society, furthermore, is an economic necessity in the matter of sheer survival. Society is man's native habitat; Hobbes's "murderous anarch" is a fiction. Historically, it is not difficult to distinguish one society from another; Hindu society from Chinese society; medieval English society from that of contemporary England and so on. Each society has unique features; none is a mere aggregate of individuals. The individuals who comprise a given society are organized into certain patterns which, although in constant flux, are recognizably different from the patterns which emerge out of societies located in other parts of the globe or in other eras. A symphony is a collection of individual notes, and if these notes were erased one by one the music would cease to be; but the symphony, nonetheless, is more than a simple sum of the notes. The notes are arranged in a particular pattern which enables us to distinguish Beethoven's Fifth from Brahms' Second.

It is analogous, but more complex, with a given individual and his society. A reflective man's society is, for him, something more than "just other people"; it is possible to develop an overview which comprehends—on the basis of study and contemplation—how this particular society came to be, how it has developed, the sources of its characteristic outlook and consensus, its mode of functioning in the political and economic sectors, its probable future, and so on.

Each person, in short, participates in a given society which occupies a certain portion of the habitable globe, at this time and not at some other. He can contract out of this society only if he joins another; he cannot contract out of society and live.

In addition to his involvement in some society, every man is part of the natural order; he is not a disembodied spirit. The material world contains living organisms of which man is one. Biological, physical, and geographic elements play their allotted role in making every person the unique person he is, but making it possible at the same time to recognize rough divisions among the peoples of the earth. A Hottentot shares many of his characteristics with the Eskimo, but no one would mistake one for the other. As a biological organism man has features in common with every other mammal, and is related in some way, however distant, to all living things. Like other mammals, he is an energy system in constant pursuit of available energy, which is scarce. He is dependent on a given quota of calories daily; he needs certain obscure food elements called vitamins and minerals; he needs oxygen diluted properly with nitrogen and other gaseous elements; and he needs to fend off other biological organisms, some large and others microscopically small, which seem to regard him as having been put here mainly to further their purposes. "My body contains so many germs," wrote Samuel Butler, "that I often wonder if it does not belong more to them than to me."

The natural order contains human beings and other living organisms, but it also contains nonliving things. Its basic ingredients are listed in the table of the elements: actinium on down through gold, iron, tin, and zinc, to zirconium. Usually we meet with these elements, not singly, but only when several of them have combined to form a compound. The oceans, lakes, and rivers, the earth beneath our feet, the stones from which our monuments have been carved and our temples built are all parts of this chemical world. Our very bodies are compounded of the dust, and sea water runs in our veins.

Life is a latecomer on the world stage. Something happened, and the earth was a hot glob of gas. It spun on its axis and rotated through space for countless millions of years, gradually cooling, gradually developing a situation hospitable to life. Before this momentous occurrence, that is prior to the appearance of living organisms, the physical universe must have existed, basically, much as we know it today. Water ran downhill and boiled at 212° Fahrenheit at sea level; iron rusted when exposed to the air; ninety-odd elements were the basic building blocks, just as they are today. The causal sequences and the natural regularities which have been transcribed into the laws of physics and chemistry were in operation then, as now, but no one was aware of them, and the laws had to wait millions of years before being formulated.

This second, or natural, order is peculiarly the domain of science. Indeed, in common speech the word science, although derived from the Greek word meaning "to know," has come to mean special kinds of knowledge only. Speak of science and an image of the laboratory drifts by; physics and chemistry are science par excellence. Study man scientifically and the connotation has to do with his measurable and quantitative aspects, that is, with anatomy and physiology. In terms of the common understanding of the matter, to speak of the science of economics, or the science of history, or the science of metaphysics, evidences a desire to incorporate more certainty into these disciplines than their nature warrants. Science, to the average man—and to many who are not average—is the magic way to understand and control the natural world, the source of the mechanical and technological wonders that still dazzle many with their promise. Many believe that the Scientific Method is the best way man has for attaining valid knowledge.

H. G. Wells was one of those so dazzled. In his *Outline of History* he concluded one of several sections on science and its fruits with these words: "Now here altogether we have such a change in human life as to constitute a fresh phase of history. In a little more than a century this mechanical revolution has been brought about. In that time man made a stride in the material conditions of his life vaster than he had done during the whole long interval betwen the palaeolithic stage and the age of cultivation, or between the days of Pepi in Egypt and those of George III. A new gigantic material frame work for human affairs has come into existence. Clearly, it demands great readjustments of our social, economical, and political methods."[1]

The world view of Mr. Wells, the scientific world view, is one shared by millions in the modern world. It is set forth, somewhat ironically and with the detachment of a sceptic, by Mr. C. S. Lewis:

> The play is preceded by the most austere of all preludes: the infinite void, and matter restlessly moving to bring forth it knows not what. Then, by the millionth millionth chance— what tragic irony—the conditions at one point of space and time bubble up into that tiny fermentation which is the beginning of life. Everything seems to be against the infant hero of our drama—just as everything seems against the youngest son or ill-used stepdaughter at the opening of a fairy-tale. But life somehow wins through. With infinite suffering, against all but insuperable obstacles, it spreads, it breeds, it complicates itself: from the amoeba up to the plant, up to the reptile, up to the mammal. We glance briefly at the age of monsters. Dragons prowl the earth, devour one another and die. Then comes the theme of the younger son and the ugly duckling once more. As the weak, tiny spark of life began amidst the huge hostilities of the inanimate, so now again, amidst the beasts that are far larger and stronger than he, there comes forth a little naked, shivering, cowering creature, shuffling, not yet erect, promising nothing: the product of another millionth millionth chance. Yet somehow he thrives. He becomes the Cave Man with his club and his flints, muttering and growling over his enemies' bones, dragging his screaming mate by her hair (I never could quite make out why), tearing his children to pieces in fierce jealousy till one of them is old enough to tear him, cowering before the horrible gods whom he has created in his own image. But these are only growing pains. Wait till the next Act. There he is becoming true Man. He

1. Wells, *Outline of History,* Vol. IV, p. 1088.

learns to master Nature. Science comes and dissipates the superstitions of his infancy. More and more he becomes the controller of his own fate. Passing hastily over the present (for it is a mere nothing by the time-scale we are using), you follow him on into the future. See him in the last act, though not the last scene, of this great mystery. A race of demigods now rule the planet—and perhaps more than the planet—for eugenics have made certain that only demigods will be born, and psychoanalysis that none of them shall lose or smirch his divinity, and communism that all which divinity requires shall be ready to their hands. Man has ascended his throne. Henceforward he has nothing to do but to practise virtue, to grow in wisdom, to be happy. And now, mark the final stroke of genius. If the myth stopped at that point, it might be a little bathetic. It would lack the highest grandeur of which human imagination is capable. The last scene reverses all. We have the Twilight of the Gods. All this time, silently, unceasingly, out of all reach of human power, Nature, the old enemy, has been steadily gnawing away. The sun will cool—all suns will cool —the whole universe will run down. Life (every form of life) will be banished, without hope of return, from every inch of infinite space. All ends in nothingness, and "universal darkness covers all." The pattern of the myth thus becomes one of the noblest we can conceive. It is the pattern of many Elizabethan tragedies.[2]

The spectacular results of an application of the methods of science in the laboratory and in the field had so captivated the imagination of Westerners by the middle of the nineteenth century that a pretended "science of society" was bound to be offered. Saint-Simon, Comte, and Marx had their innings, and their legacy is with us yet. "Each branch of knowledge," asserted Comte in a celebrated passage, "is necessarily obliged to pass through three different theoretical states: the Theological or fictitious state; the Metaphysical or abstract state; lastly, the Scientific or positive state." The inference, of course, was that mankind is even now entering the Scientific Era. John Stuart Mill fell under the sway of Comte and the Saint-Simonians, and writes in his *Autobiography* that Comte's Social Physics "harmonized well with my existing notions to which it seemed to give a scientific shape. I already

2. Lewis, *They Asked for a Paper*, pp. 154.

regarded the methods of physical science as the proper models for political."[3]

The idea was that man comes under the sway of two sets of regularities, and two only. The rigidly cause and effect realm of nature obeys the laws of physics and chemistry, and the reign of physical law which holds dominion over material particles is likewise operative within the social order. The natural sciences are necessarily deterministic, on the macro scale at any rate. If we were to attribute free will to a stone, permitting it to defy gravity, or allow a litre of water to decide when and when not to freeze, we'd be back in the age of magic. And if human beings are nothing more than natural offshoots of the natural world, they too are caught up in its deterministic rigidities. To allow for free will in human beings is to deny causal sequence—as natural science understands it—and bog down at the metaphysical or theological level. The social order is embedded in the natural order, being nothing more than one of its manifestations. Grant this dubious proposition and certain consequences follow. The laws of science summarize the inexorable workings of cause and effect in physical nature, and if society is part of nature, it follows that the social order is under the sway of laws equally rigorous; the laws of economics, perhaps, which determine production. Small wonder, then, that the Comteans scorned personal rights and the liberty of conscience. J. S. Mill, when he had recovered from his infatuation with Comte, dismissed his Social Physics as "the completest system of spiritual and temporal despotism which ever yet emanated from a human brain, unless possibly that of Ignatius Loyola."[4]

If man is merely a part of nature he cannot claim to be exempt from the deterministic sequences which rigidly constrain nature. It is difficult to see how it could be otherwise. To the extent that one is convinced that man cannot exercise free will and is not, therefore, a responsible being, to that extent is he willing to organize human societies which deliberately deny liberties of the mind and conscience. Political liberty is difficult enough to arrange for at best, even when freedom of the will is a leading tenet of the prevailing philosophy; in a scientistic ethos political liberty

3. Mill, *Autobiography*, p. 116. For a thorough account of this whole episode and its meaning, F. A. Hayek's *The Counter-Revolution of Science* (The Free Press, Glencoe, Illinois, 1955) is strongly recommended.
4. *Ibid.*, p. 149.

becomes an outcast. Nineteenth-century science denied that any reality existed outside its purview, and it was largely deterministic. As a result, social engineering began to erode both the theory and practice of political liberty.

Here is man upon the planet. How many orders is he involved in? The religious outlook holds that he must make his accommodation to the mandates of at least three orders; the social order, the natural order, and a realm which transcends both, being another dimension of reality. For religion depends, as St. Paul put it, on a conviction of the reality of things not seen. The world of time and space is transitory, but it is involved with a background that does not change. "What is seen passes away; what is unseen is eternal." (II Cor. 4:18) But now this third order has pretty well dropped out of sight, permitting André Malraux to express his gratification recently over the fact that we live in the first agnostic civilization. This does not mean that the majority of people in the advanced nations are avowed agnostics or atheists; indeed, if polled, the majority of people admit to a belief in some sort of a higher power having some sort of an indeterminate influence over their lives, and to being vaguely attracted to a dilute sort of spirituality. The civilization is said to be agnostic in the sense that, for all practical purposes, those who have a lively sense of an involvement with the transcendent and of its down-to-earth significance are a scattered minority, muted and largely uninfluential in secular affairs.

The religion of Christendom, so runs the tale, has been displaced by the dissemination of exact knowledge resulting from researches in the several sciences, and now science itself has given birth to a new faith in Man (spelled with a capital M). Whereas the Kingdom of God was a far-off, divine event beyond the realm of human attainment, the new scientific faith puts the Kingdom of Man within his grasp. A new humanity shall inherit the earth and bring it into a state of universal peace and vital equilibrium. The object of worship is no longer God; it is future humanity, and this faith for living might be and is being called humanism, in contrast to theism. Humanism has been the creed of many high-minded men since the eighteenth century, and today it is an organized movement in several parts of the world. There is an American Humanist Assocation, and humanist churches function every Sunday morning in many American cities under their own name or some other. Ethical Culturalists are closely related to them. and so are some Unitarians. A promotion booklet prepared by Edwin H. Wilson, president of the American Humanist Association, is entitled *Humanism, the Fourth Faith*. There are numerous religious sects competing for attention today, says Mr. Wilson, and "we often hear them classified as 'the three faiths'—meaning Protestant, Catholic, and Jewish. It is seldom mentioned, however, that there is in the Western World a 'fourth faith' embraced by vast numbers, a faith called humanism. This fourth faith—with such rare exceptions as the Dutch Humanist League; the Ethical Societies of England, America, and Austria; and certain Unitarian and Universalist churches in the United States—has no church to embody it. But it is a widespread movement, a movement of increasing importance."

Mr. Wilson goes on to list several earmarks of humanism:

1. "The Humanist lives as if this world were all and enough. He is not other-worldly. He holds that time spent in contemplation of a possible afterlife is time wasted. He fears no hell and seeks no heaven, save those which he and other men create on this earth."

2. "He believes in people."

3. "He believes in human equality."

4. "Freedom of thought and action is a necessary part of the Humanist's way of life."

5. "The Humanist accepts the world-view of science and the scientific method of testing truth."

6. He seeks the "cooperation of all men of good will to end poverty, war, disease, and prejudice. . . . The Humanist knows he is not 'outside' nature and that he must study and conform to nature's laws. . . . Humanists also realize that man must work with and attempt to control nature on a planetary scale under some sort of a democratic federation for the salvation of all men."

Here is a fourth faith, entertained today by large numbers of moderns. It is altogether this-worldly and humanistic, seeking to control nature and improve the human lot by an artful application of science.

Let us imagine two eccentric circles, the smaller inside the larger, the two joined at one point on their circumferences. The smaller circle is society, the larger is nature. Man, in the viewpoint

under discussion, is merely a part of nature shaped by society, and
he stands at the point where the two circles touch. This is the basic
diagram of humanism, agnosticism, and atheism. It is reinforced
by the popular understanding of what, granting the universal validity of science and its methods, it is possible for a rational man to
believe. That is to say, it is a faith which assumes that there are
no truths outside the truths of science. This viewpoint has been on
the offensive for so long, and it so stoutly takes itself for granted,
that when called upon to explain and justify itself it does poorly.

The proposition that man is involved in two orders only, the
social and the natural, is certainly incorrect on the face of it, for
the mere assertion of this proposition invokes a third realm—the
nonmaterial representation of the social and natural realms and a
mind which entertains this idea. There is society and there is
nature, and there is also an awareness of society and nature. Consciousness of a fact is radically other than the fact itself. Ideas,
representation, awareness, consciousness—all constitute the very
stuff of mind; and unless mind is numbered among the real con-
stituents of the universe it cannot be trusted to give us accurate
intelligence of that universe. The mental cannot be reduced to the
social nor to the natural without destroying the very basis of all
knowledge. The mind is either *sui generis*, or it is not a valid
instrument for the attainment of truth. If it is nothing but an
offshoot of the natural order, or nothing but an emergent from
human interactions, then it is not *sui generis;* it is a mere epi-
phenomenon. If the mind is something less fundamental than the
movement of atoms and molecules studied by physics and chemistry, something less fundamental than the relationships of people
in society, then only monstrous credulity can assert with certitude
that the deliverances of such an instrument are beyond cavil.
Sound thinking obeys the laws of logic, but these laws are not
found in a waterfall, or in a chemical reaction, or in the actions of
a crowd; and if these natural and social events typify the only
realities the universe contains, then we face a vain effort to base
sound reasoning on nonrational events as a paradigm. It will not
do.

There are certain situations where "a miss is as good as a mile"
and this is one of them. If the mind does not transcend the natural
and social order, but is rather a mere clumsy tool of the physical

organism in search of a more perfect adaptation to environment, or a tool of the subconscious, or a class instrument to rationalize exploitation, or suffers from other built-in defects which render it less than completely reliable, potentially, then we cannot wholly trust any of its deliverances. Even if we assume that the mind is 90 percent reliable and only 10 percent unreliable, then we have no way of knowing that even this assumption does not issue from the unreliable 10 percent portion. A dogmatic assertion that the mind cannot be trusted is illogical, on the face of it. It is a nonsense statement of the same order as "No man ever tells the truth." If a statement of this sort be provisionally accepted as correct, then the individual who utters it—because he belongs to a class of beings incapable of veracity—stands accused by it of wholesale error. What he says is a lie; but no one incapable of the truth could recognize a lie! We are, therefore, altogether out of the realm where truths and lies are meaningful alternatives. The statement is meaningless.

Truth and falsehood exist only for a mind. If the universe can be reduced to the dance of material particles or neutral particulars; if, that is to say, only matter is ultimately real, then true and false are meaningless categories. It is meaningless to speak of a chunk of lead being truer than a chunk of iron, or to regard a chip of glass as a diamond caught in a lie, or oxygen as being in error. Such categories as these apply to propositions entertained by a mind, and to nothing else. The proposition: "Iron has a higher specific gravity than lead," is false. If someone tells another that a piece of cut glass is really a diamond, he is guilty of a falsehood. Everything in nature is what it is; of nothing on the level of nature can it be said that it is true or false. Every natural thing reflects its own nature and, poetically, may be said to be true to itself. But some things human stand apart from nature. Human free will comes onto the scene, which is but another way of saying that men do not accurately reflect human nature, which is to say that men are fallen creatures. And this puts us in the vestibule, at the very least, of a Biblical outlook.

The big question we confront at this juncture is: How shall we account for mind? Those who would make a this-worldly religion out of science and its deliverances, that is to say, humanists of various persuasions, appear to unite in implying the paradox that

the human mind is an incompetent instrument for attaining trustworthy knowledge. Mind, in their book, is assimilated to the body
and declared to be a mere reflection of prior neural events, which
are material. A materialist of the last century asserted that the
brain secretes thought just as the liver secretes bile! Or, as John
Dewey put it in one of his early lectures, "The human mind is what
happens to the human animal in a social situation."[6] Or, action is
primary and the mind merely readies the organism for it, providing
a cloak of rationalization for personal desires. In terms of this
Weltanschauung mind is anything but a thing-in-itself—conditioned, it is true, by circumstances such as those listed but capable,
nevertheless, of transcending its limitations and providing us with
reliable knowledge of ourselves and other selves, as well as knowledge of bodies and things and values. The denigrators of mind,
amusingly enough, number some powerful thinkers among them,
but they have gone astray under the influence of a twin compulsion. Their ideology is composed, on the one hand, of unfortunate
experiences of theistic religion—for which churchmen and certain
practices of the Christian Church itself are partly to blame—plus
a salvationist faith in science which views it as the only and the
infallible way to knowledge. Under the spell of this ideology,
neither facet of which now operates with the same intensity as of
old, some of the greatest thinkers since the Renaissance have
disparaged mind.

Turn to the opening pages of Thomas Hobbes' *Leviathan*
(1651). "Life is but a motion of limbs," writes Hobbes in his
Author's Introduction, "For what is the heart but a spring; and the
nerves but so many strings; and the joints but so many wheels,
giving motion to the whole body . . . ?" But does not the mind, we
ask, lie outside this piece of mechanism?

"Concerning the thoughts of man," writes Hobbes, "singly, they
are every one a representation or appearance, of some quality, or
other accident of a body without us, which is commonly called an
object. Which object worketh on the eyes, ears, and other parts of
a man's body; and by diversity of working, produceth diversity of
appearances.

"The original of them all (i.e., thoughts) is what we call sense,
for there is no conception in a man's mind, which hath not at first,

6. Cited by Benjamin Anderson, *The Value of Money*, p. 17.

totally, or by parts, been begotten upon the organs of sense. The rest are derived from that original."

By feeling we discern such qualities as heat, cold, hardness, and softness; "all which qualities, called sensible, are in the object that causeth them, but so many several motions of the matter, by which it presseth our organs diversely. Neither in us that are pressed, are they anything else, but diverse motions; for motion produces nothing but motion."[7]

If thought be reduced to motion, and if this motion is merely the effect of a prior motion, ad infinitum, then freedom of the will is an illusion and we are caught in the meshes of determinism. "There is no free will in the human mind," Spinoza was writing in 1665 or thereabouts, "it is moved to this or that volition by some cause, and that cause has been determined by some other cause, and so on infinitely."[8]

The instrument which is uncovering these stupendous truths which are to make men the masters of creation "is nothing but a heap or collection of different perceptions," wrote that keen intellect, David Hume, in 1739, "united together by certain relations, and supposed, though falsely, to be endowed with a perfect simplicity and identity."

Philosophic materialism and mechanism, the trend under examination, which denies to mind and spirit an independent status in the universe, penetrated deeply into the thinking of the nineteenth century. Materialism, briefly defined, is the doctrine that the universe contains no entities except those which can be analyzed exhaustively in terms of physics and chemistry. It is the notion that only material particles are ultimately real, with the corollary that the realms of mind, spirit, or intellect are mere offshoots of bits of matter.

This is a kind of anti-intellectualism beside which all other varieties of anti-intellectualism—including belligerent ignorance —are child's play. A theory, however, is not a material thing; it is an idea, and an idea is nonmaterial. Materialism as a theory involves, therefore, a contradiction in terms.

Nevertheless, two seeds of materialism were sown in the year 1859, in Charles Darwin's *Origin of Species* and Karl Marx's *Con-*

7. Hobbes, *Leviathan*, pp. 19, 212.
8. Spinoza, *Ethics*, Part II, Proposition XLVIII.

tribution to the Critique of Political Economy. Marx, in his Author's Preface to the *Critique,* writes as follows: "The mode of production in material life determines the general character of the social, political, and spiritual processes of life. It is not the consciousness of men that determines their existence, but, on the contrary, their social existence determines their consciousness."

According to the internal logic of this statement, the categories true or false cannot apply to it; certain sounds are emitted by Marx who, if the statement be taken literally, is a mere mouthpiece for the material productive factors of 1859. His mind may frame the words, but it does not originate the ideas. The ideas are generated mechanically by "the mode of production in material life," with no more inherent vitality than words coming from a phonograph record.

Charles Darwin is customarily regarded as Mr. Evolution; actually, there are many theories to account for the biological and geological facts, and Darwin merely supplied the theory which survived in the struggle for existence with the other theories. Darwin eliminated purpose from evolution and admittedly made no effort to account for the inherent creativity in organisms which produced the variations upon which environment operates. Once the variations appeared, an automatic or natural selective process would occur, which preserved those variations favoring survival. Criticizing the Darwinian thesis, Jacques Barzun writes, "The sum total of the accidents of variation thus provided a completely mechanical and material system by which to account for the changes in living forms."[9]

Darwin himself, unlike many of the Darwinians, entertained some doubts. Writing to a friend, he said: "With me the horrid doubt always arises whether the convictions of man's mind, which has been developed from the mind of the lower animals, are of any value or at all trustworthy. Would anyone trust the convictions of a monkey's mind—if there are any convictions in such a mind?" In the *Descent of Man* occurs the despairing assertion: "There is no fundamental difference between man and the higher animals in their mental faculties."

John Dewey is perhaps the most characteristic philosopher of the mind-a-product-of-society school. "Mind is primarily a verb,"

9. Barzun, *Darwin, Marx, Wagner,* p. 11.

he writes. "It denotes all the ways in which we deal consciously and expressly with the situations in which we find ourselves. Unfortunately, an influential manner of thinking has changed modes of action into an underlying substance that performs the activities in question. It has treated mind as an independent entity *which* attends, purposes, cares, notices, and remembers. . . ."

The mind, in being explained, has been explained away. Psychology, literally "a doctrine of the soul," is reduced to a branch of physiology. The human nervous sytem is a bundle of physical objects—brain, spinal column, nerves—which can be seen, touched, and weighed. Like the physical organism of which it is a part, the nervous system is composed of the same common chemicals which go into the manufacture of other animals, the same elements which make up the inorganic world. This disparagement of the tool by which all learning is acquired as somehow less real than the things learned is curious indeed; it is equivalent to downgrading the eye because we cannot see *it* but are limited to seeing other things *through* it.

Mind is not extended in space so that we might locate it here rather than there; it has no dimension, no shape, no weight. Mind is not located within time. Time, as it pushes relentlessly in one direction, acts upon things by causing them to assume more random and dispersed forms. But the mind can move effortlessly backward into time's abyss and draw from memory the events of fifty years ago, or ten minutes ago; and the future, to imagination, is always present. Most significant of mind's qualities, its unique aptitude, is its capacity for knowing. The mind is not a thing, it is awareness of things; and if it is not trustworthy then nothing else can be trusted.

"I have no great quickness of apprehension or wit," wrote the gentle Darwin, "which is so remarkable in some clever men, for instance, Huxley." The clever Huxley declared that "our mental conditions are simply the symbols in consciousness of the changes which take place automatically in the organism." If the mind merely trails the organism then Huxley and the others are quite correct in denying the mind any competence in the transcendent. It is not their inference which is questionable; it is their premise. "I . . . invented . . . the title of 'agnostic,' " writes Huxley. "It came into my head as suggestively antithetic to the 'gnostic' of Church history, who professed to know so very much." This word, which entered the vocabulary in 1869, captivated the mood of the period. The feeling was widespread that humanity now had the tools to operate on the natural order for its successful control, but lacked any means for establishing contact with a hypothetical supernatural order which transcended the realms of sense. And anyway—ran the mood of the time—mankind is doing very well for itself without outside help so that no purpose would be served by making such an attempt. God was not merely unknowable; He was also unnecessary. Had not the great Laplace replied, "Sire, I have no need of that hypothesis," when Napoleon had asked where God fitted into his theories of astronomy?

Hobbes, Hume, and Spinoza are among the giants of philosophy; the towering accomplishments of science have benefited the human race beyond measure. These mighty achievements of the human mind demand a theory of mind which does not make it subservient to nature and society, even though these very geniuses seem to belittle the competence of the tool they used so magnificently, basing their demeaning of the mind on the premise that the universe has no aspects except those open to scientific investigation.

T. H. Huxley had fashioned a religion of sorts out of science. "Science and her methods," he said, "gave me a resting place independent of authority and tradition." But even as he wrote a countertrend was gathering. A tributary stemmed from within the fold of science itself, one manifestation being the appearance of a little book by the great French physiologist, Claude Bernard. The year was 1865, and the book was *An Introduction to the Study of Experimental Medicine.* Bernard's book contains little or no metaphysics, sound or otherwise; it merely tells in vivid detail how a great experimenter operates, demonstrating that good science does not necessarily demand bad metaphysics, i.e., materialism, of its votaries. Metaphysics is an overview or survey which purports to include all the facts and every branch of knowledge within its purview before assessing them and declaring the meaning of the whole. There are aspects of the universe which elude capture by the methods of science, and just as we would not pretend to give an exhaustive account of life in the sea based on what is dredged up in a net with one inch mesh, neither may we assert a priori that the universe contains nothing except what is amenable to treatment by the methods of science. We need a nonmetaphysical science as much as we need a metaphysics which takes the findings of the sciences into account.

The scientist, Bernard points out, functions now as an observer and again as an experimenter. "The observer's mind must be passive," he writes, "that is, must hold its peace; it listens to nature and writes at nature's dictation." But the situation observed is often deliberately contrived by the experimenter. When we experiment, "of necessity we experiment with a preconceived idea. . . . An experimenter . . . is a man inspired by a more or less probable but anticipated interpretation of observed phenomena, to devise experiments which, in the logical order of his anticipations, shall bring results serving as controls for his hypothesis or preconceived idea."[10] "Facts are necessary materials"; Bernard goes on to say, "but their working up by experimental reasoning, i.e., by theory, is what embellishes and really builds up science. Ideas, given form by facts, embody science. A scientific hypothesis is merely a scientific idea controlled by experiment. Reasoning merely gives back a form to our ideas, so that everything, first and last, leads back to an idea."[11] This hardly smacks of materialism!

C. E. M. Joad is on sound ground when he says that "science deals with only one kind of reality out of a variety of kinds, . . the scientific picture of the world is based upon an abstraction. For if certain aspects of reality have been abstracted for scientific treatment and others left out, we are entitled to conclude that the world picture which results from this treatment is a picture only of certain aspects of the world. If, then, we take the scientific picture of the world as giving us ultimate and complete truth, we are falling into error, precisely because we are forgetting that something *has* been left out."[12]

How, then, we may legitimately inquire, did the scientific enterprise come to be hooked up with theories which reduced the status of mind and denied the category of transcendence? In the eyes of

10. Bernard, *An Introduction to the Study of Experimental Medicine*, p. 48.
11. *Ibid.*, pp. 51–2.
12. Joad, *Philosophy for Our Times*, p. 89.

Herbert Butterfield, the scientific revolution, which reaches back as far as the fourteenth century, "changed the character of men's habitual mental operations" and in significance "reduces the Renaissance and Reformation to the rank of mere episodes."[13] It represents a breaking through the Aristotelian system which had held Western thought in thrall for more than a thousand years. The work of Copernicus closed out the old system and paved the way for the new method of looking at things. There was not merely closer observation within the framework of the older system of ideas; "a transposition in the mind of the scientist himself " was required. There had to be "an attempt to see the whole of nature as a single self-explanatory system. The object was to eliminate transcendental influences—the activity of spirits and demons working on the world from outside, or the capricious intervention of God Himself—and to seek the explanations of all phenomena within the actual system of nature, this system being regarded as self-sufficient and as working under the government of law. And not only was a new factor introduced into history at this time, amongst other factors, but it proved to be so capable of growth, and so many-sided in its operations, that it consciously assumed a directing role from the very first, and, so to speak, began to take control of the other factors. . . . What was in question was a colossal secularization of thought in every possible realm of ideas at the same time."[14]

An even more exacting study of the same period is *The Metaphysical Foundations of Modern Science*, by the contemporary philosopher, E. A. Burtt. The early investigators, Burtt says, had to reduce "nature to a system of mathematical equations and attribute causality to the motion of physical atoms in order to prevent the dissipation of their limited energies. . . . We should remember that men cannot do arduous and profound intellectual labour in the face of constant and seductive distractions. The sources of distraction simply had to be denied or removed. To get ahead confidently with their revolutionary achievements, they had to attribute absolute reality and independence to those entities in terms of which they were attempting to reduce the world. This once done, all the other features of their cosmology followed as naturally as you please. It has, no doubt, been worth the meta-

13. Butterfield, *The Origins of Modern Science*, p. 7.
14. *Ibid.*, pp. 46, 191, and 194.

physical barbarism of a few centuries to possess modern science."[15]

Professor Burtt concludes his book by restoring mind to its place
in the total scheme of things. "Let the order of nature be ever so
vast and all-absorbing—it is still but the object of rationally con-
ceiving mind. And as for purpose, do we not empirically note that
every object of mind is likewise a *means* for the realization of
further *ends?* Among the irreducible relations of a thing known,
is there not its relation to a more valuable end which it may be
made to serve? If this be the case, then purpose is an even more
ultimate function than knowledge and feeling, and mind, embracing by this term such knowing, appreciating, and purposive activity, must find its total explanation beyond the material world.
Mind appears to be an irreducible something that can know the
world of extended matter, love ardently its order and beauty, and
transform it continually in the light of a still more attractive and
commanding good. Mind has the power to feel, to idealize, to
recreate its world into something significantly better, as well as to
know it."[16]

"It is mind," Plato asserted, "that produces order and is the
cause of everything. . . . Somehow it seemed right," he continues,
"that mind should be the cause of everything, and I reflected that
if this is so, mind in producing order sets everything in order and
arranges each individual thing in the way that is best for it. Therefore if anyone wished to discover the reason why any given thing
came or ceased or continued to be, he must find out how it was
best for that thing to be, or to act or be acted upon in any other
way. On this view there was only one thing for a man to consider,
with regard both to himself and to anything else, namely the best
and highest good, although this would necessarily imply knowing
what is less good, since both were covered by the same knowledge."[17]

It is "to the eye of reason," wrote Paul, that "His invisible
attributes . . . have been visible, ever since the world began."
(Romans 1:20)

The reinstatement of mind as an independent reality, the
suggestion that men—along with their involvement in a given

15. Burtt, *The Metaphysical Foundations of Modern Science*, pp. 305–6.
16. *Ibid.*, pp. 323–4.
17. *Phaedo*, 97c and d.

society and with the natural world—participate in a radically different order, does not by itself verify religion. This step, however, does return us to the *Philosophia Perennis*, and it deprives us of an oft-used excuse for dealing frivolously with the claims of religion.

CHAPTER 9

The Climate of Liberty

ONE OF THE AMERICAN GENERALS IN KOREA VOICED HIS BIT-
TER conviction that he was fighting the wrong war, against the
wrong enemy, and at the wrong time. He meant to say, I suppose,
that the real issues of our time were not being thrashed out by
North and South Koreans in the vicinity of the 38th parallel. I
don't know what this particular general might regard as the real
issues in the conflict between freedom and its enemies in the
twentieth century; but however he might identify them, his point
was that he wanted to be in the front lines and not in some
backwater. I don't suppose that any of us would disagree with this
intention; no one wants to indulge in mere waste motion. Everyone tries to identify the main issues, so that when he does take
sides, his weight will be felt on the side of his choice. But what *are*
the most critical issues of our time? Where is the sharpest confrontation between those who are working for the collective organization of human life, and those who are striving for the free society?

Wander down to the vicinity of Union Square in New York and
the chances are that you'll encounter several men on soapboxes
haranguing the few people whose attention they have succeeded
in attracting. Here is a shabbily dressed man speaking with a
foreign accent, selling copies of *The Worker* while he runs down
the Unted States and extols the virtues of the workers' paradise.
A person does not have to be very sharp to identify this man as
a Communist. All of a sudden it becomes clear; in the person of

this man we see The Enemy. It is this man, and his counterparts in all countries, we say, who constitute the chief threat to our way of life, the free way of life. Once we have identified our antagonist, why not collect all the Communists in one place and deport them, after which America could go back to being the great country she was?

Now it is a natural human tendency to personify our troubles. Communists are likely to be troublesome folk, so we might be able to generate considerable support for the idea of getting rid of them. But let's suppose we did wave a magic wand and the last Communist vanished from our shores. Alas, we'd still find ourselves in trouble with the Socialists. American Socialists are likely to be more refined than American Communists, but the panaceas of these two groups boil down to the same thing—political ownership and direction of economic life with all that this implies. Now, Norman Thomas was a nice old man, and an old line American, and we could hardly use the same approach against him as against an alien Communist. Besides, didn't Norman Thomas say in 1954 that both major political parties had adopted more planks out of the Socialist Party's platform than he had ever dreamed would be possible? Socialistic ideas are deeply embedded in policies presently operative at every level of our political life, and in both major political parties. We might run into a few difficulties if we tried to get rid of all Republican and Democratic politicians. But suppose we did succeed in that chore; the electorate which had voted those socialistically inclined politicians into power would quickly find themselves another crew just like the first. And deporting the electorate poses some insurmountable problems. In short, this approach is not very promising.

An Englishman of about a hundred years ago is reported to have said that he could not define liberalism, but that he did know what liberalism meant—it meant Mr. Gladstone. Now, Mr. Gladstone was a remarkable man, and perhaps we might admit that insofar as a complex philosophy can be embodied in one man, he was indeed Mr. Liberalism. But liberalism as a philosophy conveys implications that no one man nor any one party can fully exemplify. Likewise, the antifreedom philosophy. It may be the case that the actual Communist is the man who has carried his anti free society premises to their logical conclusions; but it is also true that many Americans find various halfway stations to Communism very attractive.

Communism may be compared to a secondary infection—a disease that cannot find a toehold in the organism until the organism has first been weakened by some primary infection. If we can identify the primary infection and rid ourselves of it, then the secondary infection will disappear of itself, and our job is done. But if we concentrate on the secondary infection and do succeed in eliminating its symptoms we gain nothing more than temporary relief. Stop the suppressive therapy and the infection reappears.

Let's carry this disease analogy one stage further. We all feel comfortably at home with the kind of disease which results from the invasion of our tissues by germs or chemicals. We are bitten by the female anopheles mosquito which deposits the plasmodia of malaria in our bloodstream. These microorganisms can be seen, and we know that they cause the illness. We are doubly fortunate in having a specific, quinine, which knocks out this microbe. Many illnesses have an identifiable germ as their source. But there is another category of sickness where there is no invasion of the tissues by an identifiable germ or chemical; this is the category of mental illness or emotional unbalance. A mental ill is not something we catch or something we have; it is something we are. The total personality is involed in the disorientation or derangement. A whole people may be similarly afflicted, and the loss of freedom in society is a problem of this sort. The growth of collectivism is not the result of an invasion by alien armies or the consequence of the imposition of alien rule; it is a growing alienation from our traditional institutions and the roots from which they sprang. We have moved away from the ideas of limited government and the free economy only because other ideas have gained the ascendancy. The idea of a free-wheeling central government, a managed economy, and a closed society will retain its dominance unless and until a significant number of people are able to detect its fallaciousness and muster the skills required to articulate the full rationale for a free society. This means going deeper than is customary in the usual contest between liberals and conservatives. It is not difficult for a clever libertarian to hack a few branches off the collectivist tree any time a discussion develops; but unless we dig out the roots of collectivism the branches will grow right back.

It used to be said, half in jest, that Great Britain was the kind of nation which might lose every battle, but which—despite this —would invariably win the war. This great people—the myth continued—had a way of muddling through; they backed into world domination, waking up one morning to find themselves possessing a vast empire. "Never again," wrote the great philosopher, George Santayana, "will the world have so boyish a master."

Leaving the realm of pleasant mythology, everyone knows that although you can afford to lose a skirmish now and then, the only way to win a war is to win battles. On the playing field or at the gaming table it is fine to be able to lose graciously; but even at this level we play to win. The repeated advice of our college coach, when it came to sentimental talk about being a good loser, was: "Let the other fellow be the good loser."

In actual life the stakes are high; we play for keeps. The authors of the Declaration pledged their lives, their fortunes, and their sacred honor. Now it is not possible to regard this concluding sentence of the Declaration as a mere rhetorical flourish, for the signers of the Declaration were hunted down one by one and the properties and families of many were destroyed. They signed and took the consequences because they believed so keenly in the justice of their cause. A similar sacrifice may never be required of us, and this is our good fortune. But in one respect the colonials had an advantage over us: they were engaged in a fair stand-up fight with an opponent who largely shared their sentiments about liberty, justice, and self-government. *We*, on the other hand, are engaged in a shadowy sort of war in which the primary enemy is not another nation or group of men; the enemy is a set of twisted ideas, an ideology. Let me expand each of these points.

The American cause in the eighteenth century was championed just as eloquently and vigorously by Englishmen in England, and even within Parliament itself, as by Americans on these shores. The first name that comes to mind is that of Edmund Burke. Burke voiced his own sentiments, of course, in his great speech on conciliation and elsewhere, but he was not speaking for himself alone; he spoke also for his party, the Rockingham Whigs, and for the century-old tradition of Whiggism. This philosophy gained strength in the eighteenth century from the rising commercial and merchant classes who needed peace and international trade if they were to flourish. The Whigs gained an influential philosopher in 1775, the economist friend of Burke, Adam Smith. *The Wealth of Nations* appeared just about as the battles of Lexington and Concord were being fought, and in the course of the next few years—duirng the Revolutionary War—this great classic of capitalism and the market economy sold some 2,500 copies in the colonies. Even on the field of battle, the armies of Washington faced a British general, Sir William Howe, who was a Whig, and thus an admirer of the American cause. Time and again, Howe defeated colonial armies, but invariably he retired from the field without pressing his advantage. Nor can this be attributed to lack of military skill, for Howe had proved his brilliance as a general in the French and Indian Wars, and elsewhere. But in the Revolutionary War he was fighting a foe whose philosophy he largely shared, and so he had no desire to clobber the Americans. So much for ancient history. Now to the present day.

The opponent we face today does not wear a red coat, nor a black shirt, nor any other mark of identification by which we might readily distinguish him. There is, nevertheless, an invasion on, and it's under full steam. The thing we face is an ideology—a body of assumptions taken for granted, a set of specious inferences drawn from these assumptions, a sales pitch on their behalf, a variety of organizations taken in by the sales pitch, a society permeated by a plausible set of notions, and finally a gang of politicians eager to enact these plausibilities into welfare state legislation. The generic name for the development here sketched is "collectivism." Local varieties of collectivism operate under such labels as Communism, Socialism, Fascism, the New Deal, or the Great Society. These various ideologies may fight among themselves, but even the much touted hostility between Communism and Fascism is a lovers' quarrel; there is agreement in fundamentals, argument over details. Every modern "ism," with varying degrees of explicitness is, however, in implacable opposition to what Adam Smith called "the system of liberty, equality and justice"; they are opposed to the American cause articulated and fought for in the eighteenth century; they are opposed to the idea of limited government, private property, and the free market. Their opposition is sometimes explicit, as when the Communists attack the idea of private property and capitalism, or when Mussolini says he wants to expel the corpse of liberty. This kind of opposition puts us on guard; it alerts us to the presence of an enemy who wants to do us in. The more dangerous kind of opposition is implicit; it comes from people much like ourselves who profess nothing more than a desire to "save capitalism" and who justify every intervention by government on this basis. Lord Keynes pressed his remedies on us as a means of protecting capitalism from the classical economists; but after an application of Keynesian panaceas the capitalism "saved" bore little resemblance to the market economy. And in the process we were saddled with an overextended government which skirted constitutional limitations on government and rationalized every departure from traditional norms of political action in terms of the needs and demands of this or that pressure group.

The old movie Westerns have one thing in common with modern television spy dramas; both are based upon the conflict between good guys and bad guys. But with this difference: the bad guys in the old Westerns were always recognizably such; they needed a shave, they wore disreputable clothing, and they rode a black horse. The good guys, on the other hand, were clean-cut, looked you straight in the eye, and bought their Western outfits from Abercrombie and Fitch. In the modern spy drama, the good guys and the bad guys are impeccably dressed, their speech is cultured, and not until James Bond has shot him do you realize that this ingratiating character was in the employ of Dr. No. And as for James Bond himself, and the methods he employs to emerge victorious, well, he didn't get them out of the *Boy Scout Handbook*. His ends justify any means, so he has tossed away the rule book. Perhaps it is just this sort of point that constitutes the fascination of the best-selling novel, *The Spy Who Came in From the Cold:* the secret agent is in danger of cutting himself off from the society which employs him, forgetting civilized and humane values, only to lust after intrigue and deception for the sake of the perverted thrills these afford.

In short, we can no longer trust external characteristics. These are deceptive, so we must try to penetrate the facade. The older biologists of the prescientific era believed in the thing called spontaneous generation, the idea that life could spring out of the nonliving. For example, tie a knot in one end of a horse hair and put it in a barrel of vinegar and it will eventually turn into a worm.

Relatively simple experiments convincingly demonstrated that life did not appear in a sterile container, and that the seemingly spontaneous appearance of life was due to spores carried by the air to the nutrient; or to eggs deposited by some insect. The conclusion was that something does not come out of nothing, and that life comes only from life. Analogously, the something we call the free society does not come out of nothing. Such institutions as the free market and limited government are not among the marks of homo sapiens wherever he appears; these manifestations are rare events in human history. They are pretty much limited to Western civilization, and even there they come and go. The appearance of these things on the surface of social life implies that preparation for their emergence occurred below the surface, where we are mainly unconscious of them. Just as—the psychoanalysts claim—rumblings deep down within our unconscious mind may erupt into our awareness with their origins disguised.

There are things seen and things not seen. We see the institutions of our common life—free or collectivized—but we do not see the fundamental assumptions and premises about life, the universe, and man, which give rise to these institutions, and support them in both our sentiments and intellect.

Let me quote from two British philosophers a few words bearing upon this important distinction. First, Alfred North Whitehead: "When you are criticizing the philosophy of an epoch," he writes, "do not chiefly direct your attention to those intellectual positions which its exponents feel it necessary explicitly to defend. There will be some fundamental assumptions which adherents of all the various systems within the epoch unconsciously presuppose." T. E. Hulme put it this way: "There are certain doctrines which for a particular period seem not doctrines, but inevitable categories of the human mind. Men do not look upon them merely as correct opinions, for they have become so much a part of the mind, and lie so far back, that they are never really conscious of them at all. They do not see them, but other things *through* them. It is these abstract ideas at the center, the things which they take for granted, that characterize a period."

Typhoid fever is an easily diagnosible disease, but it is no simple matter to spot a Typhoid Mary. Typhoid Mary, or her male counterpart, harbors typhoid bacilli which make her the source of infection to others, even though she herself does not fall ill. Many an epidemic of typhoid has been traced to these unwitting carriers. Something analogous to this has happened in the realm of social and political philosophy. Karl Marx is regarded by many as the evil genius of this age, but long before Marx appeared on the scene, the road had been paved for him by philosophers of the utmost respectability. To show you how this thing works out, let me first offer you a schematized version of the procedure, using a familiar syllogism.

The syllogism was invented by Aristotle. It consists of a major premise, a minor premise, and a conclusion; or, put another way, it consists of two Whereases followed by a Therefore. For example:

> Whereas, all men are mortal, and
> Whereas, Socrates is a man;
> Therefore, Socrates is mortal.

This is a valid syllogism. If you want to resist the conclusion, you must challenge the major premise; you must somehow deny the proposition that all men are mortal—on some such grounds as that nobody has ever known all men, or that for all we know some man now alive might live forever. However, if you do accept the first Whereas, and don't reject the second Whereas, then your adversary has you over a barrel. No matter how much you squirm you cannot logically avoid accepting his Therefore. You may not admit it, but if you walk away in a huff you leave him in command of the field, victorious. It is my contention that collectivism gains by default in the modern world because almost everyone has unknowingly accepted collectivism's Whereas Number One, and its Whereas Number Two, and thus we fare so badly when we try to avoid embracing the collectivist conclusion, its Therefore.

Keep your eye on the Whereases and the Therefores will take care of themselves. But that's easier said than done. Now let's bring this down to earth with some words from an admired contemporary of ours who has achieved eminence in several fields, Joseph Wood Krutch. Most people don't have original ideas, and so the ideas, assumptions, and habits of thought that people of a given period take for granted are the answers to their unexpressed questions, supplied to them by thinkers whose names they may not even know. It is the task of philosophy and social criticism to confront us with the men we permit to do our thinking for us, to make us aware of our assumptions and their origins. Here is Mr. Krutch's thumbnail historical analysis of the way the mind of modern man has been shaped: "The fundamental answers which we have on the whole made, and which we continue to accept, were first given in the seventeenth century by Francis Bacon, Thomas Hobbes, and René Descartes, and were later elaborated and modernized by Marx and the Darwinians. These basic tenets of our civilization (in chronological but not quite logical order) are:

> (1) The most important task to which the human mind may devote itself is the "control of nature" through technology (Bacon);
> (2) Man may be completely understood if he is considered to be an animal, making predictable reactions to that desire for pleasure and power to which all his other desires may by analysis be reduced (Hobbes);
> (3) All animals (man excepted) are pure machines (Descartes);
> (4) Man, Descartes notwithstanding, is also an animal and therefore also a machine (Darwin);
> (5) The human condition is not determined by philosophy, religion, or moral ideas because all of these are actually only by-products of social and technological developments which take place independent of man's will and uninfluenced by the "ideologies" which they generate (Marx).[1]

Dr. Krutch in this far from exhaustive list nominates five key thinkers whose thought has been a disastrous influence in the modern world; Bacon, Hobbes, Descartes, Darwin, and Marx. With the exception of Karl Marx, these men were gentlemen and scholars, venerated during their own lifetimes, with access to the great universities and the great houses. Mostly, they were pious Christians. But they taught the world things which have contributed largely to the modern world's agony.

Let us now turn from men and ideas to the mental layers below, where abide the things we take for granted, things beyond the

1. *If You Don't Mind My Saying So*, pp. 86–7.

immediate reach of argument. Call this a deposit of sentiment, if you will, it is, nevertheless, formed around a precipitate of ideas. Change at this level is slow and tidal, and it is relatively immune to the kind of argument that might be embodied in a syllogism. The process of change here is somewhat along the lines of what happens to a man getting psychiatric treatment. If the patient's mental and emotional quirks were within the reach of rational argument a clever dialectician might be able to argue him out of them in a sitting. But the psychologist does not operate this way; rather, his treatment consists of a gradual and long continued exposure of the patient's fixations to a sounder outlook until a mutation occurs. Likewise, there is a tide in the affairs of men, building up pressures below the surface of events until an eruption finally takes place. Looking back we can pretty much agree that a great sea change took place in European affairs five centuries ago in the development called the Renaissance, a period which witnessed the emergence of new ideas, a new outlook, and a new mood. Gains and losses both are registered in an upheaval of these dimensions, but an assessment of these must wait upon a consensus as to what took place.

(1) Theism is naturalized. There is a conviction that the things which are owe their origin to, and are sustained in their existence by being rooted in, a realm beyond themselves. The world did not create itself, and cannot be explained by itself. The natural order presupposes a divine order. This is theism. It was gradually replaced by the idea that the world was not created, but simply *is;* and that a thing is adequately explained if its constituent parts are described and their causal connections traced. This is naturalism.

(2) Man is secularized. If the natural order is all there is, then man is as much its product as a tree. He is no longer considered to be divinely authored. His soul is as mythical a thing as the Creator from whom it was thought to derive and to whom man was thought to be responsible for its proper ordering.

(3) Mind is materialized. The natural order—the material universe—is all there is, which means that before man appeared on the scene there was nothing here but material particles. There was no Primal Intelligence. Organic life made its appearance, and finally man emerged, with his highly developed brain and nervous system. In association with the latter, and only there, as a sort of

unexplained secretion of gray matter, is the thing we call mind. Mind, in other words, instead of being an attribute of the Deity is merely a peculiar offshoot of material particles in the context of the human nervous system. The fundamental reality is the material body, and with its dissolution, the mental manifestations it exhibited during life disappear.

(4) Society is deified. Individuals come and go; only Society endures, outlasting the generations. There is no immortal essence in a man to link each person with the Ground of his being, God; and there is no God. It is a man's Society which gives him his identity, and he is but one of its units. Society is the supreme reality. At its pleasure it permits a kind of abstract individualism and promises its individuals rights, of a sort. But if a person is what he is only because he happens to be born into a particular society at a particular time, where will he find any inclination to resist social pressures, or a leverage to make his inclination effective? And whence could he derive his notion of a righteous man resisting unlawful power except from the outmoded cosmology?

(5) Power is democratized. There's a seeming paradox in a situation which centers power in The People at the expense of individual persons. The medieval kings ruled "under God." The Renaissance kings claimed autonomy for their power, and ruled by "divine right." The monarchical ideology was replaced by a democratic ideology and the new rulers governed by an appeal to the Will of The People. Popular sovereignty means that each is dominated by all. "We are doing it to ourselves!" But the "we" who are doing it are not the same people as the "ourselves" who are on the receiving end.

(6) Morals are relativized. The norms for human conduct were once thought to have been laid down by God; conformity with God's will was the aim. But if the natural and social orders are all there is to the cosmos, then they provide man's only clues. It is natural for man to be social, but only his society can tell him how to live within it. The society's governing agency will, therefore, lay down the commands which men must obey, and men must be conditioned to fall in step. Justifiable individual resistance to these decrees would have to be based on the assumption that each person owes allegiance to something beyond his society. This cannot be God, because God is assumed not to exist; it could only

be another society, which is treason. Therefore, no individual may justifiably resist what his society commands.

(7) Sin is socialized. The older view held that there is a stubborn hard core of unregenerate human nature which casts a shadow on man and all his works; human perversity infects every institution and society itself, and men must reckon with this perversity. Man has the capacity to ameliorate his lot, but only within limits; an earthly paradise is unthinkable, and the Kingdom of Heaven is on the other side of the grave. This outlook has been replaced by one which regards man as perfectible by education and legislation, his troubles due to a bad environment and faulty institutions. Salvation is by politics. The dogma of political messianism is that deliverance is at hand just as soon as we succeed in injecting a large dose of scientific know-how into democratic political processes. Scientific Socialism in a People's Democracy is The Final Solution of the Human Equation.

(8) Life abundant. Man is a creature of insatiable wants, and scarcity, therefore, is a fact of life, now and forever. The science of economics is premised on the fact of scarcity, its aim being to allocate goods in short supply so as to best meet human needs. Society itself is founded on the fact of scarcity and our common human need to cope with it. If all our wants and needs were met effortlessly—as they were for each of us in the fetal stage—we would be solitaries, and as solitaries we would not be human. Alone, as adults, most of us would starve. But in society with our own kind, the division of labor and exchange of specializations make it possible for great numbers to survive, and not only survive but flourish, materially and in every other way. The fact of scarcity is concealed under promises of an economy of abundance, a perfected social order, utopia. Futurism's creed is that "every day in every way things are getting better and better." Things today are better than ever before, but the future will be so much better that it justifies all the evils men are committing and submitting to now.

Nearly everyone operates a good deal within the boundary lines of the extreme logical limits of his creed; and some, in daily practice, defy their creeds. Presumably, commissars and men of "the new class" in Communist countries on occasion exhibit some of the old bourgeois virtues they profess to scorn; they are generous to friends, perhaps, and live a decent family life. The negative elements in the above eight points might be lifted out, added to, and pieced together into a platform. But who would pledge allegiance to it, for the thing defines a mood more than it articulates a philosophy. This is what we are contending against, and this is why The Enemy is so elusive, the task so difficult. This is an intellectual and spiritual infection, and the external signs of it may not be evident. The carrier of this infection may be any one of us.

CHAPTER 10

Instinct and Ethics

NEARLY EVERYONE IS A MORALIST THESE DAYS, AND A MORAL-
ist in popular caricature is one who always views with alarm. Even
the self-proclaimed immoralists of our time fall into this category,
for they denounce as "intolerant" any and all who look askance
at their weird, "beat" deviations. Disagreements are sharp at all
levels among the viewers with alarm, but the primary breach is
between those who hold that the ultimate sanction for ethical
standards must be sought in a supernatural order and—on the
other hand—those who assert that within the social and natural
orders we may find the ingredients for a viable ethic. The first
position is theistic; the latter humanistic.

The humanists, if we may be permitted this term for the second
group, admit that the moral code which prevailed in the West until
two or three generations ago was widely believed to have had its
origin and sanction in religion. But, as they view the matter, the
transcendent dimension has such a weak hold upon modern man
that to insist on a metaphysical source of moral values in these
times is to weaken ethics by tying it to a dead horse. Moral values,
they assert, are autonomous if they are anything; let them therefore stand on their own feet. Detach ethics from religion, they
urge, in order that men may be virtuous for the sake of happiness!
Men should not do right in a vain effort to please some deity, or
because they believe that God has arbitrarily commanded certain
actions and forbidden others.

These nontraditionalists tout a "scientific" or "rational" ethic. The opposite of "rational" in this context is not "irrational;" it is "theistic," "customary," or "received." No one would admit that his own ethical system or moral code is irrational, and it is obvious to everyone who has checked into the matter that there have been and are ethicists of several schools who are powerful reasoners. Not only the rationalist but every philosopher relies on reason; however, reason does tell some men that reason is not the exclusive route to knowledge of the complex reality that environs us.

A distinction which arises at this point seems to elude many thinkers. It is the distinction between reason as a means for achieving a norm, and reason itself as the norm. Perhaps the point may be clarified by analogy. "How do you propose to go to Boston?" is a question which may demand answers in two distinct categories. "By car" is one answer, which informs us that the means of transportation is not by train, plane, foot, or horse. Having settled this point, we may still need further information before the question can be regarded as answered. "By way of the Taconic, north, to the western end of the Massachusetts Turnpike, then east." This gives us the route, so that we know that the car will not proceed up the Merritt or over the New England Thruway.

Now take the serious question "How shall we validate ethical norms?" Those who answer "By reason," are really uttering a mere truism. "We're going to think about it," they are saying. And everyone who thinks about these or any other matters is using his reason. This is our only means for figuring things out, and it is not a means belonging exclusively to rationalists; it is the common means employed by everyone who philosophizes. Using this means, we seek for answers to the question of how to validate ethical norms. This has to do with the realm where the sanctions may find anchorage, whether within nature and society, or in a realm beyond the natural and social orders. Reason is our tool for operating on the problem posed; it is not itself the answer.

There are dogmatists on both sides of this controversy, and the skilled among them can and do expose weaknesses in their opponents' position. The humanist might charge his opposition as follows: The moral code is an acquired characteristic; it has to be learned anew by each generation. It is difficult enough to establish this code theoretically, even if we treat it as self-evidently useful to society and necessary for harmony in human relationships. Why, then, compound these difficulties and force things out of focus by involving ethics with metaphysics? The uncertain, in this or any other area, is shored up by relating it to the certain; but when you hook ethics up with metaphysics, you relate it to the even more uncertain, to the dubious. We don't need a transcendent sanction in order to validate or prove a down-to-earth ethics. To which the theist might respond: If you appeal to Nature to sanction human conduct, you haven't looked very far into Nature. Not even Kropotkin with his mutual aid theories denied the Darwinian struggle for existence; he merely desired to point out that it was not the whole story. But it is part of the story, and a large enough part so that we are justified in saying that Nature gives a mandate to the powerful, the fleet, the unscrupulous to live off the weaker, the slower, the innocent. And if you think to draw your ethical sanctions from society, whose society are you talking about? A society of headhunters? Nazi society? Communist society? The Great Society? As a matter of fact, if a significant number of people can be made to believe that moral conduct is merely that which is sanctioned by the society in which they live, then morality is subverted into merely customary behavior and mere legality. Furthermore, you are confusing sanctions with consequences. An ethical code resides somewhere between the sanctions advanced to validate it, and the consequences cited to justify it. If the code is put into practice the consequences may well be personal happiness, interpersonal harmony, and a prosperous society. But these results do not constitute a set of sanctions; the sanctions are on the other side of the code, in the realm of philosophy. Once we are intellectually convinced that our moral code is valid and muster enough will power to practice it, then—and only then—do we get a bonus in the form of well-being in society. But you have the thing turned around! So much for the preliminary give and take.

Evidently, each side has a case which might be spelled out at length. Is it a deadlock, or do we have here an instance of an impasse due to the hardening of the categories on either side to the point where their usefulness as conceptual tools has been impaired? And if this is so, is there an escape from the horns of the dilemma? There might be such a breakthrough if we could—

by adopting a new perspective—pose and develop a thesis which might avail itself of certain strong points in both positions. Here's such a thesis: The moral code plays a role in the life of man comparable to the role of instinct in the lower organisms, in that each functions to relate the inner nature of the respective organism to the full range of its environment.

The *Harper Encyclopedia of Science* says that "The scientific study of instinct has increased greatly in recent years, and the concept itself has regained an academic respectability it has not had since the time of Darwin." At the forefront of this research, much of it under field conditions, are Tinbergen, Lorenz, Thorne, and Barrends; Europeans all. "It now seems clear," the entry continues, "that instinct and intelligence are two quite different ways by which animals meet life's problems. Instincts are essentially prefabricated answers." In a word, an organism's instinctual equipment adapts it optimally to its normal environment. Animals —along with birds, insects, and fish—are equipped with a kind of internal servo-mechanism, or automatic pilot, which keeps them effortlessly on the beam. Instincts align the animal with the forces of life, or with the laws of its own nature. Organism and environment are thus kept "in play" with each other—except when environmental changes are so catastrophic that the automatic adjustment equipment fails, the organism perishes, and perhaps a species becomes extinct. The very perfection of automatic, instinctual adjustment may prove the undoing of organisms relying on this device; when survival depends on a creative response to novel environmental changes, something other than instinct is needed. This is, of course, intelligence. Instinct is not a mere precursor of intelligence, nor is intelligence an outgrowth of instinct; they are radically different. In order for intelligence in man to have an opportunity to flourish, the instincts had to be suppressed.

Human beings are virtually without specific instincts. There is no servo-mechanism in men which automatically keeps the human organism or the species within the pattern laid down for human life. Men have to figure things out and, by enormous effort, learn to conform their actions to the relevant norms in the various sectors of life. This absence of instincts in man constitutes the ground for man's radical inner freedom, the freedom of his will. Animal lives are fixed to run in narrow, constricted channels; they obey the will of God willy-nilly. Men, however, vary enormously from each other at birth, and the differences widen as individuals mature—each into his specialized individuality. And each person has the gift of a freedom so radical that he can deny the existence of the creative forces which produced him. This human freedom makes it not only possible but mandatory that man take a hand in the fashioning of his own life. No man *creates* himself, but every man *makes* himself, using the created portions of his being as his resources. This is what it means to say that man is a responsible being.

A magnificent animal like Man o'War is not a natural horse; he is the product of generations of human breeders and trainers of horses. They are mainly responsible for his superiority, not nature. Of all the orders of creation only man is a responsible being who can change; everything else, every horse, dog, lion, tiger, and shark is what it is. Only man is, in any measure, responsible for what he is. Man makes himself, and therefore each person is morally responsible for himself. This is possible because man has escaped from the straitjacket of instinct.

Let me quote from a once well-known Dreiser novel, *Sister Carrie*, which appeared in 1900. "Among the forces which sweep and play throughout the universe, untutored man is but a wisp in the wind. Our civilization is but a wisp in the wind, scarcely beast, in that it is no longer wholly guided by instinct; scarcely human, in that it is not yet wholly guided by reason. On the tiger no responsibility rests. We see him aligned by nature with the forces of life—he is born into their keeping and without thought he is protected. We see man far removed from the lairs of the jungles, his innate instincts dulled by too near approach to free will, his free will not sufficiently developed to replace his instincts and afford him perfect guidance. He is becoming too wise to hearken always to instincts and desire; he is still too weak to always prevail against them." Dreiser makes full use of a novelist's liberties here, but his pointer is in the right direction. Something within the tiger causes it to obey the laws of its inner nature unconsciously and easily, and, by so doing, the beast is in harmony with outer nature as well. But man's case is radically different. Does he have a true nature deep within him, and visible when the environmentally imposed camouflages are peeled off? And, if so, what are its mandates?

Once man knows the laws of his own being, how shall he muster sufficient will power to obey them while avoiding distractions and temptations that emanate from other facets of his complex nature?

My thesis is that the role played by instinct in the lower orders —keeping the organism on target—is assumed in man by the ethical code. Animals have instincts but no morals; men have morality but no instincts. An animal's instincts guarantee that he will neither disobey nor deviate from the law of his being; a fish does not seek the dry land, a robin does not try to burrow in the ground, a gibbon does not yearn to swing on the North Pole. But man fulfills the law of his being only with the utmost difficulty— if at all—and the only means at his disposal to align him with the forces of life is his ethical code. It is this code, and this alone, which may provide him with a life-giving, life-enhancing regimen.

Let me anticipate two quibbles. Instinct is sometimes contrasted with intelligence, and it is the latter, some say, on which man must rely. Or reason, as Dreiser suggests above. This is a play on words. We rely on intelligence to improve transportation, but we actually ride in automobiles or airplanes, which are the end result of applying intelligence to the problem of getting from here to there. Similarly, it is intelligence that discovers, analyzes, frames, and selects the ethical code. Which brings up the second quibble. Why *the* ethical code? Are there not many conflicting codes? Well, no —to be dogmatic. There is a hard core of similarity, almost identity, in every one of the world's developed moral codes. This is the *Tao*, the Way, referred to by the great ethical and religious teachers in all cultures. Without it, man ceases to be man. (For an expansion of this point the interested reader is referred to C. S. Lewis's *The Abolition of Man.*)

This begins to move us away from the humanistic ethics referred to earlier. Do we need to part company, and if so, by how much? The two most prominent schools of naturalistic ethics are the utilitarians and the pragmatists. It was John Stuart Mill who invented the name and argued the case for the former. He described it as "the creed which accepts as the foundation of morals, utility, or the Greatest Happiness Principle." As we saw above, it "holds that actions are right in proportion as they tend to promote happiness, wrong as they tend to produce the reverse of happiness. By happiness is intended pleasure, and the absence of pain; by unhappiness, pain, and the privation of pleasure."

Pleasure and happiness are desirable indeed, and we wish more of them for everyone. But to equate "pleasure producing" with "right" at the outset of a proposed ethical inquiry is to beg the question. There is undoubtedly a connection here, for doing the right thing has a high degree of correlation with happiness, but the connection is along the lines of the intelligence-automobile illustration above. It is as if the utilitarian were asked "What is the temperature of this room?" and he answered, "I feel chilly." Now there is some relation between this question and the answer, but the answer is not directly responsive to the question. It evades the question, implying that there is no way of finding out the temperature. There is no thermometer, perhaps. Mill and the utilitarians do not really get at the ethical question. They think they are talking about ethics when, in fact, they are discussing something else. The pragmatists present a similar case.

The pragmatists are mainly concerned with workability; it's right if it works. Here is a map of the New England states. The pragmatist follows it and drives to Boston without getting lost. "Wherein lies the virtue of this map?" you ask him. "This map is good because it works; it got me to where I wanted to go." "Why," you pursue, "do you suppose this map got you to your destination?" "That," says our pragmatist, "is a metaphysical question of the sort I cannot be bothered with." So, we have to answer the question for him. The map "worked" because it was not just any old map; it was a map which corresponded to the terrain over which our pragmatist traveled.

An eminent British philosopher of a generation or two ago, W. P. Sorley, neatly wraps up and disposes of utility-workability theories.

> It may be allowed that the relation between theory and practice does not necessitate the pragmatic explanation that the truth of the theory simply consists in its practical utility. The correspondence between theory and practice can also be explained on the view that the knowledge proves itself useful in its applications because it is true: the utility does not make it true; its truth is the ground of its utility. The former explanation is open to the fatal objection that it tends to discredit

itself; for, according to it, *the truth of the view that truth consists in utility must consist in the utility of this view.* It would be difficult to show any practical utility which the explanation possesses; but if we did succeed in showing such utility, it would be formulated in yet another proposition, whose truth again would have to consist in some practical end supposed to be served by it, and so on indefinitely. But if the truth of the proposition does not consist in or depend upon its utility, then we may hold that its utility depends upon its truth: it is useful because it expresses reality or real relations in the form of knowledge, and this brings them within the range, and possibly within the power, of the human mind.[1]

And now what about the weaknesses in the case for the theistic ethics, as that case is usually put? Fundamental to this position is the conviction that moral norms and standards are as much a part of the ultimate nature of things as the fact of the specific gravity of water. It might be convenient, at times, if water had other characteristics, but wishing won't alter the facts. The same is true of moral values. Honesty is right, and most of the time it may also be the best policy. But there are times when dishonesty would pay, where honesty makes us mighty uncomfortable; there is a conflict between what I want to do and what I know I ought to do. In order to maintain the integrity of the moral life, the ethicist champions the view that moral values are "out there," objective, as impervious to human tampering as any other fact of nature. Emphasis on their objectivity seems to imply that moral values are alien to human nature, and, if alien, hostile to man. If they are equated with God's will, God comes to seem an Oriental despot inflicting arbitrary and perverse rules upon his creatures for his pleasure and their frustration. This is, of course, a caricature.

Moral values are said to be objective in the sense that their validity is part of the system and order of the universe, of that same universe which is manifested also in persons. Neither is alien to the other, because both are part of the same reality. Sorley goes a step fruther. "The objective moral value is valid independently of me and my will, and yet it is something which satisfies my purpose and completes my nature."[2] The ethical code may come

1. W. R. Sorley, *Moral Values and the Idea of God,* p. 256
2. *Ibid.,* p. 239.

into conflict with our superficial self on occasion, precisely because it is a discipline for training and schooling our real self. Inner conflicts are a part of living, and we encounter them in all the ventures of life. Take any sport played to win. It becomes a day and night preoccupation, with hours given over day after day for years to strenuous workouts. But this is only the visible part of the story. There is also a perpetual conflict with the impulse that wants to break training, to goof off, to lead a more normal life. Then there is the agony of the contest itself, where the will to win takes over and pushes the athlete beyond his powers of conscious endurance into collapse the moment after his victory. His deepest will had attached itself to a regime for optimum functioning, overcoming the continuous static and rebellion from other facets of his personality. Similar experiences are encountered in the intellectual life, and in the moral life.

Check out the latter with a medieval theologian. Thomas Aquinas says: "If virtue were at odds with man's nature, it would not be an act of the man himself, but of some alien force subtracting from or going beyond the man's own identity." Go back to St. Paul. The Gentiles do not have the Mosaic law, he writes in his Epistle to the Romans, but "they show the work of a law written in their hearts." And Moses himself, as recorded in Deuteronomy, commends the keeping of God's commandments in order that there shall be flourishing life: "Choose life," he says. Where is this commandment, he asks rhetorically; is it up in heaven or beyond the sea? No, he declares, "the word is very nigh unto thee, in thy mouth and in thy heart, that thou mayest do it." What are we to understand Thomas, Paul, and Moses to be saying? Are they saying that to obey God's will for us is equivalent to following the laws of our own being? It's pretty close to that. And that is precisely what an animal's instincts do for him. The difference is that we are free to ignore or disobey the laws of our being, whereas no animal has that power.

In the course of several thousand generations of human beings a slow deposit has accumulated as the result of individuals here and there successfully realizing a portion of the human potential. The recipes they left behind, tested, and winnowed over the centuries, form the hard core of the ethical code. This is not a prescription for a life of power-seeking, or one of money-making, or a life devoted to fun and games, or to fame. These things are not intrinsically evil, but an inordinate attachment to any one of them breaks training, so to speak. Proper use of them, on the other hand, is part of life's schooling process.

What are we being schooled for? A clear-cut positive answer to this question is impossible, for it outruns human experience. But a pretty clear hint comes through when we contemplate the alternatives. Wealth, pleasure, power, and even knowledge, when sought as ends in themselves, begin to send up signals that they are, in reality, only means to ends beyond themselves. The space scientists "built redundancy" into their capsules, more of everything than normal requirements would ever demand. Man, too, is overbuilt, in the sense that each person has a wide range of potencies and a reservoir of untapped energy at his disposal, more than any of us ever use. Nor is man left on dead center with all this latent power. He has a chart containing the salient landmarks, and this chart is the ethical code. Let him begin to use this chart and the pieces fall into place, bits of the great design begin to emerge, the person fulfills his destiny. "The event is in the hands of God."

PART TWO

CHAPTER 11

The City of God and the City of Man

CHRISTIAN SOCIAL THOUGHT FROM ITS BEGINNING HAS BEEN
premised on the understanding that man is a creature whose destiny projects him beyond society and history. Human political
arrangements are, therefore, merely provisional and probative; the
ultimate arrangements are out of our hands. This concept has been
called, after Augustine, the idea of the two cities: the City of God
and the City of Man. Man, it is asserted, holds his citizenship
papers in two realms, the earthly and the heavenly. He is to negotiate this life as best he can, seeking as much justice and such
happiness as this world permits, but in full awareness that his
ultimate felicity may be attained only in another order of existence. "The world is a bridge," an Oriental sage remarked. "Cross
it, but do not build your houses on it."

Christian thought distinguishes between the created world as it
came from the hand of God, and the fallen world known to history
—between the world of primal innocence we posit, and the world
marred by evil, which we know. It follows from this original premise that Christian thought is nonbehaviorist; it is based on the idea
that the true inwardness of a thing—its real nature—cannot be
fully known by merely observing its outward behavior. Things are
distorted in the historical and natural order, unable to manifest
their true being. Man especially is askew. He was created in the
image of God, but now he is flawed by sin.

Some political implications may be drawn from these premises.

It has been a characteristic note in Christian sociology, from the earliest centuries, to regard government not as an original element of the created world, but as a reflection of man's corrupted nature in our fallen world. Government, in other words, is a consequence of sin; it appears only after the Fall. But if government is the result of original sin, it follows that governmental action cannot be a remedy for sin. By the same token it follows that sinful man will try to employ government for this impossible task, as well as for lesser purposes. The Christian rationale for government, in other words, is incompatible with the total state required by collectivism. When the Christian rationale for government is understood and spelled out, the only political role compatible with it is the modest function of defending the peace of society by curbing peace-breakers. When government is limited to repressing criminal and destructive actions, men are free to act constructively and creatively up to the full limit of their individual capacities.

The Christian doctrine of free will carries political overtones. Man's fall, according to theology, resulted from an act of choice —an act of disobedience, as it turned out. The kernel of this story as related in Genesis is the conviction that the God who created man gave him at the same time sufficient freedom to deny his Maker. It is but a short deduction from this belief to the conclusion that the God who gave us inwardly such complete freedom that we could either accept or reject Him wills that the relationships between men should be voluntary. The despot who repudiates individual liberty usurps a role which God even denies Himself. The despot may be a majority, but this doesn't alter matters. Outer and social liberty, in other words, is the necessary completion of inner and spiritual liberty; the free society is implicit in this reading of man's nature. Man cannot be deprived of his spiritual liberty without being dehumanized; this liberty survives under adversity, inside prison walls, and in totalitarian countries. This may be admitted, while at the same time we affirm to the hilt that man's nature is such that anything less than a free society involves a denial of some part of it.

We arrive at a similar conclusion by contemplating the second of the two Great Commandments, where we are enjoined to love our neighbor as ourselves. The bonds that should unite people, it is here implied, are those of unyielding good will, understanding, and compassion. But in collectivist theory, on the other hand, people are to be put through their paces by command and coercion. This is the nature of the means which must be and are being employed in even the most well-intentioned welfare state. In practice, every collectivized order careens toward a police state whose own citizens are its first victims. The love commandment of the Gospels brought down to the political level implies justice, parity, and freedom. There is no way whereby these basic premises may be twisted into a sanctioning of the operational imperatives of a collectivist society.

If this chapter were to have a text it would be a few lines from that great classic of both theology and political philosophy, written between A.D. 413 and 426, just after the sack of Rome; *The City of God*, by Augustine. "Two cities have been formed by two loves," writes Augustine, "the earthly by the love of self, even to the contempt of God; the heavenly by the love of God even to the contempt of self. The former, in a word, glories in itself, the latter in the Lord. . . . Two cities, for the present mingled together in body, but in heart, separated. One, whose end is eternal peace, is called Jerusalem, the other, whose joy is temporal peace, is called Babylon." Everyone knows that Augustine was not talking about ancient Babylon; he was talking about Rome. Babylon is a symbol for the human pride which puts its trust in power and temporal goods. Babylon stands for that human frailty which mistakes mere means for ends, or that willfulness which denies ends in its preoccupation with the elaboration of even more powerful and complicated means. Such was Rome, in Augustine's judgment—and much of the modern world, we might add. We too live in a secular age which is reluctant to acknowledge the dimension of transcendence in human affairs.

The ruined monuments of ancient Rome inspire awe in us even today. To the men of earlier generations this was the Eternal City. We are still living on the legacy of Rome in several fields: Latin literature, architecture, law and administration, and government. Cast your minds back to the early days of our own country. The 85 Federalist Papers were written by Madison, Hamilton, and Jay; but it is significant that they were actually signed "Publius." John Quincy Adams used the pen name "Publicola." Today, we hear more than enough about a society named after the Roman general,

Fabius. If Rome, centuries after its fall, is capable of making so strong an impression on the world's imagination, try to conceive of the stunning impact made by Rome itself—and all Rome stood for—on contemporaries.

Rome had been in decline for a couple of centuries before Augustine wrote his great book—as *we* are now able to discern. Those living in the midst of all that grandeur, however, had been blissfully unaware of the decline, until Alaric and his Goths stormed and sacked Rome in 410. Now, in the second decade of the fifth century, barbarians were walking their streets. For Romans, it was the end of the world.

While it lasted it had been a pretty good world. As Lewis Mumford writes, "Western mankind had a brief glimpse of what it would be like to live in a completely open world, in which law and order everywhere prevailed, and citizenship, in every sense, was the common human heritage." Even Augustine gives it credit: "Its joy," he says, "is temporal peace." Temporal peace and social order is an enormous accomplishment, as most people in today's war-sick world would readily agree. The Roman peace was a pretty rugged affair at times, but a Roman citizen was probably safer in any part of the known world than is a citizen of today in many parts of our large cities.

But Rome, which had been regarded as no less permanent than the hills on which the city was built, had fallen. The thousand-year-old symbol of worldly success had failed those who had put their trust in it. Augustine's immediate purpose was to absolve the Christians from blame for Rome's fall, but his book grew over a thirteen-year period, and became a philosophy of history. Its message is that human beings have a destiny which transcends history; the collapse of an earthly kingdom, therefore, need not represent ultimate failure. God's purposes for man include rightly ordered social life, but this is only the first part of the story. There is something beyond this. Man's real fulfillment is to be sought in another realm.

Augustine does not stress the point, but I think he is saying: Give Babylon its due; the City of Man *is* a genuine accomplishment—limited, but a triumph nonetheless. The City of Man is not the terminus; it points beyond itself to the City of God—or Jerusalem, as Augustine called it—as the ultimate consummation of human hopes. Man, in other words, whether he wills it or not, whether he is aware of it or not, is involved with both Babylon and Jerusalem. The two sentences, so to speak, run concurrently, but one is tangential to the other. From time to time, however, events conspire to get man bogged down, now in one realm and again in the other, to the detriment of the one neglected. The human situation is unique, for man alone among the organisms is a creature of two realms—two distinct but related orders of being. There is an order of events which is mental or spiritual; there is another order of events which is physical or material. Man bestrides, these two dimensions of reality, and if his life is to be fruitful neither must be slighted.

This point of view has room for both Babylon and Jerusalem, and we can get it into better focus if we contrast it with two contrary philosophies of life, which are also opposed to each other: Hinduism and Secularism. The first downgrades Babylon, the other despises Jerusalem. The world, as many orthodox Hindus understand it, is a trap. Nature is a deceiver, and things are not what they appear. We cannot trust our senses, for the world of matter is Maya, illusion. Deceptive external nature is evil; man's chief good is to be found in a deliberate negation of the world and life, for only by renunciation may Nirvana be attained. Why work toward such goals as improved social conditions and economic betterment when any progress we achieve is bound to be as illusory as the situation from which we start? Each person's Karma assigns him to the role he is fated to play in this round of his existence, and in future embodiments. The social outlook derived from this world view regards the festering masses at the bottom of society's pyramid with equanimity. They will have another opportunity in the cycle of birth and rebirth, and even now they may derive a vicarious satisfaction from the achievements of the Brahmins at the top of the heap. In his defense of the caste system, S. Radhakrishna, the eminent Indian philosopher and statesman said, "When the wick is aglow at the tip, the whole lamp is said to be burning."

It is difficult to see how a genuine philosophy of individualism could be derived from this outlook, which stems, in turn, from the belief that the natural world is evil. The Indian economic order is likewise hamstrung by this belief. If material things are intrinsically evil, who would urge more of them? An Indian economist, Professor B. R. Shenoy of the University of Gujerat, demonstrates with statistics that foreign economic aid has actually worsened the condition of the mass of Indian peasants. Millions of foreign aid dollars have gone into the building of dams and steel mills for which India has little economic need, but which do serve the political needs of India's rulers. The only way out of the hopeless situation in which Indians are bogged down would involve a fundamental shift in their world view, to drive the notion of Maya from their minds.

The word Maya comes from the Sanskrit "ma" or "matra," meaning "to measure, to form, to build." The Greek word, "metron," is also related to the Sanskrit "matra." The word which in Hinduism and Buddhism became Maya, denoting illusion, spawned a philosophy which resolutely turned its back on the world. For people of this culture, Babylon was a pitfall to be avoided; Jerusalem was all.

But the same Sanskrit root turned west and was transformed into the Greek "metron"—measure. "Measure" implies both a standard unit as a criterion and a reliable object to which it may be applied, that is to say, an earth which does not deceive man but challenges him to establish working relations with it. Western man set about to understand this world with his philosophies, and to control and improve it with his sciences. Western man, in one sense, is a materialist. A fundamental article of his creed is that this world is not an accident; it is the creation of a righteous God who looked out upon that which he had made and called it good. The earth was man's home, and although it terrified him at times it did not deceive him; his dispute with the world was a lover's quarrel, and it was always a fair standup fight. Individual men and whole tribes often lost—to epidemics, floods, accidents and other natural catastrophes; but the race of men gained increasing mastery over nature. Man felt increasingly at home in his planetary abode; the sense of alienation was to come later—in our time. But so long as the West was Christendom, Babylon was not permitted to exclude Jerusalem.

Christianity is the most materialist of the world's religions. Granted, there are some Platonic and Oriental elements in it, but they are not central to it. It is undeniably true that there is something finicky about Platonism, and many a Platonist appears to be chagrined to discover that his mind and spirit are ineluctably yoked to a perishing carcass which has to be fed and housed, tended when ill, and whose aches and pains interfere with his philosophizing. This should not be confused with the Judeo-Christian tradition in which most of us were reared, with its robust, earthly attitude toward the body and its concerns. "The body is the temple of the soul," wrote Paul, and being in the body is a condition of the soul's salvation. Furthermore, this religion is not concerned with the soul's immortality alone, but with the body's resurrection. The theological stance here was psychosomatic, long before that term was dreamed of.

This is the religion of the Bible, and the idea which furnishes our best clue to the central meaning of the Old and New Testaments is the concept of the Kingdom of God. In their early history, the people of Israel dreamed of a future, a golden age, an earthly kingdom in Palestine where righteousness would prevail. Then, as R. H. Charles writes, they became aware "that the earth, however purged and purified, is no fitting theatre for an eternal Messianic Kingdom. . . . This transference of the hopes of the faithful from the material world took place about 100 B.C." The Kingdom of God concept is at the heart of Jesus' message, and it became one of the dominant ideas of the Christian culture of the West. It enabled Christendom to give Jerusalem as well as Babylon its due.

The traditional religious beliefs of the West have gradually lost their hold during the past two centuries. But nature abhors a vacuum, and the spaces left by the departing religious beliefs and values have been filled by the axioms and ideas of the Enlightenment. It is the mood of the modern world to focus on human society, upon the assumption that the kingdom of heaven can be established on earth. Humanity has come of age, so runs the thesis, and now at last man is capable of taking charge of his own destiny and mastering his fate. Science has given us the tools both to know and to control, and in the democratic political processes we have perfected the means. An ideal society is just around the next corner, or the next but one, and in this environment of permanent peace and prosperity man will attain his ultimate, long promised, long deferred felicity. Confident expectations along these lines may be found in both non-Christian and Christian writers.

Leon Trotsky, in 1925, in his *Literature and Revolution* foresaw a proletarian paradise in which "the average human type will rise to the heights of an Aristotle, a Goethe, or a Marx. And above this ridge new peaks will rise." In a similar vein, the lead editorial in *The Christian Century* (July 28, 1965), declares: "It is imperative that we ask how we can turn the possibility of a Great Society from fancy and resolution into fact.

"The first answer is that we can have in this nation under federal and local governments a social order which can eliminate poverty, ignorance, disease and racial oppression—provided we do not become engaged in a global or major war."

The idea is that the problems posed by life are somehow external to man; they are something man *has*, like a suitcase he carries a while and then puts down. This is in contrast to the older and sounder view that the human condition is itself the crux of the difficulty. Man's essential nature is *the* problem, and there is no solution so long as man holds on to his humanity. This fact constitutes both the misery and grandeur of man and, typically, men wish at times to throw off the burden of their manhood. T. H. Huxley remarked somewhere that "if some great power would agree to make me always think what is true and do what is right, on condition of being turned into a sort of clock and wound up every morning before I got out of bed, I should instantly close with the offer." Had the genie granted Huxley's wish the great biologist might have made a good animal or insect or bird, but he'd have sacrificed his humanity.

Henry Bamford Parkes, the New York University historian, writes about "those dominant beliefs which have given the Western world its creativity and its sense of collective purpose." The three leading ideas which fall into this category are "ethical monotheism, natural law, and the Christian kingdom of heaven." He describes these as "the main spiritual principles of Western civilization."[1]

It would require a lifetime of effort to trace out the workings of these three ideas on the development of the institutions, outlook, and mood of the West, but at the moment we are concerned with the question of how they have fared in the modern world, where a secularist outlook is largely taken for granted.

1. *Gods and Men*, p. 3.

First, ethical monotheism. The early accomplishments of science were so breathtaking that many came to feel that the scientific method was man's only reliable means to knowledge. Formerly there was only the clash of opinions; now man had the truth. Science gave man mastery over the natural world, but it failed to reveal anything beyond the natural; its method was geared to the measurable and the quantative. In 1869, T. H. Huxley coined the word "agnosticism" for the creed that God is unknowable, as well as unnecessary. Today's scientists do not talk this way; but the mood of the science of three generations ago has seeped into the mind of today's masses, so that André Malraux—de Gaulle's Minister of Culture—could say, "we live in the first agnostic civilization." Ethical monotheism, as an operative force in men's lives today, is at a low ebb, but a renewal is taking place in our time, and theism emerges purer after its trial by fire.

Second, the natural law. Beginning with the Greek Sophists, coming down through the Stoics, Cicero, and Thomas Aquinas, to Edmund Burke and the authors of our Constitution, men have believed that a higher law was written into the nature of the cosmos, which right reason could discover, and to which the statutes of men should conform. Legislation is just if it accords with the natural law; unjust, if it does not.

The concept of the natural law was badly battered during the nineteenth century, but a heartening revival has taken place in our day. It is gaining strength as it joins forces with the current renewal of theism.

The Kingdom of God was brought to earth with a thud in the eighteenth century, and every scribbler peddled his utopian scheme. Man now was no longer merely one of God's creatures; he was lord of the planet, architect of his own fate. Scientific know-how coupled with majoritarian political processes would usher in an earthly paradise. Babylon—a perfect man-made society—was about to be achieved by human effort.

The construction of ideal commonwealths is not a native preoccupation of Asians or Africans; this aberration is limited to people of Western Europe and America. It is a secular version of the Kingdom of God, inspiring the belief in our time that a perfectly ordered social life will be possible as soon as political power is centralized and the wisest and best men are operating the government according to an ideal blueprint. The goal would have been achieved before now, were not a few old reactionaries still barring the way. They will be erased by progressive mankind.

These trends—which we might label nontheism, naturalism, and utopianism—are but three symptoms of the modern world's malaise. They are, I believe, perverse and antilife; they are not coherent, and their inconsistencies spawn feelings of alienation and despair. Men can't live by them; the map of the universe they supply is guaranteed to lead us astray. Despite all this they do represent popular trends, and thus people who are always attracted to the latest fashion in ideas climb aboard the bandwagon, and some of the bandwagons bear ecclesiastical trappings.

The Church is *in* the world, presumably, to witness to a kind and quality of life which is not wholly *of* the world; it judges the things which come and go from the vantage point of a set of values that endure. The Church is not dedicated to wealth, power, fame, or any other form of worldly success. These things are not bad in themselves, and on their own level they are indispensable. But the Church has another set of purposes, every one of which is aimed at cherishing and nourishing that elusive thing called "the soul," for whose proper ordering each person is accountable to his Maker. In terms of this main function, religion has taken on many other chores which have implications for even such seemingly remote provinces as politics and economics. These, however, are incidental to its main task—which is to remind man, in season and out, who he really is and what he may become; and this task, in every age, involves some resistance to "the world." Christianity can never be coextensive with any society, but the tension between the two is necessary for social health.

Most churches and most ministers are bending every effort in this direction; their effectiveness may be questioned, but not their intentions. But the fantastic thing is that wealthy and powerful ecclesiastical organizations, seconded by articulate theologians, are doing their utmost—which is considerable—to promote and further the currently fashionable secular trends.

Take the first point, ethical monotheism. Is the universe comprehended by a vast Purpose of Whose intentions we get occasional hints and with Whom men may hold communion; or is there nothing beyond what meets the senses? How do certain contemporary theologians deal with this fundamental question? They begin by discarding natural theology, that is to say, the use of reason to analyze the testimony of the world of nature, which reveals a preponderance of order, harmony, balance, and economy in its operations. They continue by discarding mystical theology—the effort to assess the meaning of the experience of men and women in all ages and in all countries who claim to have come into direct contact with a spiritual order of reality beyond the sensory order, that is, beyond the realm which we can see, touch, and taste. Having sawed off these two legs, our contemporary theologian is propped up on one leg only, Biblical theology. How does he understand this discipline? The name to conjure with among contemporary theologians is Dietrich Bonhoeffer, a young German pastor who was martyred by the Nazis. "God is teaching us," Bonhoeffer writes, "that we must live as men who can get along very well without him. The God who is with us is the God who forsakes us." This writer delights in paradox, speaking of a "religionless Christianity." A professor at Hartford Seminary expounds the new gospel by writing, "The entire world is empty of God; and the entire world is redeemed by God in Jesus Christ." How? "Christian love . . . is responsible action in the world, exercised in the mandates of political life, of work and friendship," and so on. "Before the cross, all talk of religion as the basis of Western civilization or democracy is silenced. The Christian['s] . . . place is with the victim—and with the rebel. . . . [Here is] the possibility of a new Christian political ethic."

What are some of the earmarks of this new political ethic which motivates the social actionist churchmen? Its keynote is power. The proponents of Natural Law theory offered legislators a set of ethical guides which governors should not overstep, but the idea of a moral order cannot survive the abandonment of natural theology. When Karl Barth came here in 1963, the man who impressed him most, he said, was an Episcopal layman named William Stringfellow. " 'Natural justice,' " writes Mr. Stringfellow, "is . . . a fiction which Americans can no longer afford. . . . Law is not some vehicle of 'natural justice', but law is an instrument of conflict." What sort of conflict? A Presbyterian official believes that modern Amercan society contains many "mixed-up, hag-ridden people [with] a virulent species of mental and emotional illness."

Do we treat these people with Christian love? Not at all. We apply "various forms of shock treatment . . . through legal, judicial and social force."

The Kingdom of God has been secularized into utopia-by-politics. The idea of the two cities, the City of God and the City of Man —Jerusalem and Babylon—has been central to Christian social thought from the earliest days. But no longer, as has been suggested already in the quotations I have used. If politicians and a few other people will only take the advice of these ecclesiastical evangels of an earthly paradise, the Kingdom of God on earth is due any minute.

Christians have always felt an obligation to improve the natural and social orders, but they have never—until now—equated even a superlatively improved social order with the Kingdom of God. This Kingdom was regarded as another dimension of existence, another realm of being—not simply an extension of our present set-up. But the late Bishop G. Bromley Oxnam told the Fifth World Order Study Conference in 1958 that we should "so change the planet that when our first visitors from Mars arrive they will find a society fit to be called the Kingdom of God."

There is a consistent pattern in the social changes which are taking place in this country and all over the world. We witness a trend toward the expansion of the political, coercive sector of the nation, at the expense of the private, voluntary sector.[2] The end result of this trend is a society run from the top by political direction and command, with no private sector remaining immune from political interventions. This is authoritarianism, benign in some countries, tyrannical in others. The tyrannical version, Communism, has attracted some ecclesiastical support, and still does; the benign version—domestic welfarism—attracts a great deal more. The aim of powerful churchmen is to mobilize the influence of religion and the churches behind every statist proposal—as if social reform and revolution were the end and religion a mere means.

The second preoccupation of contemporary churchmen, which goes hand in hand with the first, is with the machinery for worldwide ecclesiastical organization, or ecumenism. The ecumenical movement, like secular internationalism, is based on the idea that the sins of nationalism are virtues when committed by an international body.

2. See my "Painting Government into a Corner," *The Freeman*, February, 1964.

The internationalist program, secular as well as religious, works at cross purposes with itself. Domestically, it endorses the idea of a planned economy which cannot be made to work even temporarily, except on the basis of self-sufficiency or autarchy. The overall plan of a country cannot work if goods from foreign countries enter freely; each country must have tariffs, exchange controls, quotas, pegged currencies, and the like. Actions of this sort, which every controlled economy must take, will be regarded as hostile acts by every other country. International tensions must increase, and international organizations become sounding boards for the exploitation of tensions and grievances.

This makeshift internationalism commits the major powers to a foreign policy of mutual interventionism and brinkmanship; it increases the occasions for war, and brings on war itself. A given war, such as the "police action" in Korea or the fighting in Viet Nam, is a logical effect or consequence of pursuing a foreign policy that is bound to eventuate in military action somewhere under some pretext. If the war in Viet Nam is judged to be a crazy, mixed-up affair, this is just what one must expect if our nation embraces an insane foreign policy committed to global interventionism. Most liberals and most intellectuals approve the policy of global interventionism, and it is favored by powerful and articulate churchmen; but they profess to dislike its consequences. To condemn a result while advocating the course which brings it about is a pointless gesture. And if the foreign policy of global interventionism is of a piece with domestic welfarist interventionism, then the first step taken away from peace and toward war is the political act of garnisheeing a portion of people's wages—thus denying citizens full freedom to pursue their personal goals—in order that government may have the means to carry out the grandiose national goals of the liberal ideologues. Those who really want peace must give up the collectivist dream of coercively redirecting the people's energies into channels other than those of individual choice. If this is too great a sacrifice, then those who refuse to make it have opted, not for peace, but for war.

The tide of secularism has carried almost everything before it; it has even swept potent segments of the church into the flood. The ancient world was a sacral society, it was church and state in one. But there is an inherent tension between the institutions of religion and those of politics, as set forth in a celebrated sentence of Pope

Gelasius I in A.D. 494; "Two there are, august Emperor, by which this world is ruled on title of original and sovereign right—the consecrated authority of the priesthood and the royal power."

Christianity enlarged the idea of God from a family, tribal, or urban deity into a Being with universal attributes, and this development produced the kind of religious institution—the Church— which must forever confront political institutions in an atmosphere of encounter and tension. The history of Europe is in large measure polarized between the two powers; sword and scepter, crown and miter, Empire and Papacy. Such a dualism is fatal to the idea of the monolithic state. The effort of this polarization is to decentralize power and disperse authority, and there is no other way to deal with the root problem of politics—the governance of power. In addition to the division of authority between Empire and Papacy during the centuries of Europe's history, power was further fragmented among numerous kings, counts, and lesser officials. In practice, then, there were always tendencies for power to get itself deadlocked; with the result that there was a widespread enjoyment of what might be called "interstitial liberties" by the people. Men had a set of customary freedoms within the spacious nooks, crannies, and crevices of European society long before the law moved up to recognize specific freedoms based upon a sacredness in each person.

But Christianity as a conscious faith began to lose its hold on men's minds and their loyalties, in consequence, began to shift to the state. The modern world has moved toward "totalitarian democracy," in Talmon's phrase, where religion is absorbed by politics. Omnipotent government cannot abide a universal religion; it must find pliant churchmen or else construct its own domesticated variety of secularized religion.

And thus we complete another of those enormous spirals of history. Religion is stripped of its transcendent significance in order to promote social cohesion. Ethical behavior is redefined as that conduct which enhances the interests of the state. Religion and ethics and politics are now united so as to form one package, as was largely the case in the ancient world. That was a social system where, as Fustel De Coulanges put it, "the state was a religious community, the king a pontiff, the magistrate a priest, and the law a sacred formula; where patriotism was piety, and exile excommunication; where individual liberty was unknown; where man was enslaved to the state through his soul, his body, and his property."[3]

With modern man it is different. Our pilgrimage has brought us to a different turn on the spiral of history, and we have acquired a kind of sophistication that will not permit us to be reabsorbed into our societies without undergoing inner tension and conflict. This is one consequence of our lengthy encounter with Christianity. We live in a secular age. Men today may be non-Christian or even anti-Christian, but nevertheless the effects of Christian teachings have leaked into our lives to shape the modern psyche in the region of values and assumptions about the meaning of life. Our mood is mainly Christian, whatever the creed or philosophy we profess. T. S. Eliot says much the same thing when he points out that our "society has not ceased to be Christian until it has become positively something else. It is my contention," he continues, "that we have today a culture which is mainly negative, but which, so far as it is still positive, is still Christian. I do not think it can remain negative, because a negative culture has ceased to be efficient in a world where economic as well as spiritual forces are proving the efficiency of cultures which, even when pagan, are positive; and I believe that the choice before us is between the formation of a new Christian culture, and the acceptance of a pagan one."[4]

It was customary for a tribe beaten in war to adopt the gods of the victors. This does not adequately describe our situation, but as the tides of secularism have rolled over us there has been little resistance from places where most resistance might have been expected. The religion of the secular challenged the religion of the spirit and the latter's line has not only been breached in many sectors but the presumed defenders have made common cause with the attackers. The starchy old Tory, Sir James Fitzjames Stephens had a word for it: "The old ways of living. . . . are breaking down all over Europe, and are floating this way and that like haycocks in a flood. . . . The waters are out and no human force can turn them back, but I do not see why as we go with the stream we need sing Hallelujah to the river god." Nor do I!

3. *The Ancient City*, p. 389.
4. *The Idea of a Christian Society*, p. 13.

Yet there is still lots of health left in us, and a proper diagnosis of our condition is the first step toward recovery. The great French observer and thinker, Alexis de Tocqueville, paid a visit to America a century and a quarter ago and wrote a book about us which is even more cogent now than when it first appeared. America, Tocqueville wrote, although a nation of vigorous free people, was peculiarly exposed and vulnerable to a novel kind of political tyranny labeled, by him, "democratic despotism." The despotism foreseen as our fate would not be an alien dictatorship imposed from without and by conquest over a beaten but rebellious people. Democratic despotism would manifest itself as a gradual but spreading paralysis of will, as a "failure of nerve," as a gradual erosion of individual responsibility.

But listen to Tocqueville's own words from Chapter 6 of Volume II of his *Democracy in America:*

> A democratic state of society, similar to that of the Americans might offer singular facilities for the establishment of despotism; it would be a despotism more extensive and more mild than any previous; it would degrade men without tormenting them. . . . The will of man is not shattered, but softened, bent and guided; men are seldom forced by it to act, but they are constantly restrained from acting. Such a power does not destroy, but it prevents existence; it does not tyrannize, but it compresses, enervates, extinguishes and stupefies a people, till each nation is reduced to nothing better than a flock of timid and industrious animals, of which the government is the shepherd.

One of the ominous phrases of our time is "fifth column," which came out of the Spanish Civil War of the Thirties. A communique of General Emilio Mola reported that he was marching on Madrid with four columns of troops and had a "fifth column" of sympathizers inside the city. The world seized upon this phrase because it was all too familiar with the ugly reality behind the label— betrayal from within. The term "fifth column" is usually connected in people's minds with Communism, for it is this thing which spearheads the revolt against the institutions of the West. Communism, in other words, is not only an external and military menace headquartered in Moscow or Peking. It is this; but in addition, when estimating the extent of the threat, we must include the sinister fact that Communism today has willing allies and bewitched victims in every country in the world. There is a "fifth column" at work on every continent to sap and betray the religions, the morals, the laws, and the institutions which men have lived by for centuries. The revolution is total.

Communism adapts its means to its end; now gaining its way by military conquest, and now by conversion. The conquest aspect of Communism is not the primary threat—although this must not be minimized—it is the Communist success with conversion that makes it dynamic and dangerous. This repulsive creed has proven irresistibly attractive to men as far apart as a Manhattan millionaire and a Chinese coolie. For countless people around the world Communism has become a kind of ersatz religion, a religion which generates a demonic kind of fanaticism and self-sacrifice. If the Communist faith ceased to operate, Red armies would soon cease to march and their menace would be reduced tenfold.

We arm by necessity to meet the military threats of Communism, but what good are the most powerful ships, planes, and bombs if our people are intellectually and spiritually disarmed? This is the crux of the matter. It is a secularized West which is at bay, a culture uncertain of its premises and confused about its goals. Once the West recognized itself as Christendom, a society whose aspirations and norms were derived from Christianity. But our society is now organized apart from God; the religious dimension has largely dropped out of our social life, and man is regarded as his own end and goal. Much that is unintentional and implicit in our present way of life has been made explicit and intentional in the Communist creed, a fact which constitutes its main allure. The uncommitted nations are "neutral" largely because, having compared us to our adversaries they have come to feel that the Commies are just like us, only more so. If they could understand the true "inwardness" of our situation, however, they might see things differently.

One should not use the term "Christian civilization" lightly. Many contemporary churchmen condemn its use altogether. Read the history of Europe, they say, and point to one nation which exemplified Christianity in practice. Besides, they continue, Christianity transcends history; it cannot be identified with any culture, and it is idolatrous even to try. All of which is very true. But some of these churchmen then about-face and refer to Communism as a Christian heresy. It is, of course, no such thing, but accepting their terminology for the moment, let's see what is implied by what they are trying to say. Communism offers no substitutes for Christian doctrines at the spiritual level; therefore, if Communism is a Christian heresy, it must be deviant with respect to things at the social and cultural levels. The orthodox things at that level in the West are the things of Christian cultivation. Therefore, a reference to Communism as a Christian heresy implies the prior existence of Christian civilization. In short, it is impossible to examine European and American history and deny the importance of Christianity as a shaping force at every level—at least to this century. This is not to say that Christendom lived up to its aspirations; it did not, of course The nations pursued policies of power and aggrandizement in the secular order; and in the sacred, the Church periodically betrayed its Master's commission. Despite its continuing defections, we do, nevertheless, speak of "the Christian Church." By the same token we may, with propriety, refer to the West as "Chritian civilization": The West was Christian in its assumptions about man and his destiny; its aspirations were Christian.

It is the norms of that civilization that are now in jeopardy, its vision of an ideal order. In the thinking of many of our contemporaries the idea that norms have a status in the transcendent is denied. By reference to these norms we once knew what we were, and we had intimations of our destiny in eternity. But now there is widespread confusion as to what it means to be a human being, and uncertainty as regards the individual's relation to God. Our society at large can hardly be blamed for its uncertainty about these matters, when Christians themselves are so unsure. In the words of the eminent contemporary historian, Christopher Dawson: "It is the intellectual and social inertia of Christians that is the real obstacle to a restoration of Christian culture. For if it is true that more than half the population of this country are Church members, Christians can hardly say that they are powerless to influence society. It is the will, not the power, that is lacking."

The churches may point with pride to their massive structures, to their expanding membership, to their educational and church union programs, to their political influence, and so on, but if they do not address the individual person in his aloneness and lostness, the authentic religious note—which holds all the rest together—is lacking.

In modern mass states, the problem, we are told, is to fit little men into big societies. Balloting of sorts goes on in all modern states, and therefore most countries call themselves "democracies," merely because men are counted. But to be counted is not the same as to count. The individual in mass societies doesn't count. He feels himself submerged in the mass, dwarfed into insignificance except as he joins some crowd or pressure group. So long as he runs with the pack he feels secure; but a man's two legs were also given him to take a stand on. It has been remarked that if we don't stand for something, we are in danger of falling for everything. Where shall we take our stand, and for what principles?

Our ancestors believed that each man counted because they knew that each man was accountable. In the religious faith they professed, the individual had to render an account of his life before God, and therefore he was, in his own and in his fellow's eyes, a responsible being. These are the convictions we must recover; that each of us counts, that each of us is responsible, that what we do or don't do with our lives can mean victory or defeat for the things that matter most for us and our posterity. The churches which sound an uncertain trumpet here, cease to be authentic parts of the true Church. When churches speak a healing word, men may be made whole; and when men recover wholeness their societies will be restored.

CHAPTER 12

The American System and Majority Rule

THE CONSENT DOCTRINE ANALYZED IN ANOTHER CHAPTER HAS a corollary in the idea of popular sovereignty. One of the articles of faith of Classical Liberalism was that The People should participate in rule. The People would be enlightened by means of the national system of education and thus able to share intelligently in the framing and shaping of the rules under which they would live and the code by which they would be governed. The nation would be self-governed by representative parliaments whose members would be chosen from and by The People in popular elections.

As things work out in actual practice, the electorate numbers less than the total number of citizens in the nation; those who register are more numerous than those who actually vote in any given election; the number of votes cast for the winning candidates is less than the number of the total votes cast (often it is less than the sum total of the votes garnered by the several losing candidates); and finally, the number of those who are actually voted into public office is but a tiny fraction of the electorate. The figures for the 1964 Presidential Election may be of interest in this connection.

The total population in the United States in 1964 was 193,-000,000. Of this number, 113,000,000 were eligible to register as voters, or 58 percent of the population. However, only 87,000,000 actually registered, or 77 percent of those eligible, and 45 percent of the population. Seventy million persons actually voted in the presidential sweepstakes of 1964, or 80 percent of those actually registered, 62 percent of those eligible to register, and 36 percent of the total population. The winning candidate received 43,000,-000 votes, or 61 percent of the total votes cast, 48 percent of those actually registered, 38 percent of the number eligible to register, and 22 percent of the total population. An interesting and significant figure turns up if we subtract the number of votes cast on Election Day, 1964, from the total number of people eligible to be voters (70 from 113). The result is 43,000,000. In other words, there were 43,000,000 "lost voters," men and women who meet the legal qualifications for voting, but who, for one reason or another did not register—or if registered did not vote in November, 1964. By coincidence, this number, 43,000,000 is exactly equivalent to the number of votes which elected the President.

It is from procedures of this sort that something called "the majority" emerges. As the result of a sifting and winnowing process we wind up with a figure of 43,000,000, the number of men and women whose votes were sufficient to place a candidate in office. This is "the majority" which, in the eyes of some political theorists, confers a mandate on the victorious party to impose its program on the reluctant "minority" of the nation; that is, on the other 78 percent. This is the theory of majoritarianism, ardently espoused by many contemporary intellectuals and tacitly accepted by many others. But will it hold water? Does it square with traditional American political theory? Let's take a hard look.

It is standard procedure among journalists to divide the world into two camps. The Soviet bloc comprises one camp, whose member nations are run along totalitarian lines. The non-Soviet bloc, by contrast, is called the Free World. The United States, it is generally conceded by our fellow Americans, are a prime example of the free society.

Everyone favors freedom, but freedom does not mean the same thing to all people. Take a random sampling of our citizenry and ask them to explain what they mean when they declare that ours is a free society. "America is free," most of them would say, "because the People in free elections choose their own leaders. And then, by letter writing, lobbying, and delegations to Washington, the People make their opinions felt in the determination of policy. If the People do not like the government they chose in 1964 they need not revolt; all they have to do is convert a majority of voters to their way of thinking and they'll get the government they want."

Now suppose someone not in sympathy with a part of the national government's program utters some criticisms of it. He gets a standardized reaction. The customary response is: "Under our system of government the People are sovereign. The People are entitled to get from government whatever a majority of them want; free schooling, job insurance, cheap electricity, medicare, and so on. Would you deny them this right?" It is assumed that the voice of the People, expressing itself through majority opinion is, in a democratic society, the final determiner of policy, and the ultimate sanction for political conduct. The idea is that a society is free to the extent that the majority will is not frustrated.

Let me document this point of view by citing Professor James MacGregor Burns of Williams College, biographer of the late President Kennedy, and a leading spokesman for modern liberalism. Professor Burns proudly proclaims that liberals play "the numbers game." ". . . as a liberal I believe in majority rule," he writes. "I believe that the great decisions *should* be made by numbers, by forty-nine million as against forty-seven million. . . ." Or whatever number of votes was cast. Then, being asked the question as to whether there might not be some principle more basic than majority rule, to which even the majority should yield, Professor Burns says, "What does a majority have the right to do? It has the right to do anything in the economic and social arena that is relevant to our national problems and national purposes— except to change the basic rules of the game."

That final disclaimer sounds much like an afterthought, and some liberals support the majority rule idea without qualification. Professor Herman Finer, late of Harvard, writes, "For in a democracy right is what the majority makes it to be."[1] In other words, the majority has the power to carry out its will, and whatever it does is all right; its program is right, by definition.

If so, then the liberals, by winning an election, have won the right to run the country as they please—including, Burns suggests, the right to be let alone by conservatives. The liberals now have

1. Herman Finer, *Road to Reaction*, p. 60.

a majority of the nation behind them, Professor Burns asserts, and "I want the liberals of the nation to have a right to rule in what I think is their day today."

Professor Burns seems not to have noticed, but in saying this he has abandoned the majority rule idea for the more exciting notion of Winner Take All. In the politics of Winner Take All—which is modern liberalism—public office comes to be regarded as private property; the national government becomes an article of commerce whose capture is worth over two hundred billion dollars annually to those who gain possession of it. Those who win an election, even by the slimmest of margins, have a mandate from the country—provided they are liberals—to impose their program on the whole nation. It is amusing that those who begin by playing the numbers game in politics wind up with a mathematical absurdity; a majority, 51 percent, is—in their book—not only equal to the whole, 100 percent, but superior to it.

Something like this is the rationale for much of today's politicking. This is "Liberalism," and it may plausibly be argued that this is the going ideology in such circles as the following: top-flight businessmen in the Committee for Economic Development; high ranking churchmen in the National Council of Churches, and their opposite numbers in the other faiths; professors, lawyers, publicists, and others in Americans for Democratic Action; politicians in both major parties. These groups comprise the Establishment, and in the Establishment there is no philosophy but "Liberalism." These circles have set the tone in our society for a generation, but in terms of *their* actual ascendancy in the religious, the academic, the business, and the political worlds, those of a conservative persuasion are a pitifully tiny and ineffectual minority. Conservatives, nevertheless, have a case which is solidly grounded, intellectually and morally. But this makes it all the more imperative that we be perfectly clear as to the role of a creative minority in society, and that we understand the limitations of majority opinion and majority rule.

Let me pause here to stress an important point: The opposite of majority rule—or the alternative—is not minority rule. It is not one man rule, or rule by an elite. These are all in the same category, being but various forms of rule. The opposite of majority rule —or any kind of rule—is individual liberty. That's what we stand for—individual liberty within a spiritual, moral, and legal framework.

Present day assumptions about the desirability of permitting majority will free rein were not shared by the men who drafted the Constitution. To the contrary, these men worked overtime to devise ways of protecting society against the action of majorities. They knew that the phrase, "The Majority," is a technical term in politics, customarily meaning "a minority on the make." If democracy is a system of government in which every citizen is equally represented, and where policy is determined by sampling majority opinion, then the Founding Fathers tried to circumvent "democracy" and succeeded. A rather silly European Socialist, presumably with this in mind, referred to our Constitution as "very nearly a plot against the common people." The real intent of the document was quite the opposite: it was to protect the common people —which includes just about all of us—from political adventurers. Our forebears had experienced the tyranny of monarchs, but they had no intention of accepting dictation by a majority in its place. "An *elective* despotism is not the government we fought for," wrote Jefferson in 1781.

The end they fought for was individual liberty within the framework of a moral and legal order, and to this end they created a number of antimajoritarian institutions. The Senate is one instance. One senator in the state of New York represents about 8,000,000 people; but the lucky people of Nevada have one senator for every 100,000 of them. In the House of Representatives, on the other hand, New York State has forty-one votes, while Nevada has but one. Whatever one's reaction to this, he cannot call it equal representation.

To emphasize further the nondemocratic nature of the Senate, the Constitution provided that its members be appointed by the legislators of the various states, not elected by the voters. We amended the Constitution to change this procedure.

The Constitution declared that the President of the United States would not be chosen by mass vote. The legislature of each state was to determine the manner of chosing electors who, in turn, would meet and select a president. The idea was to insulate this office from the popular will.

And then there is the Supreme Court. Theoretically, a bill might have the unanimous support of the voters, be passed into law by the Congress, and then be thrown out by the Court on the grounds of unconstitutionality.

The federal republic designed by the Founding Fathers is miles away from what the average American today understands by a democracy, in which majority opinion rules directly and unfettered. Let's take a look at the men who launched this venture in political liberty. Were they armchair theoreticians, or extremists, or cranks? To the contrary, they were inspired but practical men. They were experienced with colonial charters, compacts, and self-government; and their religion conduced to individual liberty. These qualifications have been largely lost among us—although they might be restored. But until a restoration occurs, we as a people will probably continue to resort to the expedient of "majority rule" to sanction any governmental action an actual minority of the voters wants.

One hundred and eight-three years ago, in the spring of 1787, a body of delegates met in Philadelphia. They represented twelve of the thirteen colonies, Rhode Island abstaining. By September they had drawn up the Constitution and signed their names to it, and beginning in October three young men wrote a series of 85 articles urging the adoption of this document by the states: Hamilton was 30, Madison 36 and Jay 42. The series was nearing completion when the papers were collected and issued in book form as *The Federalist*. This book has long been recognized as a classic in political philosophy, and the document whose virtues it expounded, The Constitution of the United States, is still—nominally at least—the law of the land. The first Congress under the new Constitution met at New York on March 4th, 1789.

The men who drafted our basic political document and set a new government in motion represented a people who were exceedingly alert intellectually and politically. There was a population of some three million along the Atlantic seaboard in the latter part of the eighteenth century, largely rural. But they were readers and thinkers, as well as farmers and artisans, as the following instances show. Blackstone's famous *Commentaries* appeared between 1765 and 1769, and 2,500 copies sold in America before the Revolution. Adam Smith wrote his *Wealth of Nations* just as the Revolutionary War was getting started, in 1776, and despite the preoccupation of Americans with their own problems in this time of trouble, several thousand copies of the book sold here shortly after its publication in England. Tom Paine wrote his pamphlet, *Common Sense*, in January 1776, and Americans bought about 100,000 copies within a few weeks.

Many colonists were at home in the realm of ideas, and thus were ready, when the time came, with a rationale for liberty based on an acquaintance with its literature as far back as Greece, Rome, and Israel.

When the Founding Fathers sat down in Philadelphia to draw up a new constitution, the American adventure was already 180 years old. In other words, about as much time has elapsed between the settlement in Jamestown in 1607 and the Philadelphia Convention as between Philadelphia and ourselves. These men were anything but novices in practical politics. What had their experience taught them?

During the sixteenth century, individual adventurers like Sir Walter Raleigh conducted colonizing efforts at private expense, but in the seventeenth century, companies were chartered by the English Crown to establish colonies and carry on trade. The famous East India Company was organized in 1600, and was probably the model on which the Virginia Charter of 1606 was framed. This Charter created the London and Plymouth Companies which led to the settlements at Jamestown in 1607 and Plymouth in 1620. We need to take a careful look at these commercial corporations of colonization for, in structure and function, they were models used by the colonists in their later political experiments.

This fact has been noted by Charles A. Beard in his book, *The Rise of American Civilization.*[2] Referring to the Virginia Company, Beard writes: "Like the State, it had a constitution, a charter issued by the Crown . . . like the State, it had a territorial basis, a grant of land often greater in area than a score of European principalities . . . it could make assessments, coin money, regulate trade, dispose of corporate property, collect taxes, manage a treasury, and provide for defense. Thus every essential element long afterward found in the government of the American State appeared in the chartered corporation that started English civilization in America."

2. Charles A. Beard, *The Rise of American Civilization*, p. 37.

These chartered companies were also missionary enterprises. The colonizers who came to these shores were Dissenters from the Established Church in England, seeking here a haven where they might worship God according to their own convictions. They did not believe in, nor did they practice, what we have come to call "religious toleration." Theorizings about the "rights of private conscience" would have fallen upon deaf ears; the freedom they sought was freedom to worship as *they* chose, not every man's freedom to do as he pleased. They were not easy-going people, nor were they easy to live with; but perhaps it took a certain kind of fanaticism to make the ocean voyage in the first place and, in the second place, to survive in an extremely hazardous situation.

This "hardshell" aspect of Puritan and Separatist religion has no discernible political significance; history bears witness to hundreds of crusading faiths for which the adherents were willing to suffer and, upon occasion, to persecute. But there were two peculiarities of the Puritan religion which did have a direct bearing on American political theory and practice—its covenant theology and its congregational polity. Let me quote the words of a scholar, R. L. Perry, referring to the Mayflower Compact: "The document represents the application to the affairs of civil government of the philosophy of the church covenant which was the basis of Puritan theology. This theology found in the Scriptures the right of men to associate and covenant to form a church and civil government and to choose their own officers to administer both religious and civil affairs. Each member of the congregation had a vote in the election of officers, and each congregation was considered was independent and autonomous of every other and not subject to the authority of any centralized church hierarchy."[3]

Edmund Burke delivered his great speech on "Conciliation with the Colonies" in 1775. Speaking of the influence of the colonists' religion on their will to resist he said:

> Religion, always a principle of energy, in this new people is no way worn out or impaired; and their mode of professing it is also one main cause of this free spirit. The people are Protestants, and of that kind which is the most adverse to all implicit submission of mind and opinion. This is a persuasion

3. *Sources of Our Liberties*, R. L. Perry, Editor, p. 57.

not only favorable to liberty, but built upon it . . . the dissent-
ing interests have sprung up in direct opposition to all the
ordinary powers of the world, and could justify that opposition only on a strong claim to natural liberty. Their very
existence depended on the powerful and unremitted assertion
of that claim. All Protestantism, even the most cold and passive, is a sort of dissent. But the religion most prevalent in our
northern colonies is a refinement on the principle of resistance; it is the dissidence of dissent, and the protestantism of
the Protestant religion.

As a corollary of this religion the Founding Fathers posited a
higher law—the Natural Law or the Moral Law—to which the
laws of men ought to conform. Men might create statutes, or
legislation, but the Natural Law is discovered, not created; it is a
law superior to the will of human governors, and legislation is just
or unjust as it conforms to or violates Natural Law. The Natural
Law is largely unwritten, but the down-to-earth parts of it are
found in the Common Law, in "the ideas of immemorial rights of
Englishmen," and in the various charters written to implement
these rights from Magna Carta on down.

So much for the men and the political ingredients at their finger-
tips. They were acquainted with political philosophy and experienced in the art of governing. Their Dissenters' faith disposed
them to individual liberty, and in the Natural Law they had a
device to limit arbitrary rule. This was their equipment, and then
they were given an opportunity, unique in history, to draw up the
fundamental rules for a society in which men would be free. One
of them, James Wilson, wrote: "The United States exhibits to the
world the first instance, as far as we can learn, of a nation, unat-
tacked by external force, unconvulsed by domestic insurrection,
assembling voluntarily, deliberating fully, and deciding calmly,
concerning that system of government under which they would
wish that they and their posterity should live." The exuberant
Patrick Henry went even further. Cried he: "We are, Sir, in a state
of nature!"

These men, so equipped, were given a unique opportunity to
ask, and then to answer, the two fundamental political questions.
The primordial political question—in old-fashioned terminology

—is: What shall be the extent of rule? or, as we would put it today, What is the proper scope of government in society? The second and lesser political question is: Who shall rule? or, as we'd say, What devices shall we employ to choose personnel?

The first question is basic: What shall be the extent of rule? The answer of the Founding Fathers to this question constitutes a political breakthrough. Once this first question is answered properly, the second question, devising a workable device for choosing personnel, is easy. Majority opinion, as determined by balloting, is one such device. But to use majority voting in order to determine the proper scope and boundaries of government is to confuse the two categories; it is to count noses to determine a matter of principle.

The answer our forebears gave to the question: What shall be the extent of rule? is, basically, the answer of classical liberalism. It is the function of government, they said in effect, to act as an umpire who enforces the agreed-upon rules. Let government administer justice among men and otherwise keep hands off; men will be free then to administer their own affairs. When government keeps the peace by curbing peacebreakers, men may go freely about their productive and creative pursuits, cooperating and competing with one another as each of them deems best.

In giving this sort of answer, the Founding Fathers broke with a long and powerful European tradition. For many centuries the alchemists had sought for a philosopher's stone which would transmute lead into gold; but the dream which had really haunted the mind of Europe ever since Plato was not the quest for a philosopher's stone, but the search for a philosopher-king. That phrase comes from Plato, whose words are found in Book V of *The Republic:* "Until philosophers are kings, or the kings and-princes of this world have the spirit and power of philosophy, and political greatness and wisdom meet in one, and those commoner natures who pursue either to the exclusion of the other are compelled to stand aside, cities will never have rest from their evils—no, nor the human race, as I believe—and then only will this our State have a possibility of life and behold the light of day." Gorgeous rhetoric, but a baneful idea.

It reads like a self-evident truth—the idea that the human situation would be immensely improved by first creating elaborate and powerful govermental machinery, capable of running society and doing wonderful things for The People, and then finding the wisest and best men to operate this mechanism. But this ancient dream of giving the wisest and best men unlimited political power in order to accomplish social good has nightmare possibilities; the dream goes sour periodically, and the subjects who get it in the neck hope that the next king will be better than his predecessor. The Americans scrapped this machinery, lock, stock, and barrel. Government, they said in effect, is necessary in human society, but unless it is limited and kept under control, government is capable of doing great harm. And human nature is such that, if power situations are deliberately created the worst men will gravitate toward them, and such good men as are given arbitrary power will tend to be corrupted by it. Therefore, keep government limited to the administration of justice and the defense of life and property and you deprive it of its propensity for evil. Each man will then be free in society to realize his highest potential.

This is a fundamental point; let me restate it: Followers of the philosopher-king idea will try to construct a political system in which benevolent men, when they are given the power, can do the most good. The champions of political liberty, on the other hand, will try to keep government limited and its powers dispersed in order that unregenerate men will have little opportunity to do harm. The European political tradition, generally speaking, has embraced the first of these two alternatives—more or less gingerly. Modern collectivism seizes powerfully on this first alternative. The politics of collectivism is based squarely on the thesis that the State is the most effective social device for accomplishing positive good. Collectivism is doubly in error here; its first error is the notion that good can be mass-produced, and its second, the delusion that good can be mass-produced by coercion—for the State is society's legal agency of coercion. Evil can be mass-produced; unquestionably. Soviet policy in the 1930s deliberately caused a famine in the Ukraine, resulting in the death of millions of Kulaks. Ruinous wars, resulting from careless or criminal policies of rulers, issue in mass slaughter and destruction. Examples of this kind might be multiplied and lesser instances cited; evil can be, has been, and is being mass-produced. But good is accomplished on a person-to-person basis, slowly and with infinite pains. A man may be downgraded without his acquiescence, and even against his will; but a man becomes better—more skillful, more learned, morally better—only if he wills to become better. A government, to the extent that it maintains the peace and order of the community, enforces the rules of fair play and prevents people from interfering with or injuring one another, provides a neutral base from which men may seek to improve and upgrade themselves. But if government itself seeks to be their tutor, seeks to organize political life around benevolence rather than justice, harm is bound to result in the end no matter how benevolent the intentions of those who set the machinery in motion. Government, by its nature—its ultimate resource is legalized coercion—simply cannot be an instrument for the accomplishment of positive good. Government performs a unique and indispensable role in society if it can prevent injury, or provide just redress when injury has been committed.

The first choice we must make in politics—as to the scope of government—will depend upon our estimate of the nature of man, and our judgment as to what power does to him. If we are optimists and utopians we think in terms of erecting large and powerful structures of government and putting wise and good men in charge, in order to extend benefits to all. On the other hand, if we are realistic about human nature, we will want to limit the governmental machinery in order to forestall evil men from snatching control of it and doing great harm. As Jefferson said in the Kentucky Resolutions (1798): "When it comes to questions of power let no more be heard of the goodness of man, but bind him down from mischief by the chains of the Constitution."

So much then, for the moment, on the primordial political question: What shall be the extent of rule?

The second question has to do with the choice of personnel. Once you decide to limit government to policing functions, how do you go about selecting men for the jobs? Four such devices are available. The first is determination by bloodline. If your father is king, you'll be king when he dies, and your son will rule in your place, and so down the line. The second device is aristocracy, where a few families comprise the ruling caste, as in Venice. The third is called sortilege, determination by lot, drawing straws—used for a considerable period in Athens to choose judges. The fourth form is the one that seems natural to us: Impose a few qualifications for the privilege of voting, and then let the voters by balloting freely choose their representatives; the candidate who gets the majority of votes being declared the winner. This is the proper place to use majority rule, in dealing with the second of the two main political questions.

There are two distinct kinds of knowledge that we need to have. On the one hand, we want to know the plain truth of things, and we go about gaining this kind of knowledge by reasoning and experimentation, primarily. This we can do by ourselves, or in a classroom, or laboratory. The second kind of knowledge we want is information about other people's opinions and preferences. If we want to know whether people prefer Brand X to Brand Y, there is only one way to find out: ask them. Take an opinion poll. Both methods of gaining knowledge are valid, each within its own domain; but we should not confuse the categories.

The primary question: What shall be the extent of rule? can be answered or resolved on the basis of intellectual and moral criteria only—not by counting noses. No scientist would suggest that the validity of the germ theory of disease, for example, should be determined by an opinion poll; and similar considerations apply to disputed questions in history, psychology, mathematics, and elsewhere. There is no difference of opinion on this score; every scholar agrees that disputes in his field are to be settled by laboratory experiments, by field tests, or by reason and logic—in short, by weighing the relevant evidence.

The only exception is in this sector of political science. But even here, every scholar leaves himself a loophole. Ask the person who tells us that majority rule should reign everywhere if he believes that the majority in this country should decide for everyone what church we should all be forced to join. He will answer in the negative, and in disavowing this logical inference from his position he has implicitly admitted that the majority rule idea should not be permitted to upset certain principles—the principle of religious liberty, in this instance. In so doing he also acknowledges, in a sort of left-handed fashion, that majority rule is not itself a principle. Majority rule is a mere device. It is a means for accomplishing certain ends, but not others. So when someone says to us, "Don't you believe in majority rule?" we must render the question intelligible, as follows: "Do I believe in majority rule *to do what?*"

Let me, at this point, draw a distinction between "majority" and a term I have deliberately refrained from using, "consensus." A majority emerges and is recognized after a deliberate act of counting noses; but there is a consensus on basic questions, whether anyone takes a tally or not. Every society is built upon the common acceptance of certain axioms and premises by which its citizens interpret existence and affirm the meaning life has in their culture. These postulates, by and large, are taken for granted, being in the realm of "what every man knows. . . ." Everybody knows, for instance, that murder and theft are wrong, although perhaps only the philosophically minded have tried to figure out the reasons why. Members of a given society share other convictions—often below the level of awareness—and, taken together these bedrock assumptions and acceptances constitute that society's consensus. No one, at any time or place, deliberately created this consensus. A majority, on the other hand, *is* willed and shaped by conscious effort.

On certain fundamental matters, majority and consensus virtually coincide. Ninety-nine and forty-four hundredths percent of the members of a civilized society believe that murder is evil. But if some one were now to declare that murder is evil merely because a majority of citizens say so, he would be told that this puts the cart before the horse; murder is wrong per se, and the consensus acknowledges this fact. There was a consensus against murder all the time and, really, we knew this even before the count was taken.

Our language contains many "imposter terms"—to use old Jeremy Bentham's label—and the jargon of politics is particularly rich in examples. "The People" is one example of an imposter term. People obviously exist, but "The People" is a fiction introduced into a discussion to mislead. So whenever you hear anyone orating about "The People," put your hand on your wallet. Likewise, when someone sounds off about "The Public" or "The Majority." "Majority," as mentioned earlier, is a politician's or a liberal's word for "minority." A so-called majority is often nothing more than a numerical minority manufactured and manipulated by a small group of determined and unscrupulous men. Majorities for or against this or that measure are often manufactured at will. This procedure goes on today and it has been going on for a long time.

The philosopher, according to an old joke, is like a blind man in a dark room looking for a black cat that isn't there; but the theologian, so the story goes, is one who finds the cat! The people of Europe searched in vain for a philosopher-king, but never found him; we of the modern world have found our philosopher-king, and his name is The People, expressing itself through majority rule.

Government, in this view, is identified with The People; and when this belief is accepted, any constitutional, legal or moral device designed to limit government is regarded as an affront to The People, an impediment to majority rule. Such a view is fatal to liberty and to peace.

Whenever a society subordinates all if its principles to the expedient of majority rule it winds up with a political arrangement in which the winner takes all; and the politics of winner-take-all results in a society with a permanent body of second-class citizens, a servile society. If a majority of the voters, 51 percent, controls the whole society, then the 49 percent who lose the election are prevented from exercising their full citizenship rights. I do not mean to say that the losers are completely deprived of their rights, for this is not the case; but the losers—merely by coming out second best in an election—no longer have the same rights as the victors. Some rights remain, but there is no longer equality of rights, and this is the critical point.

An illustration may make this clearer, an illustration from the field of religion, where the old principle of equality of rights is still pretty much intact. Suppose that my denomination, Congregationalism, were to grow and grow until, numerically, we were to constitute a majority of the electorate. Then suppose we decided to play the game of winner-take-all politics. (We once did, as a matter of fact, and kept on doing so, in Massachusetts, until 1833.) We would win a national election and use the fact of victory at the polls to "establish" our denomination. Now that we are "established" we are able to levy taxes on Methodists, Baptists, Catholics, and Holy Rollers, forcing them to contribute to our support. We would not, of course close the doors of their churches, nor forbid them to attend services whenever they chose. All we'd do is deprive them of part of their income and property, and then we'd use *their* income and *their* property to promulgate *our* doctrines. If 10 or 15 percent of *their* income is being spent by us to further *our* purposes, it's obvious that they have that much less money to spend on their own programs.

Now, money is not everything in religion, but it is something. It takes money to build churches and maintain them; it takes money to train and support ministers; it takes money to print hymn books and text books and send out missionaries, and so on. And it is obvious that other religious programs will suffer to the extent that we force people to pay for *our* program. There is a sense in which people are still free to practice their religion, but they are not *fully* free to practice it; religious liberty has been impaired. Most people would say, as a matter of fact, that the society I have conjured up in my illustration does not have religious liberty. And anyone who argued—in defense of this arrangement—that the Methodists and Baptists shouldn't complain, but rather should work toward becoming a majority so that they too could operate a racket, would be hooted down, and properly so. The believer in religious liberty will not settle for an ecclesiastical arrangement which invariably puts minority religions at a disadvantage; he wants full freedom for all. Nor will the believer in political liberty settle for a theory which contemplates a permanent category of second-class citizenship as an intrinsic part of its operation. And yet this is prcisely what present day liberals stand for; this is what they offer us as the latest thing in politics and morals.

No majority had the right, under our constitutional system, to impose its religion on any minority, or impair its freedom of utterance, or deprive it of property. But under the new dispensation "The Majority" is almighty. All it has to do is gain control of government and then it has a legal cloak behind which an actual numerical minority of the nation uses the governmental machinery to work its will on the rest of the society. According to the theory of majority rule, the governmental machinery is always "up for grabs" for such a purpose.

Collectivist regimes act as if the apparatus of government were the private property of officeholders, through which these men exercise their virtual ownership of a country, and their power over the lives of the citizenry. The excuse offered is that "we are doing it to ourselves." What a misuse of language this is! If Methodists are doing it to Baptists, or Congregationalists to Presbyterians, it is obvious that some people are doing something to other people; "we" aren't doing it to "ourselves." The "we" who are dong it aren't the same people as the "ourselves" to whom it is done.

Those who put their trust in majoritarianism proclaim that there is no other test of the goodness of a law than its ability to muster the might of the majority behind it. Any law that has majority support is a good law, by definition, and there is no other test. By the same token, government's role is to perform whatever services a majority demands of it, and short of killing the goose, the majority is entitled to all the golden eggs it can get.

No one can read our Constitution without concluding that the people who wrote it wanted their government severly limited; the words "no" and "not" employed in restraint of governmental power occur 24 times in the first seven articles of the Constitution and 22 more times in the Bill of Rights. Why this distrust, and what was their intention? These men understood the necessity of the police power in a society. But they recognized its potential danger, as well, and so they designed the machinery for keeping their government limited to the performance of police functions. The police power is, ideally, competent to maintain the peace and order of the community, which is what the policing of a society means. If the police power, which is a major function of government, is limited to policing, then the society is free; the public sector is small and well-defined, the private sector is large enough to give peaceful people plenty of elbow room.

The Constitution designed a federal republic with territorial representation in the Senate, and numerical representation in the House. It is improper to refer to the government in Washington as "the federal government;" it is the *national* government. The federal structure is comprised of the national government plus the governments of the sovereign states. Government—to repeat—is *the* power structure of society, and federalism limits power by dividing it between the nation and its component states. The federal structure deals with the problem of power in much the same way as a Gothic cathedral handles architectural stresses. The enormous weight of the roof of one of these medieval structures presses outward against the walls and would level them, except for the flying buttresses which exert an equal pressure inward to maintain the building in a dynamic equilibrium. A national government tends to extend its sway over a whole nation unless its centrifugal force is countered by the centripetal force exerted by the states and the congressional districts.

The structural complexity of the American system of government makes sense if we understand the premises of those who created it. They were concerned to limit and cramp the style of government in order to hamstring the proven capacity of men in power to do evil. The rather awkward machinery they put together may offend against elegance, but it serves admirably the purpose for which it was designed. It is not, however, an efficient, streamlined, political mechanism, such as would be erected by those who believe government should be unfettered and strengthened in order to give the wise men who wield its power increased opportunity for doing good. This approach was repudiated in the Constitution, by some of the most sophisticated yet wisest political thinking on record.

The very structure of constitutional government, then, reflects a philosophy of man; the political machinery itself disperses power and thus limits it.

The free society, or the system of liberty, has as a counterpart the ideal of the Rule of Law; or, as we sometimes say, a government of laws and not of men. Freedom means, among other things, equality before the law, and to insure equal treatment for all citizens the law must meet certain tests. There are, to put it briefly, five earmarks of good law. In the first place, a good law makes no pretensions to perfection. No human laws are in fact perfect, and the attempts of some to apply their "perfect" laws to imperfect human beings have been disastrous. A good law will take human shortcomings into account; it will reflect our limited understanding and sinful nature.

In the second place, a good law will be written so as to correspond to what the eighteenth century referred to as the Higher Law. A good law, in other words, will not violate our ethical code; it will not try to supplant morality with mere legality; it will not try to legislate morality.

A third feature of a good law is generality. Everyone should be equal before the bar of justice, and so a good law is one which applies to all men alike and without exception. It does not specify or single out any person or class. Men are different in several important ways; some are bright and some dull; some are rich, others are poor. There are differences of nationality, color, and religion; there are employers and employees, and so on. These are important distinctions and classifications—but not before the law. The law should be blind to such differences, and any law which is general, applying to one man as to all cannot have much wrong with it.

Besides being imperfect, moral, and general, a good law is conditional; it has an "iffy" quality about it. It says, *if* you steal, or *if* you defraud, or *if* you drive on the left side of the road, you will be punished. A good law takes the side of the negative, saying "Don't," or "Thou shalt not." This means that it is theoretically possible for a man to negotiate life without adversely encountering the law, provided he sticks to the positive. The fifth and final point in this abbreviated list is something like the first; a good law reflects the customs and habits of a people—otherwise it is an attempt to reform them by law, and reformist law is bad law.

CHAPTER 13

Equality: Which Kind?

IN THE SERMON ON THE MOUNT, JESUS STRESSES GOD'S IMPAR-
tiality: "He maketh his sun to rise on the evil and the good, and
sendeth rain on the just and the unjust." (Matthew 5:45) "God is
no respecter of persons," Peter is recorded as saying (Acts 10:34);
or, "God has no favorites," as the New English Bible translates the
passage. In Christ, says Paul, "there is neither Greek, nor Jew,
circumcision nor uncircumcision, Barbarian, Scythian, bond nor
free." (Colossians 3:11) Ideas such as these will seep into secular
affairs and find embodiment in the institutions of everyday life—
in customs, conventions, and laws. Justice will be the ideal of such
a society. Christian magistracy, as a working counterpart to the
theological doctrine of God's impartiality, will seek to dispense an
even-handed justice to all men. Ideally, there will not be one law
for the rich and another for the poor, one for the powerful and
another for the weak; there will be one law for all men alike
because all men are one in God. The idea of the rule of law
emerges naturally in a Christian culture, whereas a society divided
into castes would find no theological sanction in Christian doctrine. A caste-ridden society justifies these unbridgeable caste divisions between men on the grounds that some men are now being
punished for misdemeanors in a previous existence while others
are being rewarded for good behavior.

Plato, in the Third Book of his *Republic* contrives a myth,
calling it an "opportune falsehood" and a "noble lie," in order to

justify inequality between the ranks of men and make them contented with their station in life.

> While all of you in the city are brothers, we will say in our tale, yet God in fashioning those of you who are fitted to hold rule mingled gold in their generation, for which reason they are the most precious—but in the helpers silver, and iron and brass in the farmers and other craftsmen. And as you are all akin, though for the most part you will breed after your kinds, it may sometimes happen that a golden father would beget a silver son and that a golden offspring would come from a silver sire and that the rest would in like manner be born of one another. So that the first and chief injunction that the god lays upon the rulers is that of nothing else are they to be such careful guardians and so intently observant as of the intermixture of these metals in the souls of their offspring, and if sons are born to them with an infusion of brass or iron they shall by no means give way to pity in their treatment of them, but shall assign to each the status due to his nature and thrust them out among the artisans or the farmers. And again, if from these there are born sons with unexpected gold or silver in their composition they shall honor such and bid them go up higher, some to the office of guardian, some to the assistantship, alleging that there is an oracle that the state shall then be overthrown when the man of iron or brass is its guardian. Do you see any way of getting them to believe this tale?
>
> No, not these themselves, he said, but I do their sons and successors and the rest of mankind who come after.
>
> Well, said I, even that would have a good effect in making them more inclined to care for the state and one another.

Aristotle had a place for slavery in his political scheme. It is affirmed by some, he writes in Book I of his *Politics*, "that the rule of a master over slaves is contrary to nature, and that the distinction between slave and freeman exists by law only, and not by nature; and being an interference with nature is therefore unjust." Is there, Aristotle continues, "any one thus intended by nature to be a slave, and for whom such a condition is expedient and right, or rather is not all slavery a violation of nature?"

"There is no difficulty in answering this question," Aristotle continues, "on grounds of both reason and of fact. For that some should rule and others be ruled is a thing, not only necessary, but expedient; from the hour of their birth, some are marked out for subjection, others for rule. . . . It is clear, then, that some men are by nature free, and others slaves, and that for these latter slavery is both expedient and right."

The ideal of equality before the law does not fit either the Platonic or the Aristotelian mold; the metaphysics of Christianity, however, does provide a soil in which personall liberty can take root. Of all the world's great cultures, it is only in Christendom that liberty is taken for granted; personal liberty is the exception everywhere else.

The great political battles of the modern world are associated with certain key words; words like liberty, equality, security, peace, solidarity, fraternity. The watchwords of the French Revolution, as you recall, were "Liberty, Equality, Fraternity." Talleyrand declared that he had heard so much talk about fraternity that if he had a brother he'd call him cousin!

The economist and the political scientist in their discussions have no choice but to use common, everyday words. The chemist says H_2O instead of water, and $NaCl$ instead of salt; the physicist and the mathematician use the language of numbers and symbols. But social philosophers have to use words like liberty, equality, and justice—which are in everyday use by the man in the street —so that even the experts have difficulty in agreeing among themselves as to the precise meaning and implication of these words; even if they are well intentioned—and some are not. In the George Orwell world of *1984* the language had become so debased that people were moved by such paradoxical slogans as "Freedom is Slavery," and "War is Peace."

The word "equality" has never figured as a party label, although the name has been borrowed by one or two utopian movements. "Created equal" is a phrase in our Declaration, and the misuse of the idea of equality in today's political contests demands that we clarify the contradictory ways in which the word is used. I've already cited the war cry of the French Revolutionaries, who demanded equality—in the sense of social leveling—as one of their goals. Adam Smith was no friend of the French Revolution; to the contrary, he was in the sturdy Scotch, Whig tradition. We know him best for his *Wealth of Nations*, published in 1776. In this

work, Adam Smith praised what he called "the liberal plan of
equality, liberty, and justice." It is evident from the context that
Smith believed that these three concepts—equality, liberty, and
justice—belong together and reinforce each other. It is equally
obvious that Adam Smith means by equality something quite different from what the French *philosophes* meant by the word. Present day liberalism, with its emphasis on the political management
of the economy and its professed concern for economic leveling
—equality in the sense of economic parity—may be traced directly
to the French Revolution. It has parted company with Smith and
the free economy.

Adam Smith was part of an older tradition. The old-fashioned
Whigs were the precursors of the classical liberals, and their present day counterparts are certain kinds of conservatives and certain kinds of libertarians. People of this persuasion also use the
term equality, but they give the term a meaning quite the opposite
of the French and modern liberal usage. For them, equality is the
Rule of Law, equality before the bar of justice, a government of
laws not of men. The old Whigs and Liberals confronted a society
of privilege. Engish society well into the eighteenth century—and
the society of much of Europe as well—was politically stratified
into orders of rank, caste, class, and privilege.

At the top were royalty and the aristocracy; at the bottom were
the peasants and serfs. In between were the independent yeomen,
the artisans, merchants, and those born into the servant class. The
stratification was not as rigid as the divisions in Indian society, but
nevertheless this was a society of status where people were locked
into their station in life generation after generation. You've heard
the couplet: "God bless the squire and all his relations, and keep
us in our proper stations." This inequitable social arrangement was
reinforced by a set of taboos and, when need be, was enforced by
the police power. This was a society of status, of fixed relationships; to be replaced, in the West, by a society of contract.

Hinduism provides a contemporary example of a system of
privilege. The highest caste in Indian society is the Brahman caste;
the lowest caste is the Sudra. In between are the Kshatriya and
Vaisya castes—warriors and merchants, respectively; outside the
caste system altogether are the Untouchables. Men are born into
a given caste, and that is where they stay; that's where their

ancestors were, and that's where their descendants will be. There is no ladder leading from one level in this society to any of the others. This is the system of privilege—in contrast to a society built on the system of liberty.

The liberating movement in England—part of the Puritan and Whig heritage, plus the efforts of men like Locke, Hume, Burke, and Smith—challenged the system of privilege with a set of ideas, among them the idea of equality. The idea of equality—in the political sense—means simply: no arbitrary, politically created and enforced privilege.

On this continent, the writers of our Declaration believed it axiomatic that "all men are created equal." They did not say *"are* equal," or *"born* equal,"—which would deny the obvious; they said *"created* equal." Now, the created part of a man is his soul— in terms of metaphysics—and the souls of all men are precious in God's sight whatever the individual's outer circumstances. Equality before the law appeared to follow from this premise—the idea of one law alike for all men because all men are one in their essential humanness. But right there the likeness ceased; human beings are different and unequal in every other way. Some, thank God, are women! Equality before the law is political liberty viewed from a different perspective; it is also justice, a regime under which no man and no order of men is granted a political license by the State to use other men as their tools or have any other legal advantage over them. Given this framework in a society, the economic order will automatically be free market, or capitalism. We are speaking now of the idea of equality in a political context. Later I shall return to the opposing concept of economic equality, which is incompatible with limited government and the free market. Political equality is the system of liberty, and its leading features are set forth in Jefferson's First Inaugural Address:

> Equal and exact justice to all men, of whatever state or persuasion, religious or political; peace, commerce, and honest friendship with all nations,—entangling alliances with none; the support of the State governments in all their rights, as the most competent administrations for our domestic concerns, and the surest bulwarks against anti-republican tenden-

cies, the preservation of the general government in its whole constitutional vigour, as the sheet anchor of our peace at home and safety abroad; . . . freedom of religion; freedom of the press; freedom of person under the protection of the habeas corpus; and trial by juries impartially selected,—these principles form the bright constellation which has gone before us, and guided our steps through an age of revolution and reformation.

This "liberal plan of equality, liberty, and justice" was central to classical liberalism. It was never applied 100 percent, but what was the result of a partial application of this idea? The results of abolishing political privilege in Europe and starting to organize a no-privilege society were so beneficial that even the enemies of liberty pause to pay tribute. R. H. Tawney was one of the most gifted of the English Fabians, an ardent Socialist and redistributionist. His most famous work is *Religion and the Rise of Capitalism*, but in 1931 he wrote a book entitled *Equality*, arguing, in effect, that no one should have two cars so long as any man was unable to afford even one. He wished to take from those who have and give to those who have not, in order to achieve economic equality. But he acknowledged that there was an earlier idea of equality familiar to us from the Declaration of Independence—equal treatment under the law. This is the same thing as political liberty. Political liberty from, say 1800, made the Industrial Revolution possible. Here is Tawney on the resulting benefits which emerged in those early decades:

With the abolition of restrictions on freedom of movement, on the choice of occupations, and on the use of land and capital, imprisoned energies were released from the narrow walls of manor and gild and corporate town, from the downward pressure of class status, and from the heavy hand of authoritarian governments, to unite in new forms of association, and by means of them to raise the towering structure of industrial civilization. It was not only in the stimulus which it supplied to the mobilization of economic power that the movement which leveled legal privilege revealed its magic. Its effect as an agent of social emancipation was not less profound. Few principles have so splendid a record of humanitar-

ian achievement. . . Slavery and serfdom had survived the
exhortations of the Christian Church, the reforms of enlightened despots, and the protests of humanitarian philosophers
from Seneca to Voltaire. Before the new spirit, and the practical exigencies of which it was the expression, they disappeared, except from dark backwaters, in three generations.
. . It turned [the peasant] from a beast of burden into a human
being. It determined that, when science should be invoked to
increase the output of the soil, its cultivator, not an absentee
owner, should reap the fruits. The principle which released
him he described as equality, and the destruction of privilege,
democracy, the victory of plain people . . . [It was] the end
of institutions which had made rich men tyrants and poor men
slaves.[1]

Walter Lippmann wrote *The Good Society* in 1937. Looking
back at the nineteenth century he called it "the great century of
human emancipation." "In that period," he continued, "chattel
slavery and serfdom, the subjection of women, the patriarchal
domination of children, caste and legalized class privileges, the
exploitation of backward peoples, autocracy in government, the
disfranchisement of the masses and their compulsory illiteracy,
official intolerance and legalized bigotry, were outlawed in the
human conscience, and in a very substantial degree they were
abolished in fact."[2]

All these good things are a result of the effort which began two
centuries ago to put the system of liberty—equal rights before the
law—into practice. But, of course, when men are free politically
there will be, inevitably, economic inequalities. There will continue to be rich and poor, as there have been in every society since
history began, but with this difference: the wealthy will be chosen
by the daily balloting of their peers in the market place, and the
wealthy won't necessarily be the powerful, nor will the poor necessarily be the weak. The Beatles are wealthy, but there is no correlation between their millions and any political power they have.

At this point let us introduce the word "power." As the term is
used in a social context, power means government. There is but
one power structure in a society, and that is the government of that

1. Tawney, *Equality*, pp. 119, 120, 121.
2. Lippman, *The Good Society*, pp. 192–3.

society. Government is *the* power structure. Today's sociologists
speak of "community power structures," when referring to such
things as business, social, and religious groups. Thus the fashion
setter in your local country club would be part of the power structure—in the vocabulary of certain sociologists. Well, this is to use
the word power in a metaphorical sense. Government possesses a
one-of-a-kind power in society; only government can mobilize the
police, the armies, the navies; only government can draft a young
man to serve in Vietnam; only government can tax, and so on. The
largest corporation in the land cannot force me to buy one of its
products or work for it; I can ignore General Motors, but no one
who chooses to live within these 50 states can ignore the real
power structure—which is the political agency, government.

The system of privilege, of which I gave two illustrations—
Hindu society and the older European society—ties wealth and
power together. The wealth enjoyed by the Dukes of Bedford, for
example, is not a measure of the services the family currently
renders to consumers, not at all; the wealth of the Bedfords is a
function of the political power conferred on the family centuries
ago. But the system of liberty—meaning, political equality and
equal treatment under the laws—dissociates power and wealth. In
New York State our multi-millionaire governor and I have one
vote apiece; if we park overtime we pay the same fine; there is not
one law for a Rockefeller and another for me; in theory, the law
recognizes neither rich nor poor. Now, I know what normal human frailities do to human ideals, and that there will be injustice
till the end of time. But a theory which does not have injustice as
a built-in feature of its operation is miles ahead of one which does.
The system of privilege is intrinsically unjust; the system of liberty
is just, in theory. And it is this latter system which seeks to limit
political power, government, to the function of keeping the peace
—as peacekeeping is spelled out in Whig and classical liberal
theory—and further, the system of liberty dissociates accumula-
tions of wealth from abuses of political power.

The weakening of the hold of the system of privilege in England
and America after Adam Smith and the Declaration of Independence, the rise of classical liberalism, the Industrial Revolution—
these things in combination resulted in the beneficient changes
cited earlier from the writings of Tawney and Lippmann. Political

liberty expanded, and there was increasing religious freedom. The conditions of life eased, and there was more material abundance for everyone. Mortality rates declined and health improved. But paradoxically, discontent also increased. A society increasingly free and prosperous produced a class of malcontents who ought to destroy that society, and they gained a hearing during the past century while the freest nations ever known to history—France, Germany, England, and America—were losing the spontaneous loyalty of significant numbers of their citizens. Ever since the middle of the eighteenth century the peoples of the West had been led to expect a heaven on earth—Utopia—as soon as certain old institutions were unseated and society reorganized. Democratic revolutions occurred, and social conditions became much more tolerable, but because they were not perfect they came to be regarded as *in*tolerable!

It is a peculiar thing about social evils that in their grossest forms they may last for centuries and be accepted by the masses as part of fate, rather than as curable evils. But when circumstances improve to a certain degree, that is to say, when people move up a notch or two out of poverty, filth, degradation, and disease and the means of further improvement are in sight, then circumstances come to seem unbearable. Men in the nineteenth and twentieth centuries refused to credit "the liberal plan of equality, justice, and liberty" for such improvements as they began to enjoy; instead they condemned the system of liberty for not having completed their liberation. It is as if a totally paralyzed person undertook a treatment which restored his powers of movement except for one limb; and instead of praising the treatment for what it had accomplished, blamed it for his game leg!

The system of political liberty—limited government and the free market—aimed at equality before the law and necessarily resulted in inequalities in material goods. Everybody was levered above the subsistence level, and many went from rags to riches. But nearly everyone thought he deserved better, and the political movements of the modern world reflect this mood. In the new dispensation—as the twentieth century dawned—economic inequalities came to be regarded as the intolerable bane of modern life, which it is the function of government to overcome. With the result that the political slogans of the twentieth century have played variations on the theme of soak the rich and subsidize the poor; take from some and give to others—redistribution. Present day politics is based on the redistributionist principle: taxes for all, subsidies for the few. Its alleged purpose is to elevate the low income groups by depressing the wealthy. This social leveling is supposed to bring about economic equality—or a close approximation thereto: "From each according to ability, to each according to need"—as need is determined by the politically powerful.

A certain well-known contemporary social philosopher phrases the principle of redistributionism as follows: "We are going to try to take all of the money that we think is unnecessarily being spent and take it from the 'haves' and give it to the 'have nots' that need it so much."

Several years before this statement by ex-President Johnson, a theologian of considerable reputation, Nels Ferre, expressed the same sentiments, but gave them a religious flavor: "All property is God's for the common good. It belongs, therefore, first of all to God and then equally to society and the individual. When the individual has what the society needs and can profitably use, it is not his, but belongs to a society, by divine right."[3]

Now, Dr. Ferre is a kindly and well-disposed man, almost a caricature of an other-worldly professor; benevolence oozes from his every pore. But unfortunately he, like others of his kind, is unable to distinguish a bucket of water from a pail of gasoline. Even if such a man is your best friend he's a dangerous person to have around when your house catches fire.

The rage for redistribution is upon us, and we might multiply statements similar to the ones I have quoted from Mr. Johnson and Dr. Ferre. Those who espouse this viewpoint hold the utterly mistaken notion that the distribution of rewards in a free market society, or capitalism, is analogous to the parceling out of loot to members of a robber gang, or the division of spoils after a pirate expedition. Actually, these things are as unlike as night and day; there is no comparison between them. In the free economy, a man is rewarded to the degree that he pleases consumers. His offerings of goods and services are judged by his peers—every one of whom is a consumer—in terms of their usefulness. If customers aren't pleased, they don't buy; if they are greatly pleased they buy a lot. The market does not assess the real worth of a man and reward

3. Ferre, *Christianity and Society*, p. 226.

him accordingly; passing such a judgment is God's role. No group
of Americans got together and decided, as a public act, to make
Bing Crosby rich merely because he's a nice guy; they just happened to like his voice and they paid good money to hear him sing.
The sole aim was the individual enjoyment of his music, but the
common pursuit of this aim by many people produced a pleasant
dividend for Mr. Crosby. This is the free market in operation; this
is the system of liberty. Government is not involved here except
to provide a framework of law and order. Government has nothing
to do with a man's economic status under the system of liberty;
his level of economic well-being is strictly a measure of his success
at pleasing consumers. There is more, much more, to life than this,
of course; but if the integrity of the market is not respected, consumer choice is impaired and some people are given a license to
foist their values on others. Permit this kind of poison to infect our
economic relationships and our ability to resist it anywhere else
is seriously weakened.

If we do not like the system of liberty (as many of our contemporaries do not), and are shopping around for alternatives, what
choices are open to us? At first thought we might suggest that we
have a choice between Socialism, Communism, the Middle Way
of Sweden, the Great Society of the United States of America and
several other isms. Now there are differences between these several ways of organizing society, and some of these differences may
be worth fighting for; but we should not overlook what every one
of these alternatives has in common. Every alternative to the
market economy and the system of liberty—when carried to its
logical conclusion—relates a man's economic status to his political
power; the higher he is on the political ladder the greater his
opportunities for acquiring wealth. Those without political power,
those below the bottom rung, are condemned to poverty—unless
they acquire a patron, or resort to predation.

There is only one genuine alternative to the system of liberty,
and that is the system of privilege. The privilege arrangement may
be pretty well concealed in contemporary ideologies, and there are
great differences between these ideologies and the old aristocratic
regimes. But all these superficially different systems have this element in common—they make economic status a function of political power.

To give a working example of economic status as a function of political power, go back to 1066 and the Battle of Hastings. William of Normandy had a claim, of sorts, to the English throne, a claim which he validated by beating Harold and then conquering the rest of the island. Having established his overlordship of England he parceled out pieces of the island to his followers as payment for their services. In the words of historian Arthur Bryant, "William the Conqueror kept a fifth of the land for himself and gave one-quarter to the Church. The remainder, save for an insignificant fraction, was given to 170 Norman and French followers —nearly half to ten men."[4] This redistribution of England's territory was, of course, at the expense of the Anglo-Saxon residents, who were displaced to make room for the new owners. The new owners of England, from William on down, were the rulers of England; ownership was the complement of their rulership, and the wealth they accumulated sprang from their power and their feudal holdings.

This was a fine system—from the Norman viewpoint; but the Anglo-Saxon reduced to serfdom viewed the matter quite differently. It was obvious to the serf and the peasant that the reason why they had so little land was because the Normans had so much and, because wealth flowed from holdings of land, the Anglo-Saxons reasoned correctly that they were poor because the Normans were rich. It is always so under a system of privilege, whether the outward trappings of the despotism are monarchical, democratic, or bear the earmarks of *1984*.

Economic inequalities cannot be overcome by political means —by coercive redistribution—without establishing political inequalities. Every form of political redistributionism widens power differentials in society; officeholders have more power, citizens less; political contests become more intense, because control and dispersal of great amounts of wealth is at stake. Every alternative to the market economy—call it socialism, or communism, or fascism, or whatever—concentrates power over the life and livelihood of the many in the hands of a few. Now, it is an axiom of politics that power tends to corrupt the man who wields it. The only man whom power would not corrupt is the kind of man who would not accept it in the first place. The principle of equality before the law is discarded, being incompatible with any form of

4. Bryant, *Story of England*, Vol. I, p. 164.

the planned economy, and, as in the George Orwell satire, some men become more equal than others. We head back toward the Old Regime—the system of privilege.

People in our time have accepted political inequality and the enchancement of power differentials in society because they believed that this inordinate power, under popular sovereignty, would reduce economic inequalities. But power obeys its own laws, and one of its basic laws—exemplified by political power wherever it has existed and whatever form it assumes—is *the use of political power to enhance the economic well-being of officeholders and their friends,* at the expense of the rest of the nation. Albert Jay Nock designated this perversion of government as The State, a two-headed monster comprising, on the one hand, those who wield political power—officeholders—and on the other, their friends who derive economic advantage for themselves from a wrongful exercise of political power. "Votes and taxes for all; subsidies for us and our friends," is the rationale. Every state tends to create the means of its own support—comprising citizens and pressure groups who realize their dependence on the state for such economic advantages as they enjoy. The Court at Versailles was the symbol of this under the Old Regime; the symbol in our time is a deep freeze, a vicuña coat, a television set, the relief racket, or what have you. Not to mention Billie Sol Estes, Bobby Baker, and other enterprising young men.

One of our genuine contemporary philosophers is Joseph Wood Krutch, who writes in a recent essay: "When men cannot compete for wealth they compete for position, for authority, for influence in the right places. When they cannot own a palace, four automobiles, and ten servants, they manage to get themselves appointed to jobs in connection with which these things are assigned them. More dreadful still, when these same men find themselves no longer required to pay the common man to do their work for them, they quickly discover that when the profit motive has been abolished, the fear motive affords a very handy substitute."[5]

Those of you who are fans of Lewis Carroll will remember his poem, "The Hunting of the Snark." Every time the hunters closed in on their quarry the snark turned out to be a boojum! Every time a determined group of people have concentrated power in a cen-

5. Krutch, *If You Don't Mind My Saying So,* pp. 17–18.

tral government to carry out their program, the power they have set up gets out of hand. The classic example of this is the French Revolution, which turned and devoured those who had started it. It is not so much that power corrupts, as that power obeys its own laws. Our forebears in the old-fashioned Whig–classical liberal tradition had some awareness of this, so they sought to disperse and contain power. They chose political liberty, in full awareness that in a free society the natural differences among human beings would show up in various ways; there would be economic inequalities as well as inequalities of every other kind, with one important exception—there will be no political inequality. This is political and economic realism, and practicing this realism we live in accordance with the way things are. The alternative is a servile state in which a ruling class enforces equality of poverty on the masses. To embark on a program of economic leveling is like trying to repeal the law of gravity; it won't work, and in the course of trying to make it work we defeat our efforts to attain reasonable goals that are within our reach.

CHAPTER 14

Despotism By Consent

ECONOMICS IS A DISCIPLINE IN ITS OWN RIGHT, ITS TAKE-OFF point being the disparity between the limitless nature of human demands and the scarce means for meeting them. The recognition of this science came late, because the underlying regularities in market phenomena have no opportunity to manifest themselves except under conditions of political liberty. The democratic revolutions of the eighteenth century provided wide margins in several societies for the exercise of individual free choice; regularities in economic affairs began to manifest themselves, and Adam Smith devoted his masterpiece to an explication of them.

A society has political liberty—the men and women who comprise it are free—when its government is properly limited. In an age when freedom is the popular catchword of parties and movements representing every shade of political opinion, the free society has little to fear from the ideologues of despotism who attack liberty on political grounds; the danger is from economic planners. Erosions of liberty, under these conditions, will be an unsought by-product of political efforts to redirect or control the economy. A person who has a sound grasp of economic theory knows that the free economy operating within the proper legal and moral framework has a marvelously intricate set of built-in controls at every stage of production and distribution. The situation is analogous to the human body. Volitional control of the digestion of food or the circulation of blood is impossible, and it would be disastrous if it could be accomplished. It is not needed precisely because these processes are not out of control even though they are not consciously directed.

To the extent that the economic processes of a free society are not understood, to that extent are they exposed to the blundering efforts made by some to bring them under conscious political control. Successful moves in this direction are invariably at the expense of human liberty. The free economy is a label for men and women engaged in manufacturing, buying, and selling the things they choose to manufacture, buy, and sell. Interfering with people's choices at this level of human affairs does, indisputably, curb the liberty of those involved. Furthermore, such political intervention, especially if undertaken on ideological grounds, begins to pick up a momentum which will carry the interventionist pattern far beyond what its instigators intended. The unforeseen consequences, especially the damages, of any given political interference with the economy, provide a needed excuse for another intervention to clean up the problems caused by the preceding one. And the beneficiaries of any intervention constitute a standing invitation to all those left out, to organize themselves and lobby for their fair share of government largess. Ideologically motivated politicians welcome these collisions of interest because each intervention enchances the power of the political apparatus which they manage.

A fully planned economy demands a totalitarian state as an invariable concomitant; a fully free economy is impossible except in a society which limits its government to the protection of life and propety, and the punishment of fraud and injury—as these are defined by law. Actual societies hover somewhere on the spectrum between these two polarities, but they are subject to pressures making for a trend in one direction or the other. We live in a period when the doctrine of popular sovereignty is widely held, and our observable trend toward statism occurs under its auspices. Every society seeks an ultimate sanction for political conduct, and in societies such as ours sovereignty is sought and found in the will of the people. If the majority of folk want something, or if they can be made to appear to want it, that is what they should get; government is a mere instrumentality for whatever majority gains control of it.

As we remarked above, Tocqueville foresaw this trend in democracies and, in 1835, labeled its result "democratic despotism." His disquieting prophecy is worth quoting at some length.

> [The government] covers the surface of society with a network of small complicated rules, minute and uniform, through which the most original minds and the most energetic characters cannot penetrate, to rise above the crowd. The will of man is not shattered, but softened, bent, and guided; men are seldom forced by it to act, but they are constantly restrained from acting. Such power does not destroy, but it prevents existence; it does not tyrannize, but it compresses, enervates, extinguishes, and stupefies a people, till each nation is reduced to nothing better than a flock of timid and industrious animals, of which the government is the shepherd. . . .
>
> Above this race of men stands an immense and tutelary power, which takes upon itself alone to secure their gratifications and to watch over their fate. That power is absolute, minute, regular, provident, and mild. It would be like the authority of a parent if, like that authority, its object was to prepare men for manhood, but it seeks, on the contrary, to keep them in perpetual childhood.
>
> The principle of equality has prepared men for these things; it has predisposed men to endure them and often to look on them as benefits.

How have the United States fared under Tocqueville's melancholy prophecy? The America of a former day was more than a geographical location in the Western hemiphere; it was a symbol for people everywhere of the enduring human quest for a country in which each person might be his own man. Here, people dared to dream, and the American Deam kept "alive, in human history," as Jacques Maritain has put it, "a fraternal recognition of the dignity of man—in other words, the terrestrial hope of men in the Gospel."[1] The Declaration of Independence was once the emblem of this idealism.

During the nineteenth century the defeated and the oppressed looked to America as a land of liberty and justice for all. Multitudes of them came here to find freedom for themselves and their children, and found it, in overflowing measure. It goes without

1. *Reflections on America*, p. 199.

saying that there were frustrations; reality, here as everywhere, fell short of the professed ideal. The expressed aim was equal freedom. In practice, freedom was sometimes betrayed in the treatment of some men by other men, but the idea was never wholly without influence, being inscribed in a basic national document for all to see and many to memorize. The document contains a dangerous ambiguity to be discussed later, which eventually drained away its main strength, but until that happened the Declaration of Independence was a beacon of liberty.

Let us go back and take a look at its origins. The American Revolution was really a revolution prevented, wrote John Adams at the time; the colonists were up in arms against the king's efforts to subvert their rights as men and as Englishmen. They had been fighting for more than a year before the Declaration of Independence was written, by which time it was imperative that the Continental Congress prepare a statement to bring into focus the hitherto uncrystallized thoughts and feelings of the colonists. Such a statement would also have a practical bearing on the war: It would elevate the colonies to a de jure state and thus make it "consistent with European delicacy, for European powers to treat with us, or even receive an Ambassador from us," as Jefferson put it.

Jefferson brought with him into Congress, it was said, "a reputation for literature, science, and a happy talent for composition." Thus Adams replies to a friend who asked him the reason behind the selection of Jefferson as the principal drafter of the Declaration. The story of the framing of this document is properly Jefferson's, and is best told in his own words. The delegates from Virginia to the Continental Congress, he writes, "moved, in obedience to instructions from their constitutents, that the Congress should declare that these United colonies are, and of right ought to be, free and independent states." The date was Friday, June 7, 1776. Some of the colonies, however, "were not yet matured for falling from the parent stem . . . (so) it was thought most prudent to wait a while for them." On June 8, in order to take up the slack occasioned by this necessary ripening period, "a committee was appointed to prepare a Declaration of Independence. The committee were John Adams, Dr. Franklin, Roger Sherman, Robert R. Livingston, and myself. . . . The committee for drawing the Declaration of Independence desired me to do it. It was accordingly done, and being approved by them, I reported it to the House on Friday, the twenty-eighth of June." Several days of debate ensued, closing on the evening of July 4; "the Declaration was reported by the committee, agreed to by the House, and signed by every member present, except Mr. Dickinson."

Jefferson claimed no originality for the ideas he embodied in the Declaration. His purpose as drafter was not, he writes, "to find out new principles, or new arguments, never before thought of, not merely to say things that had never been said before; but to place before mankind the common sense of the subject, in terms so plain and fair as to command their assent. . . . It was intended to be an expression of the American mind." And indeed it was. The basic political ideas embodied in the Declaration—inherent natural rights and consent of the governed—have a long ancestry and were the common coin of eighteenth-century political discussion; and they figured largely in the election day sermons of the New England clergy as well. "The strength of the Declaration was precisely that it said what everyone was thinking," wrote Carl Becker.[2]

Nevertheless, Jefferson must be credited with the originality of phrasing and composition which gave a creative thrust to ideas which had lacked political momentum till that time. He had "the coolness, forecast and capacity," said Lincoln in 1859, "to introduce into a merely revolutionary document an abstract truth applicable to all men and all times, and so to embalm it there that today and in all coming days it shall be a rebuke and a stumbling block to the very harbingers of reappearing tyranny. . . . The principles of Jefferson," he concluded, "are the definitions and axioms of a free society." This was not a unique judgment at the time of its utterance; Lincoln was doing little more than giving voice to the prevailing consensus. Many American reformers and social critics expressed similar sentiments. They were sensitive to social ills and injustices, but they traced them to infractions of the principles laid down in the Declaration—inherent, individual rights, and a limited government set up solely for their protection. Freedom was the remedy they advocated, and they knew that somebody's freedom was being impaired the moment government

2. *The Declaration of Independence*, p. 24.

exceeded its proper limits. It followed that the first reform, on which all others hinged, was to confine government within the boundaries defined in the Declaration. Only so could the rights of all persons be secured.

The philosophy back of the Constitution is substantially the same endowed-rights doctrine that is set forth in the Declaration. And social critics in the early Republic, accepting this doctrine, traced many social evils to the door of government; it was government which either legitimized violations of personal liberty—as in the case of slavery—or sanctioned violations by refusing to enforce the laws which protect person and property against predation. The remedy, they believed, was to cut government back to the limits prescribed in the Declaration—defense of the lives and property of all men alike.

The formation of the thirteen colonies into a federal union did not usher in Utopia. The noble principles of political organization set forth in the Constitution could not of themselves eliminate social evils; no charter alone can do this. But the document did pinpoint some of the evils and it did blueprint a political structure designed to minimize them. A mechanism can do no more; the rest is up to the people who operate it.

It may be reasonably inferred that the Founding Fathers, had they wanted a streamlined government, would have designed one. Instead, they created a political structure in which the national government was to be internally self-governed by three separate but balanced powers, and the several states were to retain their original sovereignty in order to act as a counterpoise to the central authority. The Constitution is most explicit when setting forth what government may *not* do. These men knew from experience the tendency of governments to go off on careers of their own and grow at the expense of popular liberty. And so, realizing that liberty implies limited government, they devised a political instrument to curb governmental action.

But if this was the ideal it must be admitted that the practice fell short, even from the beginning. To cite one example: we set up a no-privilege government—equality before the law, no politically dispensed special favors for some at the expense of others—and the first law of the First Congress (after the motion organizing itself as a body) was a tariff law. Now, whatever else may be said

about a tariff no one can deny that it has the effect of penalizing
certain consumer interests and by the same token advantaging
certain producer interests. It denies to some people the right to
buy in the markets of their choice; i.e., to make any peaceful use
they choose of their resources. And to others this political intervention has the effect of granting a virtual monopoly of certain
markets by excluding foreign competiton, thus forcing customers
to pay a price above the market price which free and fair competition would determine. In short, a tariff enables its beneficiaries to
get something for nothing; it is equivalent to a political subvention
giving some people an income for which no equivalent services are
rendered.

A political principle may be adduced from such a practice: It is
one function of government to intervene in the affairs of men so
as to benefit a segment of the nation at the expense of the nation
as a whole, or to sacrifice a portion of the people so that another
portion may prosper. This was not the kind of government we
thought we were setting up, and although government intervention steadily proliferated during the nineteenth century—each
succeeding intervention being sold as a necessary means of cor-
recting the evils caused by prior interventions—we would still
think of ours as "a government of liberty and justice for all," i.e.,
a government shorn of the power to dispense privilege. As an ideal
we still looked to the equal rights doctrine of the Declaration, and
this doctrine filtered down through popular oratory and literature.
Granted that we didn't practice what we preached, at least we had
here a plumbline of sound principle by which we could measure
our deviation from the norm. But there came a time when we
accepted the deviations as the norm and began to cast about for
a political principle to justify them. When we took this tack, such
a principle was easy to find because it too was enshrined in the
Declaration itself—as a technique—along with the natural rights
philosophy. It was the "consent of the governed" idea.

The consent of the governed idea is an implementing principle,
not a primary one. Deriving the just powers of a government
"from the consent of the governed," as the Declaration does, it is
a natural means of implementing the "self-evident" truths, "that
all men are created equal, that they are endowed by their Creator
with certain unalienable Rights, that among these are Life, Lib-

erty, and the Pursuit of Happiness." This is the primary principle, this axiom about Creator-endowed rights. But when these truths are no longer self-evident, when the belief in God-given rights dies out, leaving "consent of the governed" as the sole political expedient, then the road ahead leads to a kind of despotism. Contemporary despotism will not conform to the pattern of a divine right monarchy, which needs a different sanctioning principle; it will be —in Tocqueville's phrase—"a democratic despotism."

"Consent of the governed" introduces the majoritarian principle into politics. However useful majority rule may be as a device for choosing personnel, it is vicious when it expands into the delusion that the majority has competence in the realm of faith and morals, and has, therefore, a right to rule unrestrained except by prudential and expedient considerations. The right thing to do, politically, is whatever the majority wants done. Consent of the governed, without the restraining influence exerted by the belief in God-given rights—a belief which loosened as religion progressively lost its hold on the modern mind—has led logically, directly, and implacably to totalitarianism and the so-called Peoples' Democracies.

The word "rights" still sounds good in our ears, however, so when a United Nations commission meets to draft a list of things governments should do for "their" people the document is labeled a Covenant on Human Rights. The members of the commission gave the word "rights" a meaning it has never had in American political theory until lately. As collectivists, they believe that paternalistic government should perform certain services for people; people have a "right" to be provided with housing, education, a job, medical care, and so on. "This lengthy catalog of 'rights,' " Russell Kirk observes, "ignores the two essential conditions which are attached to all true rights: first, the capacity of individuals to claim and exercise the alleged right; second, the correspondent duty which is married to every right. . . . If rights are confused thus with desires, the mass of men must feel always that some vast, intangible conspiracy thwarts their attainment of what they are told is their inalienable birthright."[3]

The same reduction of "rights" into "demands" or "goals" is to be found in the recent National Council of Churches' *Report on*

3. *The Conservative Mind*, p. 42.

The Changing Dimensions of Human Rights. "Where formerly
human rights were limited mainly to those political rights which
governments have protected," reads the *Report,* "they now extend
their orbit to include a whole galaxy of social and economic goals
in the attainment of which people look to their democratic, representative governments as instruments." Human "rights" were
once thought of as endowed by God. "Rights" have now been
debased into demands that people may make of the State for
"social and economic goals." The State has no means of its own
for meeting such demands, so, in practice, this concept of "rights
as demands" means the creation of pressure groups to secure
favors from the State for their members at the expense of people
not so organized. This is, of course, a flat denial of the latter's
rights. That a church group should sponsor such a philosophy is
a measure of our intellectual and spiritual decline.

There was a watershed point somewhere along the line, in the
latter part of the nineteenth century. On the far side of it, social
critics harped on the wrongful interventions of government and
urged the recovery of our original principles of liberty and limited
government. On our side of that line, reformers forgot these principles in their preoccupation with the practical difficulties of applying them. The result was the gradual acceptance of the evil
principle that the State exists to dispense economic advantage to
those with political power.

This was spoken of as a new thing, the Cooperative Commonwealth of Socialism, but actually it was the age-old system of
privilege, beguilingly camouflaged, and served up with an almost
universal appeal. The idealists were trapped with the promise of
a more equitable distribution of wealth, the envious were brought
in by the prospect that their betters would be brought low, the very
rich were beguiled by the prospect that no competitors would be
permitted to rise through the ranks and challenge their eminence
(hence the phenomenon of "the millionaire socialist"), the politicians were to be the high priests of the system, the literary men
were provided with the exciting theme of social upheaval, and so
on down the line. Everybody was to be taken care of except the
independent, hard-working man who wanted no more than was
rightfully his, and who desired to live in peace with his neighbor.
Although men of this type were, and probably still are, in a

majority, they were no match for the determined minorities in-
flamed by the new philosophy. They became the forgotten men.

All this could be and was justified as: "democracy," "consent of
the governed," "the greatest happiness for the greatest number,"
and similar slogans—justified without hypocrisy, it must be emphasized, because such ideas as these are not intrinsically bad.
They are, in fact, instrumentally valuable when they work in col-
laboration with religious faith and moral idealism.

Judging by the record of history, man seems to have a natural
propensity to seek a cosmic foundation for his social way of life;
no culture of record has been wholly secular. Men posit a divine
order of reality transcending the natural world which meets the
senses. A relationship to this divine order gives added meaning
and significance to the natural order, and the divine law furnishes
the ethical and esthetic norms by which the different patterns of
behavior in society are coordinated. These norms are believed to
be anchored in the nature of things, discoverable by man, but not
created by him. They exist independently of men's awareness or
interpretation of them, and neither individual persons nor majorities can flout them with impunity.

This is not the place to argue that reality *is* so structured, with
a transcendent order imposing divine claims on the natural and
social orders. It is sufficient to point out that if men are persuaded
that the universe is God's creation they will draw up and attempt
to live by one set of sanctions; in the absence of a belief in God,
they will employ other sanctions. Until modern times men accepted the God concept and attempted to guide their lives by it, with
the result that they believed in the existence of moral norms
rooted in an order beyond human interference. This was the concept of the Natural Law, by virtue of which man was believed to
possess certain inherent rights, such as those catalogued in our
Declaration of Independence. Such a conviction kept the "consent
of the governed" idea in a secondary spot. But man, in recent
generations, has escorted God to the edge of the universe and
bowed Him off. In science, it was believed that modern man had
the means to explore all there was to be known, and by using
scientific knowledge he would gain the power to bend and control
the forces of the universe to do his bidding.

Religious knowledge was discounted as merely subjective and

the realm of which it purported to tell, illusory. With its passing went the basis for the inherent rights idea, leaving "consent of the governed" as our sole political expedient, and the "engineering of consent" as the increasing preoccupation of governments. The inevitable consequence of following the lead of majority rule and popular sovereignty was foreseen more than a century ago by Francis Lieber, professor of political science at Columbia University: "Woe to the country in which political hypocrisy first calls the people almighty, then teaches that the voice of the people is divine, then pretends to take a mere clamor for the true voice of the people, and lastly gets up the desired clamor."

John Dewey has best articulated the new mood and temper that has settled on the world, and which, in his own words, "marks a revolution in the whole spirit of life, in the entire attitude taken toward whatever is found in existence." What is this revolution? It is "a change from knowledge as an esthetic enjoyment of the properties of nature regarded as a work of divine art, to knowing as a means of secular control . . . [Nature] is now something to be modified, to be intentionally controlled. . . . Ideas are worthless except as they pass into actions which rearrange and reconstruct in some way, be it little or large, the world in which we live. . . . Modern experimental science is an art of control."[4]

The universe, according to the new picture, is simply brute fact, there are no purposes in it, but human purposes, it is devoid of all values save human values. What is to prevent man, then, from attempting to recast in his own image everything he can get his hands on? It isn't going to be easy to do much about the distant stars, but the earth is close at hand and his fellow men—millions of whom surely need improvement—are even closer. Man, under the new dispensation, can no longer be thought of as a unique being. Darwinians had convinced the learned that the origin, differentiation, and transformation of all forms of life, including the human, could be explained by the interplay of materialistic forces —in terms of physics and chemistry. Natural rights were of supernatural origin, so obviously one cannot attribute them to man any more than to an ape. "Nonsense," Bentham called the idea of inherent rights, "Nonsense on stilts."

4. *The Quest for Certainty*, (Quoted in *John Dewey's Philosophy*, edited by Joseph Ratner,) pp. 327, 342.

Before science got into orbit it took momentum from the cultural and humanistic values which helped launch it. Nature was to be controlled for the benefit of man, in order that more of the good things of life might be enjoyed, that he might be healthier and longer lived. But once science gets beyond the gravitational pull of the old norms it is inevitable that some scientists should cast themselves in the role of gods. Not man controlling nature for man's benefit, but some men using their knowledge of the natural processes to control other men. Some of the more exuberant scientists have, from time to time, hinted at their plans, none more clearly than a biochemist writing in an issue of a leading "liberal" weekly. "The revolution going on in the biological sciences, mainly in biochemistry, will make atomic energy look like child's play. . . . Therefore, and more urgently than ever, we need a revolution in our political and social institutions to cope with these findings. . . . We are even about to learn how to change ourselves. . . . I think that we are approaching the greatest event in human history, even in the history of life on this earth, and that is the deliberate changing by man of many of the biological processes. . . . With all the knowledge thus gained, we will be able to plan ahead so that our children will be what we would like them to be —physically and even mentally. At this point, man will be remolding his own being. Theologians will protest, but it is certainty itself that man will play God."[5]

This may not be madness, but surely it approaches the brink of madness of a sort. In any event, those who resist the idea of both the molding and the being remolded had better retrace their steps to the point where our path took a wrong turning. The recovery of sanity will be by a route different from the one we have been following.

Democratic despotism, we have indicated, is the inevitable consequence of the "consent of the governed" idea—unless this idea be accompanied by a virile doctrine of rights which derives them from a source beyond society. From the classical world to the time of our Declaration of Independence, this source was God. But just when the God concept found a meaningful political expression in the Declaration the concept lost its hold on the minds of men. The relationship between the explicitly articulated belief

5. Siekewitz, *The Nation*, September 3, 1958.

in equal rights of the Declaration and the God concept was that of effect and cause. When a cause finally ceases to operate, trace effects or an afterimage may linger for a time; and in the modern world the idea of inherent rights moved men even after they had cut themselves adrift from its religious moorings. The eighteenth century denatured God and deified Nature; the nineteenth century mechanized nature, and the twentieth century depersonalized man. If the universe and man really correspond to such a bleak picture, there is no place in it for anything resembling the traditional doctrine of rights.

The poet, Coventry Patmore, observed that we are the inheritors of "the fair sum of six thousand years' traditions of civility." In the course of this long human experience of living together under relatively stable conditions there gradually evolved an awareness that man is more than a thing, that there is a dignity and grandeur in the human soul because it is a portion of the divine in man, linked to that aspect of the divine interpreted as the moral order or the Natural Law. To the extent that such beliefs took hold of ancient peoples they attempted to base their political structures on the explicit consent of those involved—"those involved" numbering less than the total population which included slaves and unassimilated foreigners. Conquest and subjugation do not supply a principle of rule; rule is always based on some degree of implicit consent. Consent, in a republic, is deliberately courted. Such was the case in the Hebrew commonwealth, in the Greek city-states, and in the Roman republic. It is even more true of Christendom, which fell heir to these three strands of tradition. Christian doctrine, writes Wilhelm Roepke, "starts from man as an individual endowed with an immortal soul striving for its salvation. Before the state there is now the Person, whereas above the state there is God, His love and His justice common to all men."[6]

No complicated doctrine such as this is learned all at once; its full and varied meanings are soaked up, if at all, only after repeated exposure. By the ninth century of our era the idea of "consent" had made considerable progress. Charlemagne's enacting formula reads: "Charles the Emperor . . . together with the bishops, abbots, counts, dukes, and all faithful subjects of the Christian Church, and with their *consent* and counsel, has decreed the fol-

6. Roepke, *Civitas Humana*, p. 102.

lowing . . ."[7] This may have been little more than pious affirmation, but that little more was important. In any event, the medieval monarchies were loose-jointed affairs with power pretty well decentralized into many separate centers—secular as well as spiritual —each one being played off against the others. Kings ruled by divine grace, so long as they stayed within the common acceptance of God's ordinances; and by the same token, subjects had a right to rebel against an unjust ruler.

Cardinal Nicholas of Cusa, writing in the middle of the fifteenth century, argued that the approval or acceptance by the community is an essential ingredient of all true law; ". . . all law ought to fit the country, place, and time. . . . Since by nature all men are free, any authority . . . comes solely from harmony [with Natural Law] and from the *consent* of the subjects, whether the authority resides in written law or in the living law which is in the ruler."[8]

There are verbal similarities here, Sabine points out, to the revolutionary arguments of the seventeenth and eighteenth centuries, but there the similarity ends. Nicholas, writing at the dawn of the Renaissance, was not aiming his consent doctrine at the private conscience; his "emphasis was all on the natural freedom of the community, the society that by its own spontaneous approval generates binding practices for its members," writes Sabine. But with Nicholas began the transition from Natural Law to the natural rights theories of the later period.

Medieval monarchies were circumscribed by the rival powers of the Church, the empire, and the feudal lords. This system eventually declined, only to be replaced by Renaissance absolutism and divine right monarchies, of which Louis XIV (1661–1715) is a typical example. At the same time, however, two countervailing forces were at work. First, the various Reformation sects in England and on the Continent, glorying "in the liberty wherewith Christ hath made us free," (Galatians 5:1) entertained republican sentiments and refused full allegiances to secular rulers. As Lord Acton said, "The supremacy of the people being accepted in Church government could not be repudiated in the State."[9] And, secondly, in the English common law tradition were embedded

7. Quoted by George Sabine, *A History of Political Theory*, p. 204.
8. Sabine, *op. cit.*, p. 319.
9. Acton, *Lectures on Modern History*, Figgis & Laurence, eds.,p. 200 (Lecture entitled "The Puritan Revolution").

"the immemorial rights of Englishmen" and the idea of the Natural Law. The chief exponent of the common law, Sir Edward Coke, writes of the Natural Law in his notes in Calvin's Case (1609), "This is the eternal law, the moral law, called also the law of nature. . . . And certain it is that before judicial or municipal laws were made, kings did decide cases according to natural equity and were not tied down to any rule or formality of law."[10] The Natural Law tradition conveyed the conviction that the principles of right and justice are not at the disposal of whatever group happens to wield power in society; they are not mere expedients trumped up to meet the political exigencies of the moment, they are ingrained in the nature of things. The acceptance of the Natural Law is a curb on the ruler, who is entitled to the "consent of the governed" only so long as he does not violate the Natural Law. But the idea of Natural Law is bound to recede as the metaphysic on which it is based is increasingly ignored or displaced. When this occurs, some other device will be sought as a curb on power.

The Founding Fathers hung their case for limited government from a theological premise, although their own religious philosophies were anemic affairs and the eighteenth-century ideology which they partly shared was not hospitable to theism. The colonists, however, were a theologically minded people, and the Church played an important part in their affairs. Thus they were easily appealed to with the idea that they were supernaturally endowed with inherent rights. It is one of the end products of the religious heritage of Christendom to claim natural rights for every human being as such, and to proclaim God's sovereignty over the social and political affairs of man. These religious beliefs are reflected in the Declaration. But withdraw these religious elements from the philosophy of the Declaration and we are in trouble. The concept of God-given rights goes when belief in God is suspended. This was happening even as the Declaration was being written; it has happened at an accelerated tempo since that time. The seeds of it are found in John Locke in the latter part of the seventeenth century.

Locke argued that innate ideas do not exist; that there is nothing in the intellect except what is first in the senses.[11] On the basis of

10. Quoted in *Natural Law Institute Proceedings*, Vol. 1, p. 8.
11. *An Essay Concerning Human Understanding*

such radical empiricism it is difficult to reach so metaphysical a notion as Natural Law, a concept derived from reason and intuition, not from sensory experience. If Natural Law, which had been an impediment to absolutism, be abandoned, some other anti-authoritarian device must be found to take its place. The Social Contract idea was offered as a gambit—an idea as old as Plato, but given a characteristic modern twist by Locke who, in 1690, sought to rationalize the revolution of 1688.

There was a state of nature, Locke argued, of "peace, good will, mutual assistance and preservation." Fully endowed human beings existed in this presocietal condition, each one possessing a natural right to protect himself and his property. After a rational weighing of the personal gains to be derived from living in civil society, individual men contracted with other individuals to form one, "by barely agreeing to unite into one political society, which is all the compact that is, or needs be."[12] As history, this is, of course, pure moonshine; men by virtue of their genes, are biologically anthropoids, it is only by assimilation of their social legacy that they become fully human and members of a particular society. But Social Contract theories, which linked the ideas of natural rights and consent, were useful fictions during the political revolutions of the seventeenth and eighteenth centuries which were aimed at monarchy, and Locke furnished much of the ammunition used by our Founding Fathers. All this was fine when it came to deposing the kings—the only kind of authoritarianism which seemed to frighten the men of those centuries. But if we depose the kings only to set up a more far reaching tyranny—parliamentary absolutism or the despotism of a majority—where's the gain?

Actually, the germs of majoritarian democracy are in Locke's own theory: "And thus every man, by consenting with others to make only body politic under one government, puts himself under an obligation to every one of that society, to *submit to the determination of the majority*, and to be concluded by it; or else this original compact, whereby he with others incorporates into one society, would signify nothing, and be no compact. . . . The body [of the community] should move that way the greater force carries it, which is the *consent of the majority.*"   *(Italics supplied)*

12. John Locke, *Concerning Civil Government*, #99.
13. *Ibid.*, #97.

It was Coke's doctrine that a legislative statute should be judged sound or otherwise by testing it against the fundamental law of the land as this was received in the common law tradition. Of wrong legislation it could be said, in his words, "The common law adjudgeth a statute so far void." The "Higher Law" background of American constitutional theory owes much to Coke, as well as to English legal experience up to about the middle of the seventeenth century. English history took a revolutionary turn at this time, away from this Natural Law tradition and in the direction of the parliamentary absolutism which was established by the successful Revolution of 1688. The heat of the civil wars of this century led both royalists and parliamentarians into claims of supremacy for the king or for the parliament far beyond the limits sober judgment would dictate. The royalists lost, and "after 1688," Roscoe Pound writes, "there was no fundamental law superior to Parliament."[14] Blackstone, whose Commentaries appeared in 1765 and achieved a wide circulation in the American colonies, wrote: "So long . . . as the English Constitution lasts, we may venture to affirm that the power of Parliament is absolute and without control."[15] The governed had consented to an elective despotism.

We have been trying to follow the trail of two strands of political tradition which fused in the Declaration of Independence. On the one hand, the metaphysical concept of Natural Law, from which the doctrine of inviolable personal rights may be logically deduced; and on the other, the "consent of the governed" idea which, followed to the exclusion of any limiting principles, resulted in parliamentary absolutism in late seventeenth-century England. The scene now shifts to this continent. The colonists would have deprived themselves of their handiest weapon in the dispute with Parliament had they conceded the point about parliamentary absolutism. This was essentially a war of doctrine, with the colonists using such weapons as "natural rights," "the idea of immemorial rights of Englishmen, secured by the law of the land, and of the common law," and the "laws of Nature and of Nature's God." These phrases sprang naturally from their belief in the integrity of the human soul. But the intellectual climate of the eighteenth century was not congenial to theological concepts, not

14. Quoted in *Natural Law Institute Proceedings*, Vol. 1, p. 15.
15. Quoted by Edwin Corwin, *The "Higher Law" Background of American Constitutional Theory*, p. 87.

even to one so neutral as the idea that inherent rights are a corollary of each person's relationship to the divine order. The traditional doctrine of natural rights was progressively unhinged from any invisible means of support, being transformed in the process into secular "natural rights" deduced from an ideal, abstract man who existed as a solitary before contracting with other like units to form society. This unhistorical notion served for a time, but eventually came to be regarded as a fiction suspended from a myth. In the nineteenth century, the idea of rights in either form —as an endowment from the Creator or as a characteristic of autonomous man—went down the drain. Another sanction for political action was sought and found in the idea of majoritarianism.

A great idea which has had general acceptance never disappears all at once. It is discarded in fragments, and even after the last fragment had disappeared people are deferential to the vacuum created by its dissolution. Habits are powerful even after convictions have faded. This may explain why even Jefferson blows hot and cold in these matters. No one talked more than he about "our natural rights," or was more aware than he of the potential tyranny in the "consent of the governed" idea when reduced to mere majority rule. "An elective despotism is not the government we fought for," he wrote in 1781. But in 1787 he wrote to Madison, "It is my principle that the will of the majority should always prevail." And a year later, also to Madison: "I readily suppose my opinion wrong, when opposed by the majority." It is this phase of his thought which enabled Lord Acton to speak of "Jefferson's determined aversion to every authority which could oppose or restrain the will of the sovereign people."[16] But in 1816 the tide has come back in with the "natural rights" idea, and Jefferson writes: "Our legislators' . . . true office is to declare and enforce only our natural rights and duties and to take none of them from us. . . . The idea is quite unfounded that on entering into society we give up any natural right." But then he veered again, and in 1824 said: "All power is inherent in the people." And in his last extant letter, written ten days before his death in 1826, when the idea of inherent human rights had all but been abandoned by the

16. Acton, *Essays on Freedom and Power*, G. Himmelfarb, ed. p. 212 (Lecture entitled "Political Causes of the American Revolution").

learned, he affirmed his belief that "all eyes are opened, or opening, to the rights of man." He was quite mistaken in this, even of his own country. Seven years earlier in the epoch making Supreme Court decision in McCulloch vs. Maryland, John Marshall had written: "The government of the Union is emphatically and truly a government of the people. In form and in substance it emanates from them. Its powers are granted by them, and are to be exercised directly on them and for their benefit."

Jefferson may have been right in affirming that we didn't fight for an "elective despotism," but given the situation which existed in the eighteenth and nineteenth centuries, it is obvious to hindsight that that was what we were going to get. The tyranny of the majority is simply the unhindered application of the "consent of the governed" idea, with no restraining influence which might come from a virile belief in Natural Law and inherent rights. Edwin Corwin writes that " 'Natural Law' in the sense of 'the observed order of phenomena' has tended in recent years to crowd the earlier rationalistic conception to the wall, thus aiding the triumph of the idea of human and governmental law as an expression solely of will backed by force."[17]

The English Utilitarians in the nineteenth century, having first swallowed the premise that theological assumptions are inadmissible, tried unsuccessfully to base an ethical theory on the Greatest Happiness principle. Bentham railed against the idea of inherent rights and offered in its stead a principle which is far from self-evident: "Everybody is to count for one, and no one for more than one."[18] In naturalistic terms, the very opposite is self-evident; obviously, a person who is handsome, brave, and clever is worth more in most human scales of value than one who is ugly, timid, weak, and stupid. His market value is certainly greater and, in the absence of nonutilitarian principles to the contrary, why on earth should not the strong and clever stratify society and run the world to suit themselves?

John Stuart Mill uttered many timeless truths about liberty on the basis of the utilitarian standard that liberty provides conditions conducive to the greatest happiness. But although his rhetoric was gorgeous he didn't make his case. Of several alternative courses

17. Corwin, *op. cit.*, p. 59.
18. Quoted by William L. Davidson, *Political Thought in England*, p. 51.

of action, who will decide which one should be adopted so as to maximize happiness? Majority rule again! The decision is based on "the judgments of those who are qualified by knowledge of . . . [the consequences], or, if they differ, that of the majority among them, must be admitted as final."[19] And Herbert Spencer, who in his early writing defended the rights of man against the state, concluded somewhat sadly in his *Autobiography* (1904) that "The unlimited right of the majority to rule, is probably as advanced a conception of freedom as can safely be entertained at present; if indeed, even that can safely be entertained."[20] "The unlimited right of the majority to rule" can, in practice, mean only one thing —that a determined and articulate few will create *ad hoc* majorities for the sole purpose of ratifying minority demands.

The "consent of the governed" idea, after the disappearance of the Natural Law tradition, took possession of the field as the theory of Popular Sovereignty. This theory exercises dominion today over many nations flying the banner of Peoples' Democracies. It is a matter of record that no monarch in history, however despotic he may have dreamed of being, would have dared perpetrate the injustices and cruelties that have been condoned in the so-called Peoples' Democracies. Totalitarian tyranny, incessantly exploiting every vehicle of propaganda and using a system of compulsory voting, is given the specious endorsement of overwhelming majorities. The theoretical justification for every sort of evil is that the people will it for their own benefit. And popular tolerance of evil is increased with the thought that "we are doing it to ourselves." The modern world, by such dubious sleight-of-hand, has drawn upon the reserves of a hitherto unsuspected dimension of evil. A monarch responsible for wrongdoing can be deposed. But how do you fix responsibility on a whole people, and when responsibility is fixed, how do you depose them? An individual here and there may find the situation unpleasant, but if the people are sovereign and the government popular, the fact that it stays in power is prima facie evidence that it retains the "consent of the governed."

The totalitarian threat is two-pronged; military and ideological. Putting aside the military aspects for the moment, it is obvious that

19. John Stuart Mill, *Utilitarianism*, p. 50 (Everyman's Edition).
20. Herbert Spencer, *Autobiography*, Vol. II, pp. 512–13.

the ideological threat will not be met by those who oppose it with nothing more than a weak and diluted version of the very same doctrines which ushered in the Peoples' Democracies: "consent of the governed," majority rule, and popular sovereignty, operating in a cosmos stripped of all values, lacking a religious dimension, devoid of Natural Law.

"Consent of the governed" was an altogether inept phrase in the Declaration, out of step with the main body of the American political vision. The dream was that if men knew the right principles of social integration no one would be governed; i.e., the creature of another man's will. The society would be free; i.e., comprised of self-governing units whose social agency of arrest and restraint would serve individual liberty by maintaining the inherent rights of each person. But remove the idea of inherent rights and this structure collapses.

When the idea of inherent rights is abandoned, people will still go on using the word "rights," after distorting its original meaning. On the one hand, "rights" will be used as if the term were synonymous with "desires" or "privileges." Thus we are presented with long lists of "human rights" to such things as housing, education, medical care, a job, and so on. The source and dispenser of these "rights" is, of course, the sovereign state. On the other hand, the air is filled with talk about "civil rights," which means certain patterns of conduct permitted or enforced by the sovereign majority. The conduct in question may be ethically desirable, provided it is voluntary; but the majority has power, and is willing to use it on minorities. Members of minorities have no inherent rights, so of course they have no "civil rights" either—until they join forces with the majority.

Can we recover the idea of inherent rights? Only if we can rehabilitate the belief that man is not wholly resolvable into a social being, that part of him is inviolable, shielded always from the prying hands of either majorities or rulers. Two main lines of argument have been used to support this conviction; one religious, the other secular. According to the former, rights have a reference above and beyond society, in a transcendent sacred order. The individual is a creature of God, and therefore he is sovereign as a person in relation to his fellows. When religious belief waned, and the concept of a transcendent order was abandoned, many thinkers sought support for the idea of "natural rights" in theories of an original Social Contract. Locke, as has been mentioned, thought he could deduce rights from the nature of abstract, ideal men who were imagined to have existed as solitaries before they got together and formed themselves into societies. These two approaches exhaust the field; abandon these and the idea of inherent rights is no more than a pious wish. And we have to abandon one of them, for Social Contract theories are no longer believable. This means that the preservation of the idea of inherent rights—the only principled ground for limiting government—depends on a contemporary restatement of the ancient truth that "in the centre of his being, in that knower who is never known, man is in touch with God and even in his most wretched wandering in the wilderness of this world, is always rooted in the eternal being of God."[21] Sovereignty must reside in the Creator or liberty has no roots.

Americans, Lord Bryce observed last century, have "an aversion to the investigation of general principles as well as to trains of systematic reasoning."[22] Perhaps it may be more accurate to say that Americans have been uncomfortable with the ambiguity in their own political heritage. They have an apprehension that something is wrong without being aware of just what it is. With one part of their being they have looked to the Creator as the source of their rights, with another part they have lavishly abused those rights at the behest of now this majority, now that. The split in principles is becoming more painful and soon the choice will have to be made to ride one or the other.

It is possible for a people to live without clear-cut principles for a time, sustained by the forces of habit, custom, and convention. A man may live according to his father's code even after abandoning the faith which gave the father his code. But the grandson will have neither faith nor code. Such is, roughly, our predicament, and there is no guarantee that even a determined effort will get us out of it. But the first step in solving a problem is to face a bleak statement of it; for where there is no challenge there can be no response.

21. W. R. Matthews, *The Problem of Christ in the Twentieth Century*, p. 72.
22. Bryce, *The American Commonwealth*, Vol. II, p. 360.

CHAPTER 15

Concerning War and Peace

THE PRESUMPTION IS ALWAYS ON THE SIDE OF PEACE; IT IS A
lurch into war that needs explanation and justification. Peace,
while not the normal state of human affairs is, at any rate, normative. Even if war be regarded as the health of the state, then war
surely indicates an illness of society. The health of society consists
of the peaceful, voluntary production and exchange of goods, services, and ideas; it consists of loving families, healthy children, the
growth of individual knowledge and wisdom, the enrichment of
mind and soul, and a serene passage into eternal life. This is peace,
and a war is justified only when this peace is threatened by an
external foe; the war is justified only if victory brings about conditions of peace better than those which would obtain had the war
not been fought. The height of folly, Juvenal observed nearly two
thousand years ago, is to engage in a war which destroys the object
for which it is fought.

War is an instrumentality of a peculiar sort; it is the use of force
and violence *in extremis*. It is an apt—though not necessarily a
laudable—means for achieving certain ends; but the nature of war
itself precludes using it as a means to achieve certain other ends.
Some nations have used war to expand their territory at the expense of other peoples. War has been used to subject one people
to another, to obtain loot, maintain a dynasty, hold off the barbarians, achieve glory. War to gain territory, or to collect slaves, or to
obtain treasure is not an irrational action, however reprehensible

it may be. But wars fought to make the world safe for democracy, to guarantee universal peace, or on behalf of world brotherhood, are irrational; the nature of warfare makes it an inappropriate means for the achievement of ends such as these. Besides, such ends as these—announced goals for the wars fought within the present cycle of warfare which began in 1914—are utopian. Universal peace and world brotherhood are problematic goals at best; in all likelihood they are beyond the reach of creatures constituted as we are. An occasional human being, peculiarly gifted and intensively trained, becomes a four minute miler; but we would not think of gearing our transportation system to the assumption that this feat is within everyone's range. An occasional human being becomes a great saint, a genius in the realm of the spirit; but we cannot base our social calculations on the expectation of a general mutation which would thus transform every member of society. But even if universal peace and world brotherhood were realizable goals within the foreseeable future, they are not the kinds of ends which can possibly be reached by using war as a means.

Peace is the avowed preference of the plain man as well as the declared aim of the statesman. Never have so many declared for peace as have expressed their minds on the matter during the first half of the twentieth century. But, paradoxically, this century outdoes all previous eras in its feverish preparations for war, and in its involvement in actual warfare.

The eminent sociologist, Pitrim Sorokin, has made a study of some 967 important wars which occurred in the West from 500 B.C. to A.D. 1925. Using as his yardstick the size of the casualty list per million of the corresponding population, the war magnitude of the first quarter alone of the twentieth century stands at 52. For the entire nineteenth century the corresponding figure is 17. Writing just before the outbreak of World War II, Sorokin comments: "If, further, we add the wars that doubtless will occur from 1940 to 2000, the twentieth century will unquestionably prove to be the bloodiest and most belligerent of all the twenty-five centuries under consideration. . . . We live in an age unique for the unrestrained use of brute force in international relations."[1]

The twentieth century, then, is the century of total war. Projecting Sorokin's calculations, the war magnitude of this century will

1. Sorokin, *The Crisis of Our Age*, pp. 213, 216, 217.

be over 250, as compared with the nineteenth century's 17—even if we assume that casualties per million of the population have not and will not exceed the record first quarter. Something has gone wrong, and it is not a sudden onset of personal belligerency or a sudden admiration for the martial virtues. To the contrary, professed concern for humanitarianism and love of one's fellows is at an all time·high. But these private virtues cannot find a collective focus; they are hooked up with economic and political aberrations which translate private good into enormous public evil.

We shall examine, in this chapter, a simple economic fallacy which mistakenly hitches the fate of the economy to government spending for armaments. After showing that military spending makes us poorer in the goods we really want, not richer, an effort will be made to show that the collectivist organization of society itself contains within it the seeds of "perpetual war for perpetual peace," that a socialized society is propelled toward war by its own internal logic.

It is probably true that human beings cannot eliminate war from their affairs, but they can limit it.[2] Somewhat analogously, the achievement of proper hygiene, exercise, and diet can greatly reduce the amount of physical illness in a society, but not get rid of it entirely. On the other hand, an improper regimen and faulty conditions of sanitation can insure that illness will be endemic to a country. Similarly, *mutatis mutandis*, with social health and the social sickness of war. Human beings cannot limit war, however, so long as they mistakenly believe that economic prosperity is based on war production; and they cannot limit war if they adopt a form of political organization that, even in peacetime, takes giant steps toward war. These two questions will now be thrashed out.

Two fears hang over our world. The first fear is that war will break out, killing millions of people, destroying billions of dollars worth of property, and wrecking what's left of the institutions of once free societies. The second fear is that peace will break out and bring our vaunted material prosperity crashing to earth. There is an untenable assumption in this fear of peace, but if it be accepted, the dilemma is a cruel one. The desire for material well-being is legitimate, but the dilemma spells out into something like the following three stages: Material well-being depends on an arms

2. Cf. Major Hoffman Nickerson, *Can We Limit War?*

race; an arms race is likely to eventuate in a hot war; a hot war is a device guaranteed to end prosperity and threaten survival. Here is a series whose first term is a natural desire for well-being, but whose last term cancels everything which precedes it. This hardly sounds like progress, but if—as many people believe—the vitality of the civilian economy is so dependent on military spending that a depression looms if the spending stops, this is the logic of events. Let us examine these two fears which have so many of us walking a razor's edge, held in balance by the terrors on either side.

We are in the Cold War, we are told, and the Cold War is not war in the old sense. War used to be a thing of bombs dropping, tanks maneuvering, and infantry slugging it out in the mud; but war is now primarily an engagement in another dimension—the psychological. The aim of war, then and now, is the same—to impose our will on the enemy, or at least to resist the imposition of his will on ours—but the means have changed. Formerly, we damaged his property or the bodies of his soldiers until the enemy's will to resist was broken; but now we are done with such crudities, having discovered subtle ways of getting at the will directly to bend or break it. In the old days, a victor nation or coalition was usually one which possessed a preponderence of military might, as demonstrated in the field. On the eve of a war the question of which nation actually had such a preponderance might be a matter of debate, to be settled only by fighting it out. But the matter of preponderance is now hardly ever posed. "Preponderance" has been overcome by "sufficiency." If several nations each possess a sufficiency of military might—armament enough to clobber rival nations no matter who strikes the first blow —the possession of a preponderance confers only the most dubious of advantages. The apparatus of civilization reduced to rubble, the victor nation stands astride a bone yard.

The fear that war may break out appears to be well grounded. What about the fear that peace may break out?

The fear that peace will have a disastrous effect on the civilian economy is not a delusion of the unlettered. This fear, on the contrary, afflicts and is fostered by the sophisticated who have unlearned the capacity for taking a common-sense view of things. Turn, for example, to an article in a recent issue of the *Bulletin of the Atomic Scientists,* a journalistic outlet for writers who stress the social responsibilities of scientists. The article is entitled "The Economics of Disarmament," and opens with a question: "Can the U.S. peacetime economy maintain its high prosperity without heavy governmental spending in the arms economy?" To which, the author returns a gloomy answer. "So long as armament is not used," he says, "it serves its economic purpose in an ideal way. The income created in the development and production of arms represents a clear net gain to the total purchasing power available to sustain the consumer economy."

Good Keynesian doctrine so far, but now the catch: An arms race, the author points out, heads nations toward a disastrous military conflict which must be avoided. It is equally necessary to fend off the economic collapse which threatens if the arms race slows. What is needed, says the author, is an "economic equivalent of armament"—some prescription which promises to sustain present levels of civilian prosperity without threatening to bring on World War III. The author's remedy, increased government spending, has a familiar ring: "No stretching of the terms of this elementary discourse is needed to show that public works and public services provide the economic equivalent of armament."

Some of today's industries are totally committed to military production while others are committed in part. The "prosperity" of these segments of society is irrevocably yoked to military spending. It is easy to imagine a factory for the making of an essential weapon, the Gismo, being erected in 1942 in the sleepy little village of Ruralarea. The plant now employs 5,000 people, three times the number of citizens who responded to the town's 1940 census. The plant payroll now sustains those who work there plus bankers, butchers, teachers, ministers, and one interior decorator. Peace breaks out, military spending stops, and it is not hard to imagine what happens to Ruralarea. Admittedly, in this and similar situations, there will be hardships and some painful but necessary readjustments. But Ruralarea is not the United States, and it is not permissible to generalize its problems as if they afflicted a whole nation.The argument we are considering is that the prosperity of the society as a whole depends on national spending for arms.

This argument is a modern version of the fable of the emperor's new clothes. It contains a glaring fallacy which is easily grasped, but this fallacy in turn rests upon a faulty premise of a more subtle nature. The fallacy first: Prosperity is equivalent to an abundance of the things people consume and enjoy—houses, clothing, food, automobiles, recreation, gadgets, and so on. These items come into existence as the result of economic production. A few individuals here and there may live well on stolen goods, but society is provisioned in only one way—by human effort, augmented by tools, applied to raw materials. Thus, and in no other way, are produced the goods and services we now have in abundance and which constitute our prosperity. Our prosperity would cease if we stopped producing, and we can't produce without working. Some 72 million people are presently at work to produce the things which make up our prosperity.

Alongside this abundance of consumer goods which constitute the civilian economy are jet fighters, aircraft carriers, tanks, rockets, and the like. There is no civilian market for these items; Uncle Sam and his allies are the only customers. Even though you and I are not in the market for military hardware, some six million of our people are engaged in producing it according to the same old economic equation—by the application of human effort and tools to raw materials. While thus engaged they cannot produce goods for their own consumption. They must be supported, in this respect, by the rest of society. Furthermore, there are large quantities of machines, tools, and other capital tied up in defense projects which otherwise might be employed to make things for consumers.

Putting these two segments together, it is obvious that the total active labor force in the country is roughly 78 million people. Is it not self-evident; in the first place, that 78 million workers— other things being equal—will produce more than 72 million? Therefore, the present level of prosperity is lower than it might otherwise be by the amount of civilian goods which the six million would produce if they weren't engaged in producing arms. If the withdrawal of six million is the cause of the high level of civilian prosperity, why not withdraw 60 million and have a real boom? Thus, we would defeat our old enemy Work, that built-in curse of every economic system of the past.[3]

3. This is not to deny the need for military hardware nor to minimize the importance of our defense establishment. Perhaps we should divert twice as much manpower and capital for these purposes, but that is another argument. The only point at issue here is the

The six million now engaged in armament production are not simply off to one side, a neutral factor. They are consumers of civilian goods without producing any themselves or even producing things which might be exchanged for them. Millions of producers of food, clothing, housing, and other services work to provide these necessities for the six million engaged in armament production. Far from the arms race sustaining the civilian economy, the reverse is true; it is the incredible productivity of the civilian economy which makes it possible to spend what is necessary in military hardware. Not so many centuries ago, in subsistence days, nations called off their wars so that people could get in the harvest. Our present mastery of economic problems is so nearly complete that the productive sector of our economy can maintain a high level of civilian prosperity even though it is forced to support a swollen governmental structure along with its bureaucracies and its military establishment. Prosperity supports the arms race, not vice versa.

When things are put in straightforward economic terms without introducing the complicating factor of money, the glaring fallacy of the thesis that Americans are prosperous because their government is spending so much on armaments is obvious. It is equally obvious that such an inversion of the facts would hardly find general acceptance if men based their conclusions on primary observations of the facts. At this level fallacies are relatively easy to detect. The detection of fallacies is more difficult if the discussion is conducted at the secondary level of inferences. An inference may be incorrect, and that's that. But an inference may be correct and still conceal a fallacy if the inference is drawn from an unsound premise. The unsound premise in the present instance is based upon the supposition that the late Lord Keynes refuted Say's Law—a supposition shared by the master himself. Keynesians acknowledge this as a critical question and admit that if the validity of Say's Law be conceded much of Keynes's theory becomes untenable. So let's argue this fallacy out in terms of Say's Law— although a matter so complex can hardly be thrashed out in any space short of a book or a series of books.

Crudely put, Say's Law of Markets—named after the French
fact that manpower and capital devoted to military purposes are not available for civilian production and diminish the latter by that much. Every dollar spent for guns is a dollar less that might be spent for bread, housing, travel, and the like.

economist who advanced it in 1803—holds that aggregate supply creates aggregate demand, that purchasing power grows out of production. Benjamin M. Anderson in his *Economics and the Public Welfare* opens his Chapter 60, "Digression on Keynes," with this description of what he calls "the equilibrium doctrine":

> The twentieth century world consumes vastly more than the eighteenth century world because it produces vastly more. Supply of wheat gives rise to demand for automobiles, silks, shoes, cotton goods, and other things that the wheat producer wants. Supply of shoes gives rise to demand for wheat, for silks, for automobiles, and for other things that the shoe producer wants. Supply and demand in the aggregate are thus not merely equal, but they are identical, since every commodity may be looked upon either as supply of its own kind or as demand for other things. But this doctrine is subject to the great qualification that the proportions must be right; that there must be equilibrium.

Keynes's alleged success in disposing of Say's Law consisted in ignoring the qualification; he "refuted" a proposition which had never been seriously advanced. "Say's Law of Markets," writes Henry Hazlitt, "is based on the assumption that a proper equilibrium exists among different kinds of production, and among prices of different products and services. And it of course assumes proper relationships between prices and costs, between prices and wage-rates. It assumes the existence of competition and free and fluid markets by which these proportions, price relations, and other equilibria will be brought about."

Say's Law is not regarded as a central doctrine of classical economics, but by disposing of a fallacy it paved the way for the establishment of what Adam Smith called "the liberal plan of equality, liberty, and justice." This is the system of liberty, one of whose facets is the free market. Economics, ostensibly the study of market operations, is really concerned with the stewardship of the earth's scarce goods, such as human energy, time, material resources, and natural forces. These scarce goods are our natural birthright. Use them wisely, as natural piety dictates—that is, providently and economically—and human well-being is the result. Turn a blind eye to them and one consequence is the promulgation of such nonsense at that the arms race which makes us billions of dollars poorer is actually the cause of our prosperity. Men act upon their beliefs, even when beliefs are fallacious, and acting upon this one we career ominously toward the Total State and a hot war.

A tiny leak in the dike, if not plugged, can open up and let the flood through. What begins as a simple economic fallacy can end with a bang or a whimper.

An economic fallacy such as the one we have been considering may afflict even a free society. Even if a people endorsed and embraced the market economy way of doing business they might, nevertheless, harbor one or another of the numerous economic fallacies from time to time. But if they discard the free market–limited government way of life for the politically managed society they have adopted a militaristic mode of organization which can avoid future war only by accident. This is a hard saying, especially in view of the fact that many socialists and welfare staters are kindly and well-disposed men. But good intentions are not enough, and if the organization of society is faulty they get lost in its machinery. How, otherwise, shall we explain the paradox that the most generally educated, enlightened, progressive, and humane era known to history is also the most warlike?

The idea of peace on earth, good will to men is one of humanity's older and more enduring aspirations. It accords with the sentiments of the great religious traditions, and it is in harmony with a substantial bundle of the drives which move the individual person. History, however, is not composed of aspirations alone, else it would be quite different from what it has, in fact, been. History, as it has actually been lived and recorded, provides ample justification for the pessimist who concludes that peace is only that short interval between battles when nations are recovering from the last war and preparing for the next. Things might not be this bad, in reality, but they are bad enough to draw forth our best and most earnest efforts to understand the causes of war, in the hope of finding, if not a cure, then at least an alleviation for militaristic ills.

Assigning causation in social matters is never easy; the variables are too numerous. And in the matter of war there is an additional difficulty; the disparity between mankind's aspiration for peace and its chronic involvement in war signifies that war's causation is indirect. War, in other words, may be the unexpected by-product of pursuing policies which appear to be anything but bellicose, which are believed to be humanitarian through and through. Perhaps it is more correct to say that a war happens, than to say that a war is caused. A war may happen because a nation wants something it cannot obtain without fighting a war to get it; or, a war may happen because a people who do want peace do not want—or do not know—the things that make for peace. A policy for the reorganization of society along some idealistic line may be adopted in ignorance of the fact that the policy actually contains the germs of war. Then, when the explosion occurs, there is only slight consolation in the words, "We did not know it was loaded."

The purpose of discussing and debating social philosophies, policies, and issues is to explore the "load," to determine the direction in which the muzzle points, and at whom. If a society will not tolerate such an exchange—and ours will hardly tolerate it, so strong is "liberal" conformism—then that society may back into an era of perpetual crisis, as ours is doing.

Any man who peddles a program guaranteeing perpetual peace is a charlatan. There are few guaranteed results in human affairs, and this is not one of them. Human beings are imperfect in understanding as well as in conduct, and a war may break out even under the best conceivable economic and political system. But if there is a social philosophy which, when put into practice, sets citizen against citizen, collects people into pressure groups and ranges these against each other, creates a ruling class and pits it against the nation, then this social philosophy has readied for desperate action the country which adopts it. And when domestic economic and political conditions are bent into such a posture, the friction between nations is aggravated and the occasions for such frictions multiplied. When peoples embark on a course of this sort, war is much more likely; to the point of being inevitable.

Modern war, in other words, does not start with the act of declaring war, or at the time of marching off to war, or when the first shot is fired; it starts much further back in time. The fountainhead of war is deeply embedded in a certain variety of domestic peacetime policy where it is all but hidden from view under that policy's humanitarian guise.

The analysis of war offered in this chapter is at odds with the customary approach, which seeks to scare people into a peace-loving frame of mind. Antiwar organizations and individual pacifists recite the horrors of war, assuming that if we become sufficiently aware of what might happen to us in a hot war we will mend our ways and change course.

The typical antiwar case expounded by pacifist organizations and individuals is based on the wrong psychology. When the moralist tries to persuade us to cut down on wine, women, and song, he is seeking to turn us away from pursuits most people find immensely attractive. The moralist who would argue the *un*attractiveness of these things would waste his breath, and he knows it; so he tries to point out the harm which might accrue, in the long run, to the acting person himself and to those his actions affect. In other words, he paints a vivid picture of the evil results of yielding to present temptations. The appeal is to conscience to forego actions which sorely tempt. The expectation is that these temptations will, in consequence, lose horsepower and cease to exert their former power of attraction. But we have long known the awfulness of war, and wars have continued to recur, and they recur with increasing frequency.

They recur because war is a built-in feature of human nature. Adopting the policy is something like stepping out of a tenth-story window; as soon as we make this initial choice, other forces take over and the final consequences are not within our volition to avoid.

The purpose of war, to cite the Clausewitz doctrine again, is to impose your will on the enemy; or, at the very least, to prevent him from imposing his will on you. In a welfare state, or planned economy, the mass of men are to be guided, regulated, directed, and controlled by those wielding political power. On principle, the wills of a large segment of the nation are bent to conform to the master plan imposed on them by those in power who believe themselves competent to plan the lives of others. When this occurs in a society as a permanent peacetime policy, that society has taken the first steps of a course whose last step is war. The basic principles of the welfare state or socialism or the planned economy contain, inevitably, the germs of war.

Conscription for military service is but the more immediate application to military purposes of the control of individuals and property which is inherent in all collectivist economic planning. Some kindly collectivists do oppose conscription, but they endorse its logical counterparts; conscription, in other words, follows logically from the rest of their beliefs. These people profess aversion to the use of a lot of force on foreigners—which is war; but they advocate the use of a little force on natives in order to secure general conformity to The Plan. The catch is, that once you start doing the latter, there is no logical stopping place short of the former.

The great social drift or trend for the past hundred years or so has been in the direction of the centralized state. People in this country and elsewhere have thrust a more positive role upon government than was contemplated by the classical liberals of last century. Socialists have had a fully developed rationale for the politicalization of life ever since Marx, but as the drift gathered momentum, businessmen, teachers, preachers, writers, and people from all walks of life climbed aboard the band wagon. The upshot of this great trend has been a vast extension of the powers of government and a proliferation of government services. This costs money, so the trend has been accompanied by a skyrocketing growth in the budgets of all nations until, in our own country, the national budget alone is today over 200 billion dollars annually, out of a disposable personal income of roughly 500 billion. The latter figure represents the monetary equivalent of the goods produced annually by our labor force, which numbers about 72 million persons and has available to it the capital and the know-how resulting from the productive efforts of preceding generations.

The goods and services produced in a capitalist society are distributed in varying amounts to each man who participates, according to the value his fellows attach to his own contribution of goods and services—assuming a free market, willing exchange, and no political privileges. Government, society's police power, has all the while been exercising its constabulary function in order to protect citizens against invasions of their rights; that is to say, against such acts as assault, theft, fraud, slander, foreign attack, and the like. The cost of these policing functions is 3 to 5 percent of the gross payroll. All of which corresponds roughly to the classical liberal image of society in its economic and political sectors.

But now comes the new image. The police power, government, is no longer to play a modest policing role; it is to undertake vast national programs in response to the demands of this pressure group or that, and these programs require money. The people who produce 500 billion dollars turn 200 billion of it over to the national government, and Washington acquires new powers commensurate with its increased wealth. A vast bureaucracy is assembled, and the intellectuals—who had been telling us that life has no purpose—now have grandiose national goals to propagandize for.

It is in the nature of a government to create the means of its own support, and every dollar government spends generates a vested interest in a continuance of the spending. No government could spend two hundred billion dollars a year without benefiting certain industries, some of which would not otherwise be in business at all. Even so, it is not easy for those in power to devise spending programs which will get rid of a lot of money fast in ways which do not affront the mores and arouse popular resistance. Pyramid building takes a lot of money, but the darn things last so long. And so all governments who are trying to get rid of astronomical sums of money finally settle on "military spending, and/or space programs." Military hardware is ideal for the purposes of the planners. It accords with the mores; it costs a lot of money and whatever is not conspicuously consumed in smoke obsolesces overnight—a bottomless drain for "surplus" government money. And tragically, the same forces which are at work in some nations to swell the military budget also operate in the relations between nations to provide occasions for using it.

The first step is to deprive the people who produce goods and services, and earn an income thereby, of the right to make private decisions as to how their own incomes shall be spent. Instead, we collectivize these millions of decisions and turn the bundle over to politicians with a virtual carte blanche: "You spend this the way *you* think best." Step two is the completely ineffectual one of telling the politicians to whom we have given control that we aren't very happy with the way they exercise it. The horse has already been stolen, and it's too late to lock the barn.

To the extent that a society limits its government to policing functions which curb the individuals who engage in aggressive and criminal actions, and conducts its economic affairs on the basis of free and willing exchange, to that extent domestic peace prevails. When a society departs from this norm, its governing class begins, in effect, to make war upon the rest of the nation. A situation is created wherein everyone is victimized by everyone else under the fiction of each living at the expense of all. Power differentials in society are increased and aggravated, popular discontent mounts, and the ruling group seeks for a device to restore "unity." War is, of course, the time-honored national unifier. Similar forces are at work in all modern nations, posing similar problems for all.

The classical liberal picture envisioned peaceful competition: the free market at home and free trade with foreign nations. Domestic tensions were thus well within the competence of the local constabulary to handle, and the nationals of foreign countries were potential buyers of our goods whose trade we solicited on the premise that the customer is always right. The ideal was prosperity at home and peace abroad. Human nature distorts the practice of every social ideal; but at least this dispensation was peaceful in theory. It has been replaced by one that is destructive even *in theory*, if not in intention, and in practice has been accompanied during this century by a steeply mounting curve of actual warfare.

The welfare state or planned economy creates domestic tensions in every nation, and because the Plan won't operate at home unless foreign trade is controlled—which causes internatonal tensions to mount—brinkmanship is the inevitable consequence. As far back as 1936, H. L. Mencken described with his customary vigor the relationship between these several factors: "So long as a gang of unconscionable criminals, by inserting themselves into public office, can acquire eminent domain over the lives and property of all other citizens, we'll see exploitation and injustice at home, and homicidal adventures abroad."

Nobody, to repeat, wants the shooting war. But almost everyone, the neoliberal and pacifist most of all, wants the things which poise us perpetually, and as a matter of policy, on the brink of war.

The war-making potential of modern governments is due to the command they have assumed over the persons and resources of their respective nations. If a government did not control these vast resources, its power to make war would be reduced to manageable proportions. The first step toward war is the acceptance by almost

all men everywhere of the false assumption that political commit-
tees are competent to run people's lives. The first steps to peace
are in the direction of a voluntary society in which each person is
free to direct his own energy so long as he allows the same right
to others. There is no utopia in this direction, but in striving for
a voluntary society we may at least avoid such debacles as have
plagued our world.

God and Political Freedom

IT IS A THEME OF THIS BOOK THAT THE RATIONALE FOR POLITI-
cal liberty and the free economy cannot be constituted satisfac-
torily on naturalistic terms. The case for personal freedom cannot
rest this side of theistic belief. Three considerations make this
clear. The key idea of a society of free men is the idea of inherent
rights—rights which are "natural" in the sense of being an intrinsic
and essential characteristic of human nature. This implies the
presence in each person of a sacredness beyond that which other
men might bestow, an inviolable soul which is not derived from
the material world. A free society, in the second place, is one
which acknowledges the reality of certain moral norms which take
precedence over merely social standards and/or political fiats.
Any ethical theory which does not begin by denying the reality of
the moral categories right and wrong—a kind of ritual suicide for
ethical theory—must finally anchor the discipline in a realm which
is beyond society and beyond nature. Sound ethical theory must,
in other words, lead to or proceed from theistic premises. In the
third place, economics is a science of means, which implies that
economics does not and cannot stand alone, but needs to be completed by a discipline which deals with ends. Religion is that sector
of human thought and practice which treats of the proper ends,
aims, purposes, and destiny of human life, and economics must
eventually find accommodation within it.

The argument for basic theism has been touched upon here and there in the body of this book, but it might be helpful to bring the matter into compact focus. Some considerations bearing upon the validity of theistic belief are touched upon in this appendix. Theism provides a foundation for ethical theory, which is crippled apart from belief in God, and theism also gives validity to the idea of inherent rights.

Let us begin with the question on which every other religious question turns: Does God exist? Most discussions of this question flounder upon a lack of agreement as to the meaning of the term God. It is somewhat like asking a person ignorant of chemistry: Does H_2SO_4 exist? If the case for the affirmative assumes that H_2SO_4 is the formula for water, while the spokesman for the negative assumes that H_2SO_4 is gasoline, they'll never come to grips with the issues. There is a further stumbling block in the different meanings attached to the term "exist." If God *is*, He does not exist in time and space; He does not possess mass and extension. But neither does a thought; neither, for that matter, does time, and time is inexorably real. The issue turns on the reality or unreality of a dimension of the universe that transcends the familiar world inhabited by things we can see and touch, weigh, and measure. If God is, He is not a sensory object. Most atheists attack an idea of God that alert theists have never entertained. But the fault is not all on one side. Perhaps we can achieve a better perspective by a different approach to the question.

The argument here makes no concession to "faith"—in the usual sense of that much abused word. As the term is popularly used, "faith" means the will to believe certain propositions on nonrational grounds, or in spite of the evidence. (Faith means something else in theological discussions, but faith is not the subject of this paper.) The argument here begins with an examination of the nature of our thought processes and moves to the logical conclusion that Mind is an original ingredient of the universe. The theistic implications of this conclusion are drawn.

It has been said that we live in the post-Christian era. This may well be the case, but our age also has many of the earmarks of the pre-pagan era. Historically, paganism represents an achievement, and the virtues and pieties of ancient paganism provided one of the essential training grounds for Christianity, which appeared "in the fullness of time." It may be necessary for the race to hoist itself up to the level of paganism again before biblical religion can be judged on its merits. In any event, this essay merely seeks to carry the argument from pre-paganism to paganism.

Our age is one which habitually concentrates on change; everything appears to be in transit, nothing remains the same. In terms of the evolutionary outlook of the past century the familiar world is in flux; no fixed points, nothing enduring, everything evolving into something else. Things now complex were once simple: the powerful gasoline chariots of today evolved from the early horseless carriage of Henry Ford, the electronic marvels of today's science had their simple beginning when Ben Franklin tapped the lightning, primitive cultures gradually developed into today's civilizations, and so forth. A modern film depicts "in poetic form the exhilaration of modern man, as well as his bewilderment, in a world where the only permanent factor is change." Such is the modern temper.

Other generations have viewed the world through different lenses, and to break the spell of our exclusive preoccupation with the transitory we need to be reminded that some things are now what they always have been and always will be.

For example, the multiplication table. This did not evolve out of some proto-arithmetic which had a different answer for the product of seven times six. Seven times six has always been forty-two, even before men appeared on the planet to make the calculation. This is simply the way things are, and they will always remain thus even if men conspire to repeal the result and gain unanimous consent for the error.

For another example, take the matter of atomic number. The atomic number of nitrogen is seven; there are seven protons in its nucleus. Was the atomic number of nitrogen one on the first day of creation? No, for then it would have been hydrogen. Will the atomic number of nitrogen evolve into eight in a billion years? No, for in that case it would be oxygen. The nitrogen atom is today what it always has been and forever will be; if it acquired additional protons it would not be changing its nature, it would cease being itself.

It is similar with the logical categories of the mind. Ludwig von Mises speaks of "the immutability and universality of the categories of thought and action." He goes on to declare that the logical structure of human reason is common to all men: "The idea that A could at the same time be non-A or that to prefer A to B could at the same time be to prefer B to A is simply inconceivable and absurd to a human mind. We are not in a position to comprehend any kind of prelogical or metalogical thinking. We cannot think of a world without causality and teleology."[1]

Human persons are involved in the realm of nature, nature being defined as the material universe apart from man and his works. Nature is an orderly realm of interlocking cause and effect relationships; it is the realm studied by the natural scientists. Nature is said to be understood when the regularity of connections between events is seen to be inevitable and the sequence is framed in a scientific law. The laws in the natural order are typified by those of physics and chemistry. It is orthodox Marxist doctrine that "The world by its very nature is material . . . [and] develops in accordance with the laws of the movement of matter. . . . The material, sensuously perceptible world . . . is the only reality." Many who are not Marxists nevertheless entertain similar views, believing that such a view of the universe—which regards nature as all there is—is the only view compatible with the scientific outlook.

Some students of these matters differentiate between the natural sciences and the social sciences. In addition to the scientific laws governing the movement of bits of matter, there are, they say, the laws of the market, the laws of human action. This is praxeology, and although it reveals inexorable connections in human action, the nature of these relations distinguishes them from the subject of the natural sciences.

The universe, on this reading, consists of two orders and two only—the natural order and the social order. No one can deny that human beings live in a given society, nation, country; the social order is an undeniable aspect of reality. Nor can anyone deny the reality of the natural order and that men are part of nature. A human body is mass extended in space and time; it is a laboratory for performing elaborate feats of chemical engineering; its proportions exhibit certain mathematical relations; and so on. The individual human being is most certainly joined to the natural and social orders, but is this the extent of his connections and external

1. Mises, *Human Action*, p. 33.

relationships? Or does man—as theism contends—participate in an order which transcends the social and natural orders? He is part of nature, but is he also apart from nature?

Those who declare that there are no regularities except scientific laws and economic laws are saying that there is no *order* beyond the natural and social orders. If there is anything beyond it is chaos, without recognizable or discoverable regularities. This is a-theism in seemingly intelligible form, or, as some might prefer to call it, Humanism, or Naturalism, or Positivism.

The man who says that there are only two orders, the natural and the social, must assume a mind that knows this, a mind capable of knowing this, a mind capable of discovering true relations in the two realms outside itself. What a marvelous instrument this mind is! How shall we account for it? Most people, of course, take the mind for granted—as they take almost everything else for granted. Paradoxically, while there are many highly trained minds seeking to explain just about everything in the natural and social orders, it never occurs to them that the mind itself needs explaining.

When "explanations" are offered, they go something like this: There was a time when the planet was a hot blob of flaming gas. Life had not yet appeared, and, of course, there was then no mind —no knowing, no awareness, no consciousness—nothing mental. The earth cooled, nonlife gave rise to life, and with the appearance of man life became conscious of itself. The nonmental gave rise to mind, the nonrational issued in rationality. There was now meaning and purpose where before there had been neither meaning nor purpose. Up to a given point in time there were only things; at the next moment there were thoughts as well as things. Mind somehow, according to this account, "emerged" from matter at a late stage in planetary history, like a chick from an egg. As orthodox Marxist doctrine has it: "Our consciousness and thinking are the product of a material, bodily organ. . . . Mind itself is merely the highest product of matter. The world is a picture of how matter moves and how matter thinks."

We are being asked to accept the proposition that intelligence happened by accident as the unintended result of a chance arrangement of atoms, material particles, electrical charges, or what have you. And we are expected to believe that the instrument assembled so haphazardly is one we can trust to obtain true and certain knowledge.

We usually associate thought with the mind. For the materialist, however, thought is simply a reflex of material changes occurring in the body. "The brain secretes thought as the liver secretes bile," wrote a nineteenth century evangel of this doctrine. Now bile is of the same order as the liver; it can be seen, handled, weighed, measured, packaged, analyzed. So can the brain. The brain is a material object extended in space and time; it obeys the laws of physics and chemistry. Not so a thought. What color is a thought, how long is it, how heavy, what's the chemical formula? Speaking of the brain, it is incoherent to inquire if this organ is true or false. But thought may be erroneous, and the most relevant question to put to a line of reasoning is to ask: "True or false?" The distinction between mind and brain is clear enough.

Error occurs when a line of thinking does not conform itself to the laws of logic. An inference or a conclusion may be false as well as true, and we become aware of the error only because we can be simultaneously aware of a pattern of reasonable relationships which is somehow "out there" and other than the line of reasoning which is being tested.

Is the action of thinking under the sway of scientific laws or the laws of praxeology; or is valid reasoning known to be such because it conforms to the laws of logic? It appears to be self-evident that the laws of economics and the laws of physics and chemistry are the products of the reflective intelligence; and not the other way around. Thought is either (a) random and chaotic, or (b) obedient (when true) to the laws of logic (or laws of thought). It follows that men are not creatures of the social and natural orders only; they participate in an order which is nonmaterial and nonsocietal, an order which is mental. In the case of the higher organisms—such as man—mind does indeed inform matter—the human nervous system; and the mind's activity is evident in social structures. But mind is not identifiable with either matter or society.

The man who declares that there are but two orders only, the natural and the social, has implicitly admitted—by that very declaration—the existence of ideas, and ideas constitute a third order which can't be assimilated to either of the other two. An awareness of nature and society immediately invokes the realm of mind—or consciousness or thought. If thought does not constitute an independent order of existence—but merely reflects nature or society —it cannot be trusted. No one can diiscredit the mind in any way and at the same time affirm the validity of the conclusions reached by it. Either thought is genuine and reality is threefold, or thought is not genuine and we are thus forever back of the starting line in any effort to comprehend society and nature.

The idea of a physical object is easily distinguishable from the object itself. A thought about the Rock of Gibraltar cannot possibly be confused with the solid rock itself. It is not only different, it is radically different, wholly other. Rocks are different from trees, and the thought of a rock can't be confused with the thought of a tree; but the category of thoughts is of a different order than the category of things. To assert that thinking is merely the movement of material particles, (or of atoms, or of electricul charges, or waves, or neutral particulars) or a "reflection" of that movement, or an emergent upon that movement is easy enough to say; it is impossible to believe. What did you figure it out with? Not a mind, not an instrument capable of reaching even *that* truth! Energy is always dissipated in the movement from antecedent to consequent; cause is greater than effect; producer is superior to product. If the movement of material particles produced mind the mind is the lesser, and the lesser comprehends the greater. Deny the existence of mind, or discount mind in any way, and you undercut every conclusion presumed to be reached by it.

A mere collection of dirt, trees, water, and assorted chemicals cannot be said to be rational; it is nonrational or irrational. If we perceive that there is a radical disjunction between the rational and the nonrational, we must conclude that there is no logical way that the latter could give rise to the former, and this is to admit that mind did not simply "emerge" out of matter.

But perhaps mind is a product of the social order, as John Dewey affirmed; "The human mind is what happens to the human animal in a social situation." There are many different kinds of societies; does this mean an equal number of different minds? Does it mean that the kind of truth discoverable in a particular society is only *its* kind of truth? And anyway, does not this position get the cart before the horse? Is it not likely that a society or a culture reflects the operations of minds, rather than mind being a reflec-

tion of society? And note, finally, the unphilosophical ambiguity and lack of clarity in the Dewey statement. The "human animal" is never found except in a "social situation"—in some society. It is a truism to say that human minds are manifested where people are, and not elsewhere. But Dewey wants us to believe that the merely organic gives rise to the mental, when certain organisms associate with others of their own kind. Mind, on this view, is reduced to a mere instrument to aid in social adaptation and thought is no longer autonomous. A variant of the Dewey doctrine suggests that the mind developed as a result of speech (instead of human speech developing because man has a mind). There's indeed a reciprocal relationship between speech and mind—but why hasn't every organism possessing vocal chords taken to speech and come into possession of a mind as a result?

To sum up: If mind is not the result merely of a fortuitous combination of complex hydrocarbons, nor the consequence of social intercourse, then it follows that mind must be an independent reality in the universe. Awareness of ourselves as creatures of the natural and social orders demands that we validate that awareness. If we know anything at all, we know that we know; we are conscious of our awareness; we have an immediate intuition of a third order. Mind is *sui generis*, it is fundamental, primary, not a mere derivative of something nonmental. When all is said and done, however, anyone is still free to declare that *his* mind is basically nonmental!

An important inference is yet to be drawn. The natural order is real, the social order is real, and our instrument for discovering these two truths must be at least as real as they, or we've pulled the plug on ourselves. Furthermore, if mind is an instrument capable of discovering truths about the world outside (the realms of nature and society), there must be a sort of resonance between mind and the realms outside. Mind is rationally structured, else it could not reason; and reason could not come into possession of truths about the world outside unless that world also were rationally structured. The world is intelligible to human intelligence, and there must be an explanation for this curious circumstance. ("The eternal mystery of the world," wrote Einstein, "is its comprehensibility.") Three possibilities: This is either (a) an accidental parallelism, or (b) mind is a product of nature, or (c) the human intelligence and the intelligible world are rooted in the same Source. One accidental parallel is luck, two would be miraculous, two billion—out of the question! No one accepts (a) because the laws of probability are overwhelmingly against it. The second alternative is the popular one; it is fashionable today to regard mind as an offshoot of nature or society. But sufficient objections have already been raised against this position so that we can discount it. We are left, then, with position (c). This is the only position which grants the independent integrity of the mind; it is, therefore, the only rational position. This is theism.

Atheism is really a denial of the reality of mind; it denies mental or logical regularities or subsumes them under the category of scientific laws or economic laws. Agnosticism amounts to the same thing; it cannot decide whether mind is real or not. Both positions put themselves out on a limb and then saw it off. The mind, in the nature of the case, cannot possibly construct a solid case against itself; such a "disproof" really proves the opposite, for it displays the mind's unique ability to marshal the evidence and draw valid inferences. That which doubts the existence of mind is mind itself. The more logical and elegant mind's case against itself, the more eloquent the testimony on behalf of mind.

If thought is not a mere reflection of bodily events but constitutes an independently real order of the universe; and if valid knowledge of that universe results from accurate reasoning about it, then there is something back of this universe which (or Who) is more akin go the minds we possess and experience with than to anything else we know. Beyond the social and natural orders there is, then, something like Conscious Intelligence. Reflect on the nature of intelligence and on the intelligible universe and it is impossible to deny that a third order transcends the natural and social orders. This third order partakes of the nature of what we know as mind, consciousness, awareness; and it is of the essence of mind that it can be an ordering intelligence working out its purposes. This is, basically, what thoughtful men understand by God.

The demonstration that our minds cannot be plausibly conceived as merely emergents upon nature or society is to identify mind as an independent reality, an original constituent of the universe. But if we reason from our minds to Mind are we not bridging an unthinkable gap? Indeed we are. This is a mystery beyond the power of our finite minds to grasp. But no less a mystery is what philosophers refer to as the Mind–Body Problem, one of the perennial and unsolved problems of philosophy. We know that the mind and body interact, but we do not know how they affect each other. When the body ingests too much alcohol the thinking processes become confused; when the thinking is warped bodily symptoms such as ulcers may appear. The mind and body do interact, but no philosopher has ever succeeded in explaining this phenomenon to the satisfaction of all other students of the problem. If we cannot explain how the mind gets along with the body we should not feel undue pressure to explain how the mind could get along without the body (immortality), or the connection between our finite minds and Infinite Mind, or God.

If we were working out a campaign slogan or devising a rhetorical flourish we might, at this point, be tempted to paraphrase Descartes: "I think; therefore God exists."

So much for an instant profile of theism, a glimpse of one of its outlying provinces. The next step would involve tackling such a book a A. E. Taylor's little classic, *Does God Exist?* (Macmillan, 1945); then the more substantial volumes mentioned in "Lord Gifford's Legacy" (*The Freeman*, March, 1966).

What, now, is theism's relevance to the struggle for human liberty? Are not some of the greatest champions of the free market and limited government nontheists? The answer is, of course, yes. A lot of atheists believe in capitalism whereas a lot of theists don't; and vice versa. This is history; our concern here, however, is with theory. The distinction between theory and history is both important and elusive. A poll of the likes and dislikes of twentieth-century atheists would turn up some data of possible interest; some would like capitalism, others apple pie. This would be history. Theory, on the other hand, would inquire whether the argument for the free society can make its case if the universe has no other reality than the natural and social orders.

It goes without saying that technical questions in economics have no more relevance to theism than similar questions in mathematics or chemistry. Furthermore, it can be pretty well demonstrated that the free market economy results in maximum production–minimum wastage of scarce resources, and therefore

in the greatest possibly prosperity for the entire society. But economics per se cannot say that people ought to pursue these goals;
the word "ought" does not belong in the vocabulary of anyone
except when he is wearing his moralist's hat. Economics is a
science of means; it is not for the economist to say what ends
people should seek. And it is obvious that John Doe, with the
rarest of exceptions, does not pursue the goal of maximum production–maximum prosperity for his society with the same singleness
of purpose displayed by a brooding hen who has no other thought
but to sit on her eggs. John Doe is frequently content to live off
the fruits of others' production, as predator or parasite, as the best
available way for him personally to realize his economic ends.

Those who insist that economics is a science of means are really
implying that the case for liberty can *not* be made in terms of
economics alone. A "means" standing all by itself is meaningless.
It is like that zany Zen question which has to do with the sound
made by the clap of one hand. A "means" is defined only in terms
of its end, and the science of economics is like a tool which can
be put to more than one use. If a people aspire to the goal of a free
and prosperous nation the economist can offer sound instruction;
if a people want an interventionist economy the economist can tell
them what will happen. He cannot, in either case, tell them which
they should prefer, or what they ought to do. Not unless he assumes the role of moralist—which most of them are only too eager
to do.

In ethical inquiry the familiar terms are "the moral order," or
"the moral law," or "the categories of right and wrong." But if
reality consists only of the natural order and the social order and
nothing more, then there is no independent moral order possessing
a claim to its own integrities. If the only regularities are scientific
laws and economic laws, there are no moral laws—except in a
Pickwickian sense. The categories "right" and "wrong," one hears
it said, are outmoded categories, of no more contemporary relevance for today's moralist than the ancient categories of clean and
unclean beasts for today's biologist. The moralist, therefore, is in
disrepute; his entire subject matter has been jerked out from under
him. Right and wrong have been shorn of their ethical meanings
and reduced—as the occasion demands—to legal and illegal, conventional and unconventional, taboo and permitted, and even
"want" and "don't want."

Now, an ethical code must be rooted somewhere, or anchored to something. And if there is no dimension of reality which transcends the natural and social orders, then the ethical code must find lodgment either within nature or within society. What *are* nature's imperatives? Nature, when put to the test, reveals no clear-cut ethical mandates; nature has its mercies and mutual aid, but it is also "red in tooth and claw." We raise animals for food and keep them as beasts of burden; does nature's code demand that we give up these practices or that we extend them—when the occasion warrants—to human beings? If we recoil in horror at the suggestion and answer both questions in the negative, it is not nature per se that supplies the cue. Nature is the realm of what is; ethics is the realm of what ought to be. The two are unmistakably different. Even those who maintain that "whatever is, is right" have conceptually separated the two realms and must find some way of accounting for the realm of moral obligation. They won't find it in nature.

Positivists and naturalists may try to argue that an ethical code doesn't have to be "rooted" anywhere, that an ethical code is simply a set of rules men have devised in order to reduce the frictions of interpersonal relations. But an ethial code is not merely descriptive of the way things are—as are scientific laws; it prescribes what ought to be—it is normative. An ethical imperative says: "Do this, because. . . ." It is when the naturalist or positivist seeks to argue on behalf of his "because" that he is in trouble; as he carries his argument back step by step he must come at some point to his end term, and it is a mere physical event or material object. The man who desires to systematize his ethical inquiry must seek a final sanction for his recommendations; and the positivist vainly tries to root them in nature. Otherwise, he is merely expressing his preferences. Should he attempt to spell out his ethics from his reading of *human* nature we are back to the futile effort to derive *that* from physical nature and/or society. The natural order is like a stage on which the drama of ethics is played out; the author must be sought offstage.

The only other place to seek rootage for our ethical code—if we give up nature and deny the reality of a transcendent order—is in society. But which society? Only historic societies exist; society with a capital S is an abstraction. Today there are Communist societies, welfarist societies, tribal societies, caste societies, mo-

narchical societies—each with its own "good." And some of these
"goods" are mutually exclusive. The chief "good" of one society
might be scholarship, of another saintliness, or sports, or war, or
wealth. If it be asserted that some of these societies are better than
others, and one is best of all, we are bound to ask where the moral
yardstick came from. (You might say, "I prefer this society to
that," but preferences are not moral judgments. And we must be
cautioned against using "good" in a merely instrumental sense; a
tribal society is "good" for witch doctors and medicine men, a
democratic society is "bad" from the viewpoint of the royal
family, and so on.) If each society has its own "good" and "man
is the measure of things," then there is no good-in-itself, nothing
to which the individual conscience can appeal against the pressure
of the mass. If fifty million Frenchmen can't be wrong, then there
are no inherent or natural rights pertaining to individuals; might
makes right and there is no moral right of dissent. If each society
is its own arbiter of what is "right"—meaning by "right" whatever
is socially useful or beneficial to the country—then some organ of
that society must assume the task of defining socially useful actions, enforcing them on citizens, and punishing violators. The
only social agency in a position to undertake such a job is, of
course, the state. But before the state embarks on this task it must
throw off the restrictions placed around it by the traditional ethical
code. The state becomes completely amoral; whatever *it* decides
is socially useful or beneficial to the nation becomes "moral" by
definition. Given such a theory, it is irrelevant to pass a moral
judgment against the Communists for their liquidation of the
Kulaks or against the Nazis for their treatment of the Jews. Within
the terms of each system these policies are "moral." The mind
recoils from the diabolism of such a thought, but this conclusion
is forced upon us if we accept the premise that each society has
a free hand to decide what course of action "benefits the community."

Suppose we recommend self-interest and appeal to the individual conscience? There is an ambiguity in all such exhortations,
because those who take this approach are seldom aware of the
framework within which their appeal is made. Such an appeal may
be made within a theistic framework, or within a framework which
is nontheistic. In the former case, a man is being told that his true

interest consists in seeking to please God rather than himself, conforming his self-will to God's will. In the latter case, the rule book has been thrown out; there are only the conventions of society and the regularities of nature, and each individual is to pit himself against these (except insofar as he can use them) and against every other individual (except insofar as he can be useful). To discard the theistic framework is to abandon the idea that there are any standards (except prudential ones) to which the individual unit should conform. It is fatuous for A to urge, in one breath, that B pursue his own self-interest, and then to try, in the second, to instruct B as to what his proper self-interest is. How should A know this better than B? And a fundamental contradiction is involved: B cannot simultaneously pursue his own self-interest and let A define it for him, for in that case B would be pursuing A's interest rather than his own.

There is no ethical situation which can be boiled down to you and me; it's always you, me, and the rule book. Throw out the rule book, urge each individual to pursue his own interest and might overcomes right; ascendency is given to the strong, the clever, the devious, the unscrupulous. It is similar with an appeal to the individual conscience. The conscience schooled in the ethical code is a fairly reliable guide, at least to the extent that disobedience to it is likely to lead one astray. But it does not follow that one who obeys his conscience is always right; his conscience might be untutored and, when the theistic framework is abandoned, it is certainly unmonitored. Even when monitored and tutored the conscience is not infallible, as witness the religious and ideological persecutions of past and present.

Most societies of record have acknowledged that human destiny is somehow linked with unseen powers; people believed that they participated in an order of reality which transcends the world of time and space. Crude versions of this position have been entertained by simple people, but the philosophy has been worked out by some of the most powerful and sophisticated minds ever known. And there have been all stages in between. This worldview gave meaning to individual life and sanctioned the ethical code. Ethical living by people trying to practice the code had beneficial results; people could live together peacefully, they could trust one another. This made for social utility; the community benefited, and the persons involved were happier, by and large. The ethical code was sanctioned by virtue of its being rooted in the transcendent, it was God's moral order, His will for men; the good results—personal as well as social—followed. The ethical imperative was: Do what is right—because it is right! Murder is wrong, even though you may gain a throne thereby. Stealing is wrong, even if you can get away with it. Lying is wrong, even when it saves your hide. Social well-being is served and persons are happier if the country of Rubarbaria has a low incidence of murder, theft, and lying; but this is a consequence of moral actions, not the sanction for them. The three levels are (a) sanctions, (b) actions, and (c) results. The simple distinction between sanctions and results, between what comes before and what follows is often overlooked, in what may be a disastrous oversight. When the transcendent dimension of human life is denied or ignored, the traditional ethical code loses its historic sanctions. If the premise is that men participate in two orders only, nature and society, then the only logical conclusion is that human actions cannot be tested on the basis of antecedently existing norms and judged to be right or wrong; they can be validated only in terms of results. The stress may be on public results—such as social utility, community well-being, or national policy; or on private results—such as personal happiness, individual advantage, or larger income. Either way we become "results-minded," this is to embrace the notion that the end justifies the means.

If we concentrate on public results we face the possibility of the diabolical consequences we cited earlier, as found in Communist and Nazi ideology—and elsewhere. If we concentrate on private results, each individual will decide—according to his own tastes, preferences, and drives—what ends he wants to attain, as well as who and what he will sacrifice to attain them. Each man writes and rewrites his own rules, and who is to say him nay? If "ought" and "should" and "moral obligation" are merely meaningless sounds, no one is in a position to tell anyone else what he "ought" to do —either in terms of his ends or the means he employs to gain them. This is self-evident. If there are no moral norms there is no yardstick by which to test either means or ends, whether they be right or wrong. Means can only be instrumentally good or bad, that is, efficient ways to achieve a specified end, or inefficient. And each end, in turn, becomes the means to a further end, and so on ad infinitum. The Communist cannot logically say that advancing the Party is a good end; it is merely the end *he* seeks, and any means that furthers this end—murder, theft, deceit included—is "good" by definition.

Let us be reminded again of the distinction between theory and history. It will be pointed out that even though our third order, the transcendent dimension, has largely dropped out of modern life, most people still live very decent lives; some, exemplary lives. Granted: "The fair sum of six thousand years/ Traditions of civility" will see to that—or mere habit and inertia. But we are discussing theory, not history. If the universe is nature and society and nothing more—man assumed to be nothing but a product roughed out by nature and polished by social relationships—then there is no moral order existing in its own right. Nor is there a source from which inherent rights are derived.

Whence does John Doe derive his rights? From society? From nature. Or from some source beyond nature and society? Let's take these questions in order. To suggest that John Doe derives his rights from society boils down, in practice, to saying that he has certain government grants of privilege—to a good education, decent housing, a job, and so on. But these are not "rights" as libertarian usage understands the term; they are claims against other men, politically enforced. Perhaps rights are from nature, then? It is obvious that men cannot derive their rights from nature unless nature has them first. Nature is the entire material world, and rights are certainly not material things, although there are rights *to* material things. We cannot plausibly talk about the rights of trees when we need lumber, or the rights of fish when we need food, or the rights of sheep when we need wool. A sound natural piety acknowledges our kinship with nature, but this is not to attribute "rights" to nature.

Sometimes a slightly different tack is taken. Man, it is said, does not get his rights from anywhere; he just has them, they are inherent in human nature. But human nature is not an original ingredient of the planet. If there are but two orders, nature and society, then every facet and aspect of human nature is reducible, ultimately, into its natural and social components. If there is no third order—a dimension which transcends both nature and society—

then man and his nature are produced by natural and social forces alone, and there cannot be anything in the final product which was not in the original blend. If we cannot locate the origin of rights in nature or society then it follows that rights cannot be inherent in human nature—not unless human nature itself participates in the third order, as I have argued that it does.

Moral experience, and the human mind itself, link man to an order of reality which is beyond both nature and society. This is the realm of the mind and spirit, and as it interpenetrates the sensory order it generates an awareness of a sacredness in the human person that gives rise to the idea that John Doe has certain rights and immunities which his fellows must respect. Rights are natural attributes of the person within the framework of theism, but the idea of individual rights is utterly incompatible with atheism—defined as the belief that reality consists of the natural and social orders only.

If men really do participate in an order that transcends society and nature, but deny or ignore this fact, they not only stunt their personal development in this dimension, but disable themselves from operating with optimum effectiveness in the social and natural orders as well. Widely held convictions about the inherent rights and immunities of persons, with corollary duties stemming from the moral order, provide the only foundation for the free society. Freedom in human affairs is not for the asking or the wishing; it is won only as we fulfill the necessary conditions.

These necessary conditions are both seen and unseen. Among the visible features of the free society are: a political agency limited by both the written *and* the unwritten law to administering justice and maintaining the public peace; and a market economy. The free society, or the classical liberal order as some prefer to designate it, is a rare development in human affairs, appearing only when its requirements are met. "A liberal order," writes Hayek in his 1966 Mt. Pelerin lecture, "has arisen only in countries in which, in ancient Greece and Rome no less than in modern Britain, justice was conceived as something to be discovered by the efforts of judges or scholars and not as determined by the arbitrary will of any authority." Justice, conceived to be there prior to its discovery by men, is beyond both society and nature, existing in a dimension which transcends these two orders. It is akin to the moral order, and to the idea of inherent rights which gives each individual within society a protected domain and equal rights under the laws. The thoughtful rehabilitation of the transcendent dimension of human existence will not, of itself, generate political wisdom and economic knowledge. But the free society never has and cannot now take root unless the ground is prepared for it.

Some Axioms of Economics

1. Work must be performed if human life is to be sustained.

The raw materials of the planet cannot be consumed as is, except in rare instances. Human energy must be expended on the earth's resources in order to convert them into a form men can use. Work confers title of ownership; the product belongs to the producer.

2. Goods are scarce.

The things men want are in short supply and so men must be economical in their use. Economics is the discipline which aims at the efficient rationing and allocation of the planet's scanty resources.

3. The market is the primary labor-saving device.

Primordial scarcity drives men into a social arrangement which permits specialized production. Division of labor demands an arrangement, the market, for the exchange of the fruits of specialization. Civilization is inconceivable without the market.

4. Goods and services are exchanged for goods and services.

No one voluntarily gives up even a single unit of something he values, including his own labor, except for something he values more. All parties to this kind of exchange gain from it.

5. Money possesses intrinsic value.

No one gives up something he values for a mere piece of paper, or for a mere token; he gives up value only because he expects value in return. He relinquishes something for a mere token only if he believes the token's promise to buy him what he really wants. Money substitutes are not money; gold is money.

6. Production begets production.

No one produces beyond his own needs (as almost everyone in a division-of-labor economy does) unless he anticipates exchanging his surpluses for the variety of goods he wants. X increases his output of wanted goods and services, and this induces A, B, and C to increase their productive efforts in order to obtain them. The economy does not need more "purchasing power" to stimulate general productivity; it needs more production.

7. Capital is the key to increased productivity.

An economy's output expands as more and better tools and machines are used. Increasing the quantity of capital in proportion to population makes more goods available.

8. Supply and demand are alternate facets of the same thing.

The present stock of shoes, for instance, constitutes at one and the same time a supply of shoes and a demand for wheat, typewriters, houses, and so on. The supply of wheat, in turn, constitutes a supply of itself, and a demand for all the other things which owners of wheat might wish to obtain for it in exchange.

9. Customers set wages.

In the free economy, each person is rewarded in terms of the value his peers attach to his offering of goods and services. If his offering excites large numbers of consumers, he is rewarded handsomely; on the other hand, if his product is little valued, his wage is low. Wage rates tend to guide people into lines where their services are wanted.

10. Customers also determine prices.

A man might set a figure for his labor or his product, but if there are no takers this figure is not a price. The price of an item is what the item exchanges for on the market; that is, what the item is worth to some one. High prices attract labor and capital from lower priced trades, directing production into line with demand.

11. The entrepreneurial decision is the spark.

Technology and engineering play an important role in production, but their role is secondary. Economic production is set in motion and given direction by the entrepreneurial decision. This is the creative act which combines the correct means (men, machines, and resources) in the right proportion for the attainment of the ends envisioned. Once the entrepreneur properly marshals the factors of production the engineer and technician tool up for manufacture. The entrepreneur operates in a dimension akin to that of the artist.

12. Economics is only a part of life.

The free economy presupposes a high level of moral action. People do not enter into long-range deferred exchanges or make contracts unless they are accustomed to trust one another, and this trust does not exist unless people have generally proved their trustworthiness in the past. It presupposes also a high degree of intellectual competence. "Consumer acceptance" is a good test for makers of shoes, or vacuum cleaners, or gadgets of various kinds. Ideas, however, must be submitted to another kind of test. An idea may be true or false, and its truth or falsity has little or no correlation with its popularity. A man who continues to make high button shoes for which there is no market is an eccentric; but it is a matter of honor for a man to stand for what he believes to be true and right even though his ideas have no takers.

Bibliography

Acton, John E., *Essays on Freedom and Power*, Gertrude Himmelfarb, Ed., Boston: Beacon Press, 1948, 452 pp.

Anderson, Benjamin, *The Value of Money*, New York: Macmillan, 1917, 610 pp.

Barzun, Jacques, *Darwin, Marx, and Wagner*, New York: Doubleday, 1942, 1958, 373 pp.

Baumer, Franklin L, *Religion and the Rise of Scepticism*, New York: Harcourt, 1960.

Beard, Charles, *The Rise of American Civilization*, New York: Macmillan, 1930 (One Volume Edition).

Becker, Carl, *The Declaration of Independence*, New York: Knopf, 1942.

————, *The Heavenly City of the Eighteenth Century Philosophers*, *New Haven, Connecticut: Yale, 1932.*

Belloc, Hilaire, The Crisis of Our Civilization, London: Cassell, 1937, 249 pp.

Bernard, Claude, *An Introduction to the Study of Experimental Medicine*, New York: Collier, 1966.

Beston, Henry, *American Memory*, New York: Farrar and Rinehart, 1937, 497 pp.

Böhm-Bawerk, Eugen, *Capital and Interest*, 3 Vols., South Holland, Illinois: Libertarian Press, 1958 (1884).

Bredvold, Louis I. and Ross, Ralph G., *The Philosophy of Edmund Burke*, Ann Arbor: University of Michigan Press, 1960, 276 pp.

Broad, C. D., *The Mind and Its Place in Nature*, London: Kegan Paul, 1925, 674 pp.

Bryant, Arthur, *The Story of England*, Vols. I and II, Boston: Houghton Mifflin, 1954.

Bryce, James, *The American Commonwealth*, New York: Macmillan, 1893 (Two Vols.).

Burnham, James, *Suicide of the West*, New York: John Day, 1964, 312 pp.

Burtt, E. A., *In Search of Philosophic Understanding*, New York: New American Library, 1965, 327 pp.

————, *The Metaphysical Foundations of Modern Science*, New York: Doubleday Anchor, 1954, 352 pp. (1924).

Butterfield, Herbert, *The Origins of Modern Science*, New York: Collier Books, 1952, 250 pp.

Carlyle, R. W. and A. J., *A History of Medieval Political Theory in the West*, (Six Vols.) London: Blackwood, 1908–1936.

Chamberlain, John, *The Roots of Captialism*, Princeton, New Jersey: Van Nostrand, 1959, 222 pp.

Chambers, Whitaker, *Witness*, New York: Random House, 1952, 808 pp.

Chodorov, Frank. *One Is a Crowd*, New York: Devin-Adair, 1952, 176 pp.

————, *The Income Tax*, New York: Devin-Adair, 1954, 116 pp.

————, *The Rise and Fall of Society*, New York: Devin-Adair, 1959, 168 pp.

Cochrane, C. N., *Christianity and Classical Culture*, New York: Oxford, 1940, 1957, 523 pp.

Corwin, Edward S., *The "Higher Law" Background of American Constitutional Theory*, Ithaca, New York: Cornell, 1955, 89 pp. (1928).

Dampier, William C., *A History of Science*, New York: Cambridge University Press, Fourth Ed. 1949, 527 pp.

Dawson, Christopher, *The Dynamics of World History*, J. J. Mulloy, Ed., New York: Sheed & Ward, 1956, 489 pp.

————, *Enquiries into Religion and Culture*, New York: Sheed & Ward, 1933, 347 pp.

————, *Religion and the Modern State*, New York: Sheed & Ward, 1936, 154 pp.

Demant, V. A., *Religion and the Decline of Capitalism*, New York: Scribner's, 1952, 204 pp.

————, *Theology of Society*, London: Faber & Faber, 1947, 268 pp.

Eliot, T. S., *The Idea of a Christian Society*, London: Faber & Faber, 1939, 99 pp.

Ferrero, G., *The Principles of Power*, New York: Putnam, 1942, 333 pp.

Friedman, Milton, *Capitalism and Freedom*, Chicago: University of Chicago Press, 1963, 202 pp.

Fustel de Coulange, Numa Denis, *The Ancient City*, 1874, 1956, New York: Doubleday Anchor, 373 pp.

Hayek, F. A., *The Constitution of Liberty*, Chicago: University of Chicago, 1960, 570 pp.

————, *The Counter-Revolution of Science*, Glencoe, Illinois: The Free Press, 1955, 255 pp.

————, *The Road to Serfdom*, Chicago: University of Chicago, 1944, 250 pp.

Hazlitt, Henry, *Economics in One Lesson*, New York: McFadden, 1946, 1961, 143 pp.

————, *The Failure of the "New Economics"*, Princeton, New Jersey: Van Nostrand, 1959, 458 pp.

————, *The Foundations of Morality*, Princeton, New Jersey: Van Nostrand, 1964, 398 pp.

————, *What You Should Know About Inflation*, Princeton, New Jersey: Van Nostrand, 1960, 152 pp.

Heard, Gerald, *Man the Master*, New York: Harper, 1941, 334 pp.

————, *Source of Civilization*, New York: Harper, 1937, 431 pp.

————, *The Third Morality*, London: Cassell, 1937, 318 pp.

————, *The Human Venture*, New York: Harper, 1955, 310 pp.

Herberg, Will, *Judaism and Modern Man*, New York: Harper, 1951, 313 pp.

Hoffman, Ross J. S., and Levack, Paul, Eds., *Burke's Politics*, New York: Knopf, 1949, 536 pp.

Howard, Irving, *The Christian Alternative to Socialism*, Arlington, Virginia: Crestwood Books, 1966, 153, pp.

Huxley, Aldous, *Ends and Means*, New York: Harper, 1937, 386 pp.

————, *Grey Eminence*, London: Chatto and Windus, 1941, 278 pp.

Inge, William Ralph, *Christian Ethics and Modern Problems*, London: Hodder & Stoughton, 1930, 402 pp.

————, *God and the Astronomers*, London: Longmans, Green, 1934, 308 pp.

Ingwalson, Kenneth I., Ed., *Your Church—Their Target*, Arlington, Virginia: Crestwood Books, 1966, 275 pp.

Joad, C. E. M., *Matter, Life and Value*, New York: Oxford University Press, 1929, 416 pp.

————, *Philosophy for Our Times*, London: Nelson, 1940, 367 pp.

————, *Philosophical Aspects of Modern Science*, London: Macmillan, 1932, 344 pp.

Jouvenel, Bertrand de, *On Power*, London: Batchworth, 1945, 320 pp.

Kirk, Russell, *Beyond the Dreams of Avarice*, Chicago: Regnery, 1956, 339 pp.

————, *Program for Conservatives*, Chicago: Regnery, 1954, 325 pp.

————, *The Conservative Mind*, Chicago: Regnery, 1953, 458 pp.

Knight, Frank R., *"Conflict of Values: Freedom and Justice" in The Goals of Economic Life*, A. D. Ward, Ed., New York: Harper. 1953.

Knox, Ronald, *Enthusiasm*, New York: Oxford University Press, 1950, 622 pp.

Krutch, Joseph Wood, *If You Don't Mind My Saying So*, New York: Sloane, 1964, 402 pp.

————, *The Measure of Man*, New York: Bobbs Merrill, 1953, 261 pp.

Kuehnelt-Leddihn, Erik von, *Liberty or Equality*, Caldwell, Idaho: Caxton, 1952, 395 pp.

Lax, Albert, *Consumer's Capitalism* (Edited, with an Introduction by Edmund A. Opitz), Chicago: Hallberg, 1969, 192 pp.

Lewis, C. S., *Miracles*, London: Geoffrey Bles, 1947, 220 pp.

————, *Mere Christianity*, London: Geoffrey Bles, 1952, 177 pp.

————, *That Hideous Strength*, New York: Macmillan, 1947, 459 pp.

————, *They Asked for a Paper*, London: Geoffrey Bles, 1962, 211 pp.

Lippmann, Walter, *The Good Society*, Boston: Little, Brown, 1937, 402 pp.

Lowry, Charles W., *Communism and Christ*, Rev. Ed., New York: Collier, 1962, 215 pp.

Maitland, F. W., *The Constitutional History of England*, New York: Cambridge University Press, 1919, 548 pp.

Maritain, Jacques, *The Social and Political Philosophy of Jacques Maritain*, James Evans and Leo Ward, Eds., New York: Doubleday Image, 1965, 354 pp.

Martineau, James, *Types of Ethical Theory*, Two Vols., New York: Oxford University Press, Third Edition 1901, 1108 pp.

Menger, Carl, *Principles of Economics*, Glencoe, Illinois: The Free Press, 1871, 1950, 328 pp.

Mill, John Stuart, *Utilitarianism, Liberty, Representative Government*, New York: Dutton, Everyman's Library.

————, *Autobiography*, New York: Columbia, 1924, 240 pp.

Mises, Ludwig von *Human Action*, Chicago: Regnery, 1948, 1967, 907 pp.

————, *Socialism*, New Haven: Yale, 1951 (1922), 599 pp.

————, *Theory and History*, New Haven: Yale, 1957, 384 pp.

————, *Theory of Money and Credit*, New Haven: Yale, 1953 (1912), 493 pp.

Montague, William Pepperell, *The Ways of Knowing*, London: Allen & Unwin, 1925, 427 pp.

Moore, G. E., *Principia Ethica*, New York: Cambridge University Press, 1960 (1903), 232 pp.

Morley, Felix, *Freedom and Federalism*, Chicago: Regnery, 1952, 274 pp.

————, *The Power in the People*, Princeton, New Jersey: Van Nostrand, 1948, 292 pp.

Morrall, J. B., *Political Thought in Medieval Times*, New York: Harper Torchbook, 1962, 152 pp.(1958).

Mosca, Gaetano, *The Ruling Class*, New York: McGraw-Hill, 1939, 514 pp.

Mumford, Lewis, *Technics and Civilization*, New York: Harcourt Brace, 1934, 495 pp.

————, *The City in History*, New York: Harcourt, Brace World, 1961, 657 pp.

Murray, John Courtney, *We Hold These Truths*, New York: Sheed & Ward, 1960, 336 pp.

Nef, John U., *The United States and Civilization*, Chicago: University of Chicago Press, 1942, 421 pp.

Nickerson, Hoffman, *Can We Limit War?* New York: Stokes, 1934, 317 pp.

————, *The Armed Horde*, New York: Putnam, 1942, 427 pp.

Niebuhr, H. Richard, *Christ and Culture*, New York: Harper Torchlight, 1951, 259 pp.

Oakeshott, Michael *Rationalism in Politics*, New York: Basic Books, 1962, 333 pp.

Opitz, Edmund A., Ed., *The Kingdom Without God*, Los Angeles: Foundation for Social Research, 1956, 196 pp.

Opitz, Edmund A., *The Powers That Be*, Los Angeles: Foundation for Social Research, 1956, 104 pp.

Orton, William Aylott, *The Liberal Tradition*, New Haven: Yale, 1945, 317 pp.

Parkes, H. Bamford, *Gods and Men*, New York: Knopf, 1959, 489 pp.

Paterson, Isabel, *The God of the Machine*, New York; Putnam, 1943; Caldwell, Idaho: Caxton, 1964, 292 pp.

Perry, R. L., Ed., *Sources of Our Liberties*, Chicago, American Bar Foundation, 1959, 456 pp.

Read, Leonard, *Anything That's Peaceful*, Irvington, New York: Foundation for Economic Education, 1964, 243 pp.

————, *Elements of Libertarian Leadership*, Irvington, New York: Foundation for Economic Education, 1962, 183 pp.

————, *Deeper Than You Think*, Irvington, New York: Foundation for Economic Education, 1966, 208 pp.

————, *The Free Market and Its Enemy*, Irvington, New York: Foundation for Economic Education, 1965, 67 pp.

Robbins, Lionel, *An Essay On the Significance of Economic Science*, New York: Macmillan, Second Ed. 1952, 160 pp.

Roepke, Wilhelm, *Civitas Humana*, London: Hodge, 1948, 235 pp.

————, *The Humane Economy*, Chicago: Regnery, 1960, 312 pp.

————, *Economics of the Free Society*, Chicago: Regnery, 1963, 273 pp.

————, *The Social Crisis of Our Time*, Chicago: University of Chicago Press, 1942, 260 pp.

Ruggiero, Guido de, *The History of European Liberalism*, Boston: Beacon Press, 1959 (1927), 476 pp.

Rushdoony, R. J., *The American System*, Nutley, New Jersey: Craig, 1965, 181 pp.

————, *This Independent Republic*, Nutley, New Jersey: Craig, 1964, 172 pp.

Sabine, George, *A History of Political Theory*, New York: Holt, 1937, 797 pp.

Scherman, Harry. *The Promises Men Live By*, New York: Random House, 1938, 492 pp.

Schumpeter, Joseph, *Capitalism, Socialism, and Democracy*, New York: Harper, 1942, 381 pp.

Sidgwick, Henry, *The Methods of Ethics*, Seventh Edition (1874), Chicago: University of Chicago Press, 1962, 528 pp.

Smith, Adam, *The Theory of Moral Sentiments*, (1759) Bohn's Standard Library, 1871, 538 pp.

————, *The Wealth of Nations*, (1776) New York: Modern Library.

Sorley, W. P., *Moral Values and the Idea of God*, New York: Cambridge University Press, 1918, 527 pp.

Stanlis, Peter J., *Edmund Burke and the Natural Law*, Ann Arbor: University of Michigan Press, 1958, 311 pp.

Tawney, R. H., *Equality*, New York: Harcourt, 1931, 280 pp.

————, *Religion and the Rise of Capitalism*, New York: Harcourt Brace, 1926, 1962, 337 pp.

————, *The Acquisitive Society*, London: Bell, 1922, 242 pp.

Taylor, A. E., *Does God Exist?*, London: Macmillan, 1945, 190 pp.

————, *The Faith of a Moralist*, London: Macmillan, 1930, 872 pp.

Temple, William, *Nature, Man and God*, London: Macmillan, 1934, 530 pp.

Troeltsch, Ernst, *The Social Teachings of the Christian Churches*, Two Vols., London: George Allen and Unwin, 1931, 1019 pp.

Trueblood, D. Elton, *General Philosophy*, New York: Harper & Row, 1963, 370 pp.

————, *Philosophy of Religion*, New York: Harper, 1957, 324 pp.

Tocqueville, Alexis de, *Democracy in America*, Two Vols., New York: Knopf, Vol. I 434 pp., Vol II 401 pp., 1945.

Weaver, Richard, *Ideas Have Consequences*, Chicago: University of Chicago Press, 1948, 187 pp.

————, *Life Without Prejudice*, Chicago: Regnery, 1965, 167 pp.

————, *Visions of Order*, Baton Rouge: Louisiana State University, 1964, 167 pp.

West, Charles C. *Communism and the Theologians*, Philadelphia: Westminster Press, 1958, 399 pp.

Whitehead, A. N., *Science and the Modern World*, New York: Cambridge University Press, 1926, 296 pp.

Wicksteed, Philip, *The Common Sense of Political Economy*, London: Rutledge and Kegan Paul, Two Vols. 1931, 871 pp.

Wormser, René A., *The Story of the Law*, Rev. Ed., New York: Simon & Schuster, 1962, 606 pp.

Name Index

Acton, John, 258, 262
Adams, John, 248
Adams, John Quincy, 195
Albright, W. F., 23
Anderson, Benjamin M., 70, 71n, 159n, 274
Aquinas, Thomas, 19, 189
Aristotle, 91, 95, 123, 147, 165, 175, 232
Augustine, 12, 34, 113, 127, 193, 195, 196

Bacon, Francis, 176
Barth, Karl, 33, 203
Barzun, Jacques, 161
Batista y Zaldívar, Fulgencio, 31
Beals, Carleton, 31
Beard, Charles A., 218
Beccaria, Cesare Bonesana, 123
Becker, Carl, 96, 249
Bennett, John C., 28, 30, 31
Bentham, Jeremy, 121, 122, 123, 124, 225, 255, 263
Berggrav (Bishop), 34
Bernard, Claude, 163, 164
Blackstone, William, 217, 261
Böhm-Bawerk, Eugen, 124
Bonhoeffer, Dietrich, 203
Bryant, Arthur, 242
Bryce, James, 266
Burke, Edmund, 171, 219
Burns, James MacGregor, 214, 215
Burtt, E. A., 117, 140, 140n, 165, 166
Butler, Samuel, 92, 150
Butterfield, Herbert, 165

Caesar, Julius, 91
Calvin, John, 38n
Carroll, Lewis, 243
Castro, Fidel, 31
Charlemagne, 257
Charles, R. H., 199
Childe, V. Gordon, 121
Clark, Fred G., 55
Cobban, Alfred, 18
Coke, Edward, 259, 261
Comte, Auguste, 153
Copernicus, Nicolaus, 164
Corwin, Edward S., 261n, 263
Coulanges, Fustel de, 206
Crusoe, Robinson, 32, 74

d'Abro, A., 142
Dampier, William Cecil, 141
Darwin, Charles, 160, 161, 162, 176
Davidson, William L., 263n

Demant, V. A., 1
Descartes, René, 139, 176, 291
Dewey, John, 159, 161, 255, 288, 289
Dreiser, Theodore, 185

Einstein, Albert, 289
Eliot, T. S., 207
Engels, Friedrich, 22, 97
Euclid of Alexandria, 138, 143

Ferenczi, S., 60
Ferguson, Adam, 74
Ferre, Nels, 240
Finer, Herman, 214
Fitch, Robert, 34
Franklin, Benjamin, 248
Friedman, Milton, 99, 100n

Galbraith, John Kenneth, 108
Galilei, Galileo, 140
Garaudy, Roger, 23
Gelasius (Pope), 206
Gill, Theodore, 26
Gladstone, W. E., 169
Goedel, Kurt, 143
Goldsmith, Oliver, 88

Handy, Robert T., 30
Hayek, F. A., 65, 74, 81, 102, 143, 154n
Hazlitt, Henry, 274
Headlam, Stewart D., 6
Heard, Gerald, 120n
Heisenberg, Werner, 142
Henry, Patrick, 220
Hobbes, Thomas, 139, 159, 160n, 163, 176
Hooker, Richard, 113
Howe, William, 172
Hromadka, Joseph, 26
Hulme, T. E., 174
Hume, David, 160, 163
Huxley, T. H., 119, 147, 162, 163, 200, 201

Inge, Dean, 19, 27, 36

Jefferson, Thomas, 81, 216, 223, 235, 248ff, 262, 263
Joad, C. E. M., 123n, 124n, 164
Johnson, Lyndon B., 240
Judin, A., 24
Juvenal, 267

Kant, Immanuel, 89
Keynes, John Maynard, 173, 274
Kingsley, Charles, 21

Subject Index*

Absolutism, 258, 261
Abundance, 108, 179, 272
Agnosticism, 113, 155, 157, 162, 201, 290
American Humanist Association, 156
American Revolution, 248
American system and majority rule, 212–30
Amsterdam Assembly, 39
Anglo-Saxons, 242
Animals, 119, 183, 185
Arms race, 271, 273
Atheism, 22, 114, 153, 156, 290

Babylon, 195, 197
Battle of Hastings, 242
Behaviorism, 4n, 5n, 120, 128
Biochemistry, 256
Boom or bust, 58
Boston University School of Theology, 26, 28
Brotherhood, 40
Business cycles, 55, 58

Calculation, economic, 107, 146
Capital. *See* Wealth
Capitalism
  beneficiaries of, 41
  Christianity and, 5, 42
  communism and, 39
  criticism of, 43
  historical, 42, 47
  production and, 41, 301
  rise of, 7
  supporting, 173
  terminology, 1, 6n
  see also Market economy
Caste system, 234
Cause and effect, 127, 257, 276
Change
  evolutionary, 140, 151, 161
  predominance of, 284
  process of, 176
  social, 204
Charity, 46, 90
Choice-making, 44, 223
Christianity
  capitalism and, 5, 42
  communism and, 23, 210
  culture in, 207
  doctrine of, 6, 257
  government and, 206
  kingdom of heaven, 27, 95
  significance of, 19

socialistic, 6, 15–36
sociology, 193
Church
  communism and, 21
  labor and, 27
  purpose of, 202
  world and, 37–59
  see also Religion
City of God and City of Man, 12, 92, 193–211
Class struggle, 97
Clausewitz doctrine, 278
Cold War, 270
Collectivism
  growth of, 169
  ideology of, 33
  modern, 17
  politics of, 221
  public tastes in, 82
  varieties of, 171
  victims of, 195
  war and, 269
Colonialism, 43, 218, 248, 259
Commonwealths, 201
Communism
  American, 167
  capitalism and, 39
  church and, 21
  Christianity and, 23, 210
  criticisms of, 41
  fifth column, 208
  philosophy of, 7
  Russian, 22
Computer magic, 72
Consciousness, 125, 157, 160, 162, 290
Conscription, 278
Consensus, 225
Consent doctrine, 245, 251
Constitution, U. S., 216, 228, 250
Consumers, 52, 71, 73, 272, 301
Continental Congress, 248
Covenant on Human Rights, 252
Cuban Revolution, 31

Declaration of Independence, 93, 171, 235, 247
Deity, will of, 122
Democracy, 35, 178, 208, 214, 247, 264
Depressions, 55, 58
Despotism, 35, 91, 208, 245–66
Destiny, 69, 92, 96, 104, 232, 295
Divine right, 258

East India Company, 218
Ecclesiastical developments, 34

* Prepared by Vernelia A. Crawford